THE MODERN UTOPIAN

THE MODERN UTOPIAN

ALTERNATIVE COMMUNITIES OF THE '60s AND '70s

BY **RICHARD FAIRFIELD**
CONTRIBUTIONS FROM
**TIMOTHY MILLER,
ALAN WATTS, NICK TOSCHES**
AND THE **UNDERGROUND
PRESS SYNDICATE**

PROCESS

contents

9

THE M☯DERN UT☯PIAN

UTOPIA, U.S.A.

$3.95

foreword

by Timothy Miller

THE COUNTERCULTURAL COMMUNES ARE THE QUIET GIANTS of the 1960s, receiving far less attention than the politics, sex, drugs, and rock and roll, even though they helped define the era. There were thousands—probably tens of thousands—of them, and hundreds of thousands of young counterculturists lived in one commune or another at some point.

Richard Fairfield was unusually perceptive in seeing the importance of the new communes and tracking their trajectories. By publishing The Modern Utopian he compiled a record unlike any other, a chronicle of daring ventures in cooperative living. His extensive lists and directories let communards know that they were part of a surge in communal living, the largest such surge in American history. Fairfield's magazines and the books based on them are a priceless contemporary window into a period in which huge numbers of young Americans rejected the traditional American way of greed-based and emotionally isolated living and searched for a new life path that embodied sharing, mutual caring, and openness. Although not all communes achieved their idealistic goals, their very existence represented a yearning of the human spirit for something better than the status quo and a courageousness to act upon these convictions with direct action and sustained efforts.

Communes have a history in the United States much older than the 1960s-era counterculture. One might define a commune as a group of like-minded persons who withdraw from the dominant culture and seek to create a micro-culture in which people live together and share resources while striving for common goals. Groups fitting that definition go back centuries. Many historians identify the first American commune as Plockhoy's Commonwealth, or Swanendael, which was established at what is now Lewes, Delaware, by a group of Dutch Mennonites in 1663. Other similar experiments followed; a century later the Shakers began to develop what became an interconnected group of 20 or so villages that constituted one of the largest and longest-lived communal movements in history. The nineteenth century saw the founding of many substantial communal movements, including the Harmony Society, the Amana Colonies, and the Oneida Perfectionists. The communes of that era were a diverse lot: alongside the many Christianbased ones were enclaves based in Spiritualism (which claims that we can communicate with the dead) and other innovative religious movements. There were also a great many secular communes—socialist and anarchist ones, to name just two of the many varieties. As would be the case in the 1960s era, the communal scene of the nineteenth century was richly varied.

There was no precise beginning to the communes of the 1960s era; they emerged organically from the many communes and communal movements that had gone before. Communes dedicated to radical political activism, to mystical spiritual pursuits, to self-sufficient living, and to liberated sexual behaviors all existed long before the appearance of the 1960s counterculture. But things began to change in the early '60s. Two open-land communes, from which no one would be turned away, had appeared by 1963. Informal communities whose members explored inner space with newly available psychedelic drugs developed on the east and west coasts at about the same time. Interest in Asian religions was beginning to stir among young spiritual seekers in the early '60s, and new ashrams began to show up. In Detroit a commune with its own rock band was combining cuttingedge arts with political activism as early as 1964.

All of these new and tentative probings into innovative social structures were pointing the way toward a new wave of communes by 1965, when Drop City suddenly appeared on the southern Colorado plains and attracted both visitors and publicity. The original Droppers—Clark Richert, Gene Bernofsky, and Jo Ann Bernofsky—were visual artists who met in Lawrence, Kansas, and took their creativity in unconventional directions. Eventually they decided to start their own new civilization, and on a six-acre goat pasture began to build wonderfully unconventional structures—domes constructed from scrap lumber and covered with car tops cut out of junkyard relics. The crazy-quilt domes were pictured in magazines from coast to coast. Something new was clearly going on, whether American society was ready for it or not.

More communes were not far behind. In Southern California the Hog Farm began to take shape when its founders were offered the use of a house and land in return for tending the owner's swine. Later the Hog Farmers took to the road, staging light shows and cultural events; they were catapulted to international renown when they operated as the "please force," feeding the crowds and taking care of the sick and distressed at the Woodstock festival in 1969. Meanwhile, the Diggers were taking shape in San Francisco, practicing "garbage yoga"—gathering food and other necessities of life and providing them, free, to all, and operating several communal residences in the city.

The new culture began to stir in the countryside north of San Francisco about the same time it did in the city. Lou Gottlieb, bassist with the popular folk music group called the Limeliters, bought a 31-acre former chicken farm and apple orchard, and in the spring of 1966 his friends began moving onto the property. Gottlieb refused to turn anyone away, and by the summer of 1967, the Summer of Love, hundreds were living there in makeshift shelters. When local officials directed Gottlieb, as owner, to expel the residents, he tried to deed the land to God. The authorities were not amused, and in due course they bulldozed Morning Star Ranch four times. Many of the open-land communards moved to Bill Wheeler's much larger nearby ranch, where again they lived in simple but happy poverty until the code-enforcement agents brought it all to an end in 1973.

But by then—long before that, really—communes were popping up all over the country. In mid-decade some idealists who were enthralled with B.F. Skinner's utopian novel Walden Two began to experiment with enacting Skinner's vision, and in 1967 some of them moved onto a farm in Virginia that became Twin Oaks, one of the largest countercultural communes and one still thriving more than 40 years later. 1967 also saw the founding of the New Buffalo commune near Taos, where young counterculturists sought self-sufficiency and emulated American Indian culture. Soon Taos became a notable communal magnet, with dozens of such undertakings in the area, and also the scene of some of the worst social conflict surrounding communes, as some of the local residents took offense at what they considered an invasion of undesirables. The New Mexico communal scene eventually waned, although pieces of it have survived, and New Buffalo itself has recently been revived under new leadership.

Meanwhile, another cluster of communes took shape in the late 1960s a hundred miles or so north of Taos, in southern Colorado. Drop City, located just outside Trinidad, was still in its heyday then, but visiting artists Dean and Linda Fleming, who arrived in the area in 1967, wanted a more remote and stable community. They, with Dropper Peter Rabbit, in 1968 ended up founding Libre, where members built domes and other creative structures and pursued their art. Libre, true to its name, was free, but members had to be responsible enough to build their own homes and to survive winters at 9,000 feet. Within a few years around a dozen other communes were in operation within a few miles of Libre; some of them, including Libre, are still very much alive today.

New England also had a strong cluster of communes for several years. In western Massachusetts in the late 1960s a group of young seekers gathered around a young visionary named Michael Metelica, who in turn received guidance from a local trance medium named Ellwood Babbitt. The Brotherhood of the Spirit, as the group was called, quickly grew to perhaps 300 members. Renamed the Renaissance Community, it survived until the 1990s, and some of its descendants continue to live as neighbors. A short distance farther north, in Guilford, Vermont, several veterans of radical journalism dropped out of that frantic scene to settle at Packer Corner, better known (after the title of member Raymond Mungo's bestselling book) as Total Loss Farm. The literary success of Mungo and some of his fellow new settlers helped pay the bills for the farm. Other communes popped up nearby: Red Clover, Montague Farm, Mayday Farm, Tree Frog Farm, and many more.

One important theme of the countercultural 1960s era was spiritual searching. The largest communal manifestation of the quest was what became known as the Jesus Movement, populated by born-again Christians who affected hippie styles (exotic clothing, long hair, disdain for material luxuries). Most conventional churches found the Jesus freaks, as they were known, repulsive, but a few accepted them and, in the spirit of the time, helped them find cheap communal living. One network of Jesus-Movement communes was known as Shiloh; at its peak it had over 175 communal houses as well as extensive property holdings and businesses. It lasted until 1989, when its headquarters land was seized for back taxes. Other Jesus freaks built more stable communities, however. The Children of God, for years the focus of a great deal of controversy for their unconventional sexual practices, among other things, have become a stable network of communes with thousands of members. Meanwhile, the more than 400 members of Jesus People USA, established in Chicago in 1974, continue their common life in an old hotel building.

1965 was a turning point for Asian religions in the United States. Changes in immigration laws in that year meant that Asian spiritual teachers could come to the U.S. much more easily than previously. And come they did, in many cases gathering their followers into intentional communities. Swami A. C. Bhaktivedanta, later known as Prabhupada, arrived from India in 1965 and soon was organizing his followers in the International Society for Krishna Consciousness into urban temple communes and rural farm communities. Arriving in the West from India in 1971 at age 13, the Guru Maharaj Ji attracted thousands of followers to his Divine Light Mission, and many of them lived communally in the movement's ashrams. Similarly, Buddhist teachers from Japan and Korea inspired their followers to live communally in dozens of American cities and in many rural enclaves as well. Sun Myung Moon, whose Unification Church embodied a Korean version of Christianity, made a notable American splash in the 1970s, with many of his followers living in communal homes. A group of American Sufis founded an intentional community in an abandoned Shaker village in New York state.

Independent spiritual teachers whose followers lived communally also abounded. Perhaps the most noted of them was Stephen Gaskin, whose message drew on elements of most of the world's major religious traditions. Gaskin, originally an instructor at San Francisco State College, began delivering his hip spiritual teachings in the city in the late 1960s and soon was attracting crowds of thousands to large ballrooms and dance halls. When, in 1970, he announced that he would go on a speaking tour, his eager adherents asked to go along, and eventually a caravan of perhaps 70 vehicles snaked its way across the United States. In 1971 the tour came to an end in southern Tennessee, where the young settlers founded a commune known simply as the Farm. Until a major reorganization in the early 1980s the Farm strove for self-sufficiency and maintained a completely communal economy, its members working hard, having a lot of babies (delivered by Farm midwives), and, occasionally, enhancing the spiritual search with marijuana and other substances. Sometimes calling themselves "Technicolor Amish," the Farm members at their peak numbered some 1,500. The Farm's population is smaller today, but the Farm is very much alive and well.

As had been the case in earlier generations, not all communes were religious in orientation. Many were dedicated to social change, sometimes involving radical political action. Trans-Love Energies, led by the energetic John Sinclair in Ann Arbor and Detroit, combined radical political activism, advocacy of marijuana, underground newspaper publication, and all kinds of cultural work, including a nationally known rock band, MC5. Taking a slightly different tack, Black Bear Ranch was established in a remote area of northern California as a sort of revolutionary redoubt, a place where firearms practice could be conducted out of view (and earshot) of law enforcement and where draft resisters and other political refugees could hide. It soon shifted into a more typical, and less radical, countercultural lifestyle, and as such it has continued ever since.

A different sort of social change was sought by the members of Kerista, a commune that thrived in San Francisco for more than 20 years. Kerista was a group marriage in which one's sleeping partner changed every night. Members supported the group with a series of businesses, especially a successful computer business in the early days of personal computers. Only in the 1990s did it dissolve amid internal discord.

Yet another theme for many communes was healing. Perhaps the largest of the health-and-wholeness-oriented communities was Synanon, which started in California in 1958 as a drug rehabilitation program. In the late 1960s nonaddicts began to move in, and soon Synanon had many communal homes, with private schools, communal kitchens, and dormitories for members. It all lasted into the early 1990s; the crushing final blow was a huge bill for back taxes that the community couldn't pay.

This quick overview barely skims the surface. No one could possibly list all the communes that existed in the 1960s era, or characterize the bewildering variety of purposes they embodied and members who made it all happen. Populated by hippies, radicals, potheads, witches, organic farmers, mystics, eccentrics, dropouts, sexual liberationists, feminists, bikers, artists, clowns, ascetics, spiritual seekers, runaways, and so many more, uncounted thousands of communes came and went leaving few or no traces. But what is undeniable is that they collectively had a huge impact on the culture of the 1960s era, the greatest period of cultural change in recent history.

Richard Fairfield has preserved priceless snapshots of the emerging countercultural world. The Modern Utopian came on the scene just as it all was heating up, and it (and its short-lived successor, Alternatives Newsmagazine) persevered until Communities magazine came along to take up the baton. We are indebted to Richard for his pioneering work, and this volume presents some of his best vignettes. Enjoy this excursion into a wild and crazy and brilliant time in our recent past. ∎

Timothy Miller is a Professor of Religious Studies at the University of Kansas. He is a historian of intentional communities. Among his books are The 60s Communes *(Syracuse University Press) and* The Hippies and American Values *(University of Tennessee Press).*

THE COMMUNAL ALTERNATIVE

by Herbert A. Otto

[This article, reprinted in The Modern Utopian, *was originally seen in* The Saturday Review, *April 1971 issue. Author Herbert A. Otto was chairman of the National Center for Exploration of Human Potential, La Jolla, and author of* Love Today: A New Exploration *and* Total Sex: Developing Sexual Potential.*]*

OVER THE PAST FEW YEARS, THE COMMUNE MOVEMENT HAS grown at an unprecedented and explosive rate, and there is every indication that this is only the initial phase of a trend that is bound to have far-reaching implications for the function and structure of our contemporary society. Some traditional institutions are already beginning to feel the impact of this explosive growth.

The commune movement has passed far beyond its contemporary origins in hippie tribalism and can no longer be described as a movement for youth exclusively. There are a rapidly growing number of communes composed of persons in their mid-20s to upper 30s. A source at the National Institute of Health has estimated that more than 3,000 urban communes are now in operation. This figure closely corresponds to a recent New York Times inquiry that uncovered 2,000 communes in 34 states.

Certain common viewpoints, almost a Weltanschauung, are shared by members of the contemporary commune movement. First, there is a deep respect and reverence for nature and the ecological system. There is a clear awareness that 70 percent of the population lives on one percent of the land and that this one percent is severely polluted, depressingly ugly, and psychologically overcrowded. Commune members generally believe that a very small but politically influential minority with no respect for the ecological system or the beauty of nature exploits all of the land for its own gain. Surpassing the credo of conservationist organizations, most commune members stress the rehabilitation of all lands and the conservation of all natural resources for the benefit of all the people.

Antiestablishment sentiment is widespread, as is the conviction that a change in social and institutional structures is needed to halt man's dehumanization and to give him an opportunity to develop his potential. Considerable divergence of opinion exists on how social change is to be brought about, but there is general agreement that the commune movement contributes to change by bringing man closer to himself and to his fellow man through love and understanding.

Communes widely accept the idea that life is meant to be fundamentally joyous, and that this is of the essence in doing, and enjoying, what you want to do—"doing your thing." Work in this context becomes a form of joyous self-expression and self-realization. Many commune members believe that existence can be an almost continuous source of joyous affirmation. They usually trace the absence of authentic joy in contemporary society to the confining nature of many of our social institutions, the stifling of spontaneity, and the preponderance of game-playing and of devitalized artificial ways of relating socially.

A strong inner search for the meaning of one's own life, an openness and willingness to communicate and encounter, coupled with a compelling desire for personal growth and development, are hallmarks of the movement. A strong anti-materialistic emphasis prevails; it decries a consumption-oriented society. In many communes, what does not fit into a room becomes commune property. A considerable number of communes aim for the type of self-sufficiency through which they can exist independently of "the system."

There is a strong trend toward ownership of land and houses by communes. Leasing arrangements have not proved satisfactory; in too many instances, landlords have cancelled leases when community pressures were exerted. The non-urban communes I have visited are strongly aware of ecological factors, and, because of this, members usually had consulted with local health authorities concerning the construction and placement of sanitary facilities. Among the urban communes, toilet and bath facilities were in most cases short of the demand.

Marked preferences for vegetarianism and for organically grown food are noticeable in the commune movement. Many individual members also experiment with different health diets. Roughly, 40 percent of the communes I visited were vegetarian; 20 percent served both vegetarian and non-vegetarian meals. The remainder served meat when available—usually two to six times a week. This third group, although not vegetarian by choice, liked their vegetarian meals and expressed very little craving for meat. Whenever possible, communes concentrate on growing and raising their own food. An estimated 60 percent of the urban communes are now purchasing some or most of their supplies from health food stores or similar sources.

Not surprisingly, the commune has become the repository of repressed man's erotic fantasy. I was continuously told that visitors who come not to learn and understand but to peek and ogle invariably ask two questions: "Who sleeps with whom?" and "Do you have group sex?" There appears to be much fantasizing by outsiders about the sex life in communes.

Although there is considerable sexual permissiveness, I found a high degree of pairing with a strong tendency toward interpersonal commitment in a continuing relationship. Nudism is casual and accepted, as is the development of a healthy sensuality, and natural childbirth, preferably within the commune, is encouraged. Group sex involving the whole commune occurs quite rarely, although there may be sexual experimentation involving two or more couples or combinations.

The research team of Larry and Joan Constantine has studied multilateral (group) marriage for the past three years. They have written and published more studies in this area than other behavioral scientists, but have found only one commune practicing group marriage. Most likely, there are others. About two dozen independent families are known to be engaged in multilateral marriage, taking as their model Bob Rimmer's novel Proposition 31, which presents a case for group marriage. Many others prefer to keep their arrangement totally secret for fear of reprisals. According to an article by the Constantines entitled "Personal Growth in Multiple Marriages," failure rate is better than one out of two, because "group marriage is a marathon that does not end—it takes a real commitment to genuine, substantial, and unrelenting personal growth to really make it function and work."

Interest in spiritual development is a dominant theme in most communes. Study of and acquaintance with Eastern and Western mystics and religious philosophies is widespread. Religiosity and denominationalism were seldom encountered. On the other hand, I was struck by the deep commitment to spiritual search of so many members in all the communes I visited. Many members were trying different forms of meditation, and books on Eastern religions and mysticism were prominent on shelves.

I find that although there is some overlapping of functions and categories, a number of distinct types of communes can be recognized and are found in operation:

The Agricultural Subsistence Commune
The main thrust is to farm or till the soil (mostly organic farming) so that the land will provide most, if not all, needs and make the commune independent and self-supporting. Many of these communes cultivate such specialized crops as organically grown grain, vegetables, and other produce, which are then sold to health food stores, health food wholesalers, or supermarkets.

The Nature Commune
Emphasis is on supporting the ecological system and on the enjoyment of nature. Buildings and gardening or farming plots are designed to fit into the landscape to preserve its natural beauty. Everyone "does his own thing," and economic support for subsistence usually comes from such varied sources as sale of produce and handicrafts, wages from part-time work, welfare support, etc.

The Craft Commune
One or several crafts, such as weaving, pottery making, or carpentry (including

construction or work on buildings outside the commune), occupy the interest of members. They often spend considerable blocks of time enjoying the exercise of their craft with the income contributed to the commune. Many of the craft communes sell directly to the consumer as a result of local regional or sometimes national advertisements and publicity. Profit margins vary since the vast majority of such communes do not subscribe to the amassing of profits as the primary aim of their enterprise. Included in this category are the multimedia communes that specialize in light shows, videotape, and filmmaking.

The Spiritual Mystical Commune

The ongoing spiritual development of members is recognized to be of primary importance. There may be adherence to a religious system, such as Buddhism, Sufism, or Zen, and a teacher or guru may be involved. Studies of various texts and mystical works, use of rituals, a number of forms of meditation (such as transcendental meditation), and spontaneous spiritual celebrations play key roles in the life of the commune. Several of these communes also describe themselves as Christian and have a strong spiritual, but not denominational, emphasis.

The Denominational Commune

There is a religious emphasis with membership restricted to those of a particular denomination.

The Church-sponsored Commune

Such a commune may be originated or sponsored by a church. There is usually a religious emphasis, but denominationalism is not stressed.

The Political Commune

Members subscribe to or share a common ideology. They may identify themselves as anarchists, socialists, pacifists, etc. Emphasis is on the communal living experience with others sharing the same viewpoint. This is seen as fostering the individuals' political development. The commune is rarely engaged in direct social action in opposition to the Establishment.

The Political Action Commune

Members are committed and practicing political activists (or activists in training) for the purpose of changing the social system. Classes are conducted, strategy formulated and carried out. The commune may be identified with a minority cause or be interested in organizing an industry, community, or ghetto neighborhood. It often identifies itself by the single word "revolutionary."

The Service Commune

The main goal is social service. Emphasis is on organizing communities, helping people to plan and carry out community projects, offering professional or case-aid services, etc. Some of these communes include members from the helping professions. There are several such communes in the Philadelphia and New York ghettos; another example is the Federation of Communities, which services several locations in the Appalachians.

The Art Commune

Artists from different fields or the same field come together to share in the stimulating climate of communal artistic creativity. As compared with the craft commune, members of the art commune are often painters, sculptors or poets, who usually sell their art works independently rather than collectively. There are poetry and theater communes in Berkeley and San Francisco.

The Teaching Commune

Emphasis is on training and developing people who are able both to live and to teach others according to a particular system of techniques and methods. Communes whose purpose or mainstay is to conduct a school or schools also fall into this category.

The Group Marriage Commune

Although members may be given the freedom to join in the group marriage or not, the practice of group marriage plays an important and often central role in the life of the commune. All adults are considered to be parents of the members' children.

The Homosexual Commune

Currently found in large urban areas, with admission restricted to homophiles. The aim of these communes is to afford individuals who share a common way of life an opportunity to live and communicate together and to benefit from the economies of a communal living arrangement. Some of the communes subscribe to the principle of the homophile liberation movement.

The Growth-centered Commune

The main focus is on helping members to grow as persons, to actualize their potential. There are ongoing group sessions; sometimes professionals are asked to seek out new experiences and methods designed to develop the potentialities of its members.

The Mobile Gypsy Commune

This is a caravan, usually on the move. Cars, buses, and trucks provide both transportation and living quarters. Members usually include artists, a rock group, or light-show staff. The mobile commune often obtains contributions from "happenings" or performances given in communities or on college campuses.

The Street, or Neighborhood, Commune

Several of these communes often are on the same street or in the same neighborhood. Ownership of property is in the hands of commune members or friendly and sympathetic neighbors. Basically the idea is of a free enclave or free community.

Among the major problems faced by all communes are those involving authority and structure. Ideally, there is no one telling anyone else what to do; directions are given by those best qualified to do the job. In practice, strong personalities in the communes assume responsibility for what happens and there is a tendency toward the emergence of mother and father figures. There is, however, a clear awareness of this problem and continuing efforts toward resolution. At present, opposition to any form of structure, including organizational structure, is still so strong that communes have found it almost impossible to cooperate with each other in joint undertakings of a major nature. Interestingly enough, communes with transcendent or spiritual values are the most stable and have the highest survival quotient. It is my conclusion that the weekly or periodic meetings of all commune members, which are often run as encounter groups, have a limited effectiveness in the resolution of interpersonal problems and issues. Although trained encounter leaders may be present as facilitators, their effectiveness is often considerably curtailed due to their own deep involvement in the issues that are the subject of confrontation.

It is difficult to determine to what extent narcotics represent a problem for communes precisely because their consumption is as casual, widespread, and accepted as is the downing of alcoholic beverages in the business community. Marijuana and hashish are widely enjoyed, while use of such hard drugs as heroin is seldom encountered, especially in the non-urban communes. In a number of communes where drug use was extensive, I noticed a general air of lassitude and a lack of vitality. I also had the distinct impression that "dropping acid" (LSD) was on the decline; among commune members there seemed to be a general awareness of the danger of "speed," or methedrine. A number of communes are totally opposed to the use of narcotics, especially those with members who were former drug addicts. In most communes the subject of drugs periodically comes up for discussion so that changes in the viewpoint of the commune flow from the experience of the members. Similarly, problems of sexual possessiveness and jealousy appear to be less critical and are also handled by open group discussion. I noticed a tendency toward the maintenance of traditional sex roles, with the women doing the cooking and sewing, the men cutting lumber, etc. Upon questioning this, I repeatedly received the same answer: "Everyone does what they enjoy doing."

Another major problem in most communes is overcrowding and the consequent lack of privacy and alone time. Rarely does a member enjoy the opportunity of having a room to himself for any length of time. The common practice is to walk off into the woods or fields, but this is an inadequate substitute for real privacy. Community relations remains a major and critical problem since many communes are "hassled" by authorities or are located amid unfriendly neighbors. As one member described it, the emotional climate in a hassled commune is "full of not-so-good vibes—you don't know what they will try next, and you keep looking over your shoulder. That takes energy." Today's commune members generally have a clear awareness of the importance of establishing good community relations.

Many of the communes that have got underway this past year or are now being organized are beginning on a sound financial basis. This trend appears to be related to the strong influx of people in their mid-20s, early or mid-30s, and beyond. These individuals have financial reserves or savings and are, for the most part, successful professionals and businessmen with families.

An unprecedented number of people want to join communes. In all but a few instances, I was asked to conceal the name and location of the commune to make identification impossible. "We don't know what to do with all the people who come knocking on our door now," I was told repeatedly. In every commune, I heard of people who had recently left either to start a new commune or to join in the founding of one.

There is considerable mobility in communes, which is symptomatic of an epidemic wanderlust and search. If people have to leave for any reason, once they have been exposed to communal living, they tend to return. They like the deep involvement with others in a climate of freedom, openness, and commitment. This feeling of belonging has been described as both a "new tribalism" and a "new sense of brotherhood." One young woman with whom I spoke had this to say about her commune experience: "When a white man walks into a room full of other whites, he doesn't feel he is among brothers like the black man does. In the communes, we are now beginning to feel that man has many brothers. There is a new sense of honesty. You can say things to each other and share things like you never could in the family. I never had so much love in my whole life—not even in my own family." She also indicated, however, that commune living is highly intense and possibly not for everyone: "In the commune, there is nothing you can hide. Some people can't take it. They get sick or they leave."

It would be a mistake to characterize the commune movement as a collection of dropouts who are content to exist like lilies in the field. A considerable number of successful people from all walks of life are now involved; they have merely shifted their sphere of interest and the nature of their creative contribution. We are dealing with a massive awakening of the awareness that life holds multiple options other than going from school to job to retirement. The commune movement has opened a new and wide range of alternative lifestyles and offers another frontier to those who have the courage for adventure. It is the test tube for the growth of a new type of social relatedness, for the development of an organization having a structure that appears, disappears, and reappears as it chooses and as it is needed. Communes may well serve as a laboratory for the study of the processes involved in the regeneration of our social institutions. They have become the symbol of man's new freedom to explore alternative lifestyles and to develop deep and fulfilling human relationships through the rebirth and extension of our capacity for familiar togetherness. ■

back to
the land

CHAPTER 1

ARE COUNTRY COMMUNES ESCAPIST?

by Mason Dixon

"There is no escape—either into rural communes or existential mysticism—from this dynamic of world confrontation."   *—Tom Hayden in Ramparts*

I'VE HEARD IT ALL BEFORE, AND HAYDEN'S LANGUAGE IS TYPI-cal—communes are escapist, **A** political cop-out. As one friend succinctly put it when I told him I was moving to B.C. [British Columbia]: "What you are doing is a purely private act without interesting social consequences."

After a year and a half in the bush, Mr. Hayden, et al., I beg to disagree.

To be sure, communes are escapist, in the sense that their participants are escaping a polluted and pathological urban environment. But, it is my thesis that a return to the land does not necessarily mean turning our backs on the North American political landscape. Rural communes do and will have a role in proto- and post-evolutionary North America.

In the first place, someone is going to have to feed the cities now, and in the future. And quality of food is an important factor in the quality of life overall. By next summer we hope to be able to ship free vegetables to Vancouver to be distributed by YIPPIE! or the VLF. Good spuds are not as spectacular as Molotov cocktails, perhaps, but one does what one can.

Second, a hefty percentage of North America's population still remains in rural areas where reaction to any sort of revolution is most severe. (As an old Nebraska boy, I know whereof I speak.) It is more difficult to categorically censor hippies if you have to relate to them every day at the store, pub, or gas station, than if you merely read about their antics in Life or the Province.

So, if heads on the land are responsible to their environment and its inhabitants (and not all of them are), then potential opponents at the barricades may have second thoughts.

Thirdly, heads in the backcountry can and should be organizing their areas. In our valley, for instance, B.C. Hydro [energy company] planned to spray 2, 4-D [herbicide related to Agent Orange] along its tower right-of-way. But someone axed their defoliant stockpiles one night, and several days later when they tried to bring more in, several ranchers met the Hydrochoppers with shotguns, and refused to allow storage of the stuff on their land.

We seized upon this natural issue and printed a protest letter which we distributed up and down the valley, pointing out that the spraying demonstrated ecological irresponsibility, and was intended to get more profits to Hydro stockholders, at the expense of whoever happened to live along the transmission lines. Hydro finally dropped the spraying idea in our vicinity, grumbling about "too many angry farmers."

Keep in mind, too, that most rural inhabitants seem to have a streak of stubborn individuality and dislike of restraint that rivals our own. (After all, I was a Goldwater supporter in '64 for much the same reason.)

But I know the mental set that Hayden is talking about—the beautiful dream of moving into the promised land with a few beautiful people, chanting "OM" over the garden, and everything's gonna turn out all right.

Wrong. I'm all for good vibes, but if you think they're going to stop Hydro's D-9s from plowing up your greens about the time you're 60 and looking forward to a bucolic organic old age, brothers, forget it.

More than any place, B.C. is a heavy land-rape scene. And they think BIG. I've talked to too many old-timers who have found themselves in housing developments because Hydro wanted to build dams on their traplines or Cominco [mining company] found a nice copper deposit.

There is NO place, repeat, NO place, you can go and be assured of living in peace. Lest we forget, on our own farm there are four high-voltage power lines buzzing across our land to remind us that this is not the best of all possible continents.

I don't know, maybe it was the old civics bullshit about "responsible citizenship" being drilled so deep, but I still feel a responsibility to my community, and not just the hip one, either.

Anyway, Hayden, we're here, we're staying, and one of these days you may even be glad. Right? ∎

COLD MOUNTAIN FARM
by Richard Fairfield

IN JULY 1967, I CAME ACROSS THE FOLLOWING NEWS ITEM IN the East Village Other, one of the first underground newspapers:

A small group of Lower East Side people have moved to the country, both to get away from the City and to provide free, organically-grown food for the East Side Community. Operating now with a nucleus of six, Cold Mountain Farm (RFD 1, Hobart, New York) is making great progress, but needs more people willing to work.

The farm covers 400 acres of black, rich valley land, which has always been farmed organically. Local farmers, interested to see young city folks getting together to work, have been assisting by giving instruction and providing some equipment.

Living off the land, the Cold Mountain people are putting together macrobiotic meals from local roots and flowers. They live in a twelve-room house, provided with fresh spring water and free electricity. Their plans envision a larger, self-sufficient community complete with school for the kids.

That was the first and last time I heard of Cold Mountain Farm until a friend of mine, Elaine, handed me a copy of a long paper written by Joyce Gardiner. The paper was then edited and published in The Modern Utopian magazine vol. 2, no. 6, Sept. 1968, as follows:

Given: 450 acres of land—12 usable for farming or pasture, the remainder being old, neglected apple orchards (also pear, plum, and cherry trees) and young woods, in a mountainous, upstate New York dairy-farming area. A beautiful piece of land, with three running streams in the springtime, but only one good spring for water in the summer close to the five-bedroom house. The farm is one mile off the main road, at the end of a rugged dirt road, a mile from the closest neighbor. There is no rent, no electricity, no telephone, and to acquire any of these would be extremely costly.

The Group: Anarchists. Mostly in their 20s with children under 6. A fluctuating population, up to 30. About four couples and one or two single people consider this home. Mostly former residents of NYC, but some from other parts of the East Coast. Interrelationships have existed for as long as five years.

History: Goes back two and a half years, to NYC, where a communal loft once existed, with shared dinners and other occasions. Or back three years, when at least two families shared an apartment together for a few months. Or to last spring and summer, when a group of NYC anarchists used half an acre of a friend's land to farm on weekends.

More concretely, June 1966, to a Community Conference at the School of Living in Heathcote, MD, out of which emerged a new community—Sunrise Hill—at Conway, Mass. At least one person, loosely connected with NYC anarchists, went to live there.

The rest of us continued to farm our friend's land on weekends during the summer, meeting at least once a month at different places in the country during the winter—living together for a few days, getting to know one another better, and making plans to start our own farm the following spring. Some people from Sunrise Hill also attended these meetings.

We finally located this place through a friend. About that time, Sunrise Hill was suffering its final collapse due to internal conflicts and four people from there eventually would join us.

On to the Land

Starting a community farm is an incredibly difficult thing. We didn't fully realize this when we began. Setting up a new farm—or rather, rehabilitating an old and neglected one—was at least a season's work. Not to mention compensating for the work which should have been done the previous autumn.

It was still cold, there was occasional snow, the house was difficult to heat, and no one was prepared to move in. The dirt road was all but impassable, we walked the mile through snow, and later mud, carrying babies, supplies, bedding, etc.

Meanwhile we had to find a tractor immediately to haul manure for compost heaps. They should have been started the year before as they require three months' time to rot properly and we wanted to farm organically. We'd have to prune the neglected fruit trees within a month, since pruning too late in the season would shock them.

On the many rainy days we had to make the house livable: build shelves, worktable, bookshelves, a tool shed, a mailbox; install a sink; acquire tools and materials. Somehow, whatever needed to be done, there was always someone who knew how to do it or who was willing to find out how. But with each person having some particular responsibility upon himself there wasn't time to work on group projects.

Well, we had a farm, didn't we? All we had to do was go there when it got nice and warm, plow the land, plant our seed, and wait for the vegetables to come. We didn't even have to pay any rent! It was so simple. No rush to get out there while it was still so cold.

Consequently, the farm was completely deserted until the end of April. Then news got out fast (we couldn't help but brag a little), and we found we had hundreds of friends who wanted to "come to the country." So we had to bite our tongues and violate all the laws of Lower East Side hospitality to avoid creating a youth hostel or country resort. We lost a lot of friends that way.

Meanwhile, in NYC, an infinite number of conflicts existed growing out of two difficult years of coexistence, trying to work out an ideology based on anarchism-community-ecology-technology in an environment that presented a constant contradiction to it.

We had discouraged the city people. No one came. The land cried out to be tended, but people were preoccupied with their own personal grievances. The farm was all but deserted. The work fell entirely on the shoulders of a few people. Without telephone and often without car, we waited daily for friends and supplies to show up, waiting for reinforcements. Finally three friends arrived from Conway [Massachusetts] reassuringly bringing all their worldly goods. The man started out at once, hooking up running water in the house, pruning some apple trees, then driving to a nearby town without a license or proper registration and spending three days in jail. Soon he bought us a much-needed tractor. It was precisely this tractor (to this day still only half paid for) which shuttled up and down the one-mile dirt road, hauling cow shit (from neighboring farmers, who proved surprisingly friendly) and transporting little children to the nearby town and then, as the time to plow grew nigh, flatly refused to budge.

There was absolutely nothing anyone could do. We had to wait for our friend from Florida to return. He was our only mechanic. Days passed and finally a few people started digging their own gardens, such a pathetic task for a farm that hoped to support some 30 people and then give out free food in the city.

But all this time there were small compensations. We had an opportunity now to explore this incredible land, watch the seasons change, see the snow melt and trees slowly push forth buds, see birds moving in and laying eggs; spy on porcupines each night loudly chomping on the house, make friends with cows and four wild horses grazing on neighboring fields, start to know one another in that unique way that comes only from living together.

Tribal Feelings

Now a few more old friends began to arrive. There was an incredible feeling of warmth, of family. We were becoming a tribe. There were long, good discussions around the fire, into the night. Slowly, things were beginning to take shape. In those days I loved to look into the "community room" and see a bunch of people sprawled out on cushions around the floor, all so brown, their bodies so well-developed, their faces relaxed, naked or wearing clothes often of their own making. You could always spot someone from the city by the whiteness of their flesh, the tenseness of their body.

It was my dream and certainly no one openly disagreed with me to become a tribe, a family of "incestuous brothers and sisters." Unfortunately, living so close, we probably made love less than when we lived in separate apartments in the city. And there was so much fear and tension in the air about potential affairs that actual lovemaking all too seldom took place, and even physical contact became a rare thing. Even though we created our own environment at the farm, we still carried with us the repressions of the old environment, in our bodies and our minds.

While others were not actually opposed to these ideas, most people didn't feel quite ready for them, and certainly no one else bespoke the same vision. If we could find a form by which our visions could be shared...

Incredible Tractor

Waiting for the tractor to be fixed (it took about a week and a half of hard labor), living our usual lives, making our own bread and yogurt, etc., we spoke to a nearby farmer and learned of a barn full of manure, which he paid men to haul away for him. We offered to do it for him free, in exchange for manure to use as compost. He was so overjoyed that he offered to come up and plow our land in exchange for our labor. We thought he was joking, but a couple days later we heard a loud and unfamiliar motor coming up the hill, and there was that huge, incredible tractor. "Well, where do you want it?" And that's how we got six acres of land plowed and harrowed (later, we would plow a couple more acres ourselves). A couple of days later we got our own tractor fixed in order to start hauling manure and planting at a furious pace, trying to get the crops in before it was too late. We were already at least a week behind most everyone else in the area... in a place with a very short growing season.

These people were so overwhelmingly happy to finally have the tractor, after weeks of frustrated waiting and digging by hand, that one person actually planted some 40 mounds of zucchini and 80 mounds of acorn squash and several rows of corn in one day, by hand! Then he devised a method whereby he could dig five furrows at a time by building a drag with teeth for the tractor and installing three women as weights on the drag, where they could drop onion sets into the rows. That last part didn't work so well (all the onion sets had to be spaced again, by hand), but nonetheless by the time the other folks got home about a week later, close to an acre of land had been planted.

Now that there were more of us, we were not so close. There was no real sense of community between us. There was good feeling, but no center, no clear-cut purpose. Some of the men felt an unfulfilled need to fight. The women felt an unfulfilled need to love.

About this time we undertook or were overtaken by what I consider one of our most challenging feats: trying to assimilate a young lawyer and his family, including two girls ages four and six. Many a group meeting centered around the problem of "the kids." Because they were breaking out of a sick environment, their parents felt they needed a maximum of patience and love and understanding. Others felt they needed simply to be treated as human beings and that their mother should not repress the anger and frustration which she obviously felt.

35

Most of us felt we should in fact try to let them work through their hang-ups and hopefully eventually come out the other side. Let them yell "penis" and "vagina" at the top of their lungs. Let them throw Raggedy Ann into the cellar and elaborate upon her tortures while chanting "No, you can't come out of the cellar!" all day long. But what no one seemed to be able to endure were the howls and wails which rose from the lungs of one sister after the other, particularly on rainy days, of which there were many, when we were all locked up with them in the house all day long.

Apparently we just weren't strong enough nor healthy enough ourselves to be able to cope with these children. And their parents, who had had such great hopes of finding in us a healthy environment, soon had to build their own shelter in order to remove themselves from our environment.

By this time the house had become so generally unbearable that everyone else as well had decided to move out. Just before then, there had been 20 adults and 10 children living so close together in that house, with only three or four adults and one child sleeping outside. It seemed absurd to try to keep the house clean (anarchism does not necessarily mean chaos). And the flies were so bad that if we hung five strips of flypaper fresh each day in each room, by evening they were dripping with puddles of gooey flies. It was just barely possible to exist in the midst of all these copulating multitudes. (We didn't like the idea of using poison sprays, with all the cats and babies.) And so, in a burst of desperation to escape the noise, children, chaos, flies, tension… everybody dropped everything and for a few days did nothing but work on their own shelters. The house was almost deserted.

People who get into community too often forget about the importance of solitude. And we were lucky enough to have plenty of land so that everyone could have their own shelter. But personal possessions (especially kitchen stuff), which had originally been pooled with a great sense of communal enthusiasm, were righteously carted off to their owners' shelters.

Hostile Outsiders

About this time we started coming into conflict with the outside world. Ever since it got warm, we had all been walking around more or less nude most of the time. Unfortunately, we had to discontinue this most pleasant practice when neighbors started to mention casually that they could "see everything" from their property on the hill and that "people were talking." Our local reputation was getting progressively worse. There were too many articles in the mass media about hippies, often loosely connected with legalizing marijuana. The local people, who had originally just thought of us as "strange" and had then begun to accept us as old-fashioned organic farmers, could now call us "hippies" and forbid their kids to have anything to do with ours.

The local sheriff began to take an interest in us. Whenever we went into town we were stopped by the cops. And a friendly gas station attendant told us the highway patrol had been told to watch us. It was easy to be paranoid, to imagine their trying to take our kids away for nudity. It was terrible to compromise, but most of us began to wear clothes again. That was a great loss.

I suppose our first and worst economic argument was whether or not to buy chickens. At first, it was incredible how little a problem money had been. Whoever came just threw in whatever they had—$100 or $200 perhaps—and we'd live off that until someone got a tax return, a welfare check, or whatever. We never did spend more than $25 a week on food even when there were 30 people. But the chicken crisis involved all sorts of things. Did we eat the eggs (wasn't wheat germ good enough)? Was it morally right to take eggs from chickens; wasn't it cruel to keep chickens caged—but if we didn't cage them how would we keep them out of the garden? Were we really saving money on eggs, if we had to spend money on the chickens, chicken wire, and all kinds of feed? Who was going to plant an acre of millet and an acre of corn to feed them? Who would build the chicken coop? This was the first time I remember hearing anyone say, "Well, I won't give any money for chickens," using money as a weapon, a personal source of power. And it wasn't long before money again became a personal possession.

Bad Times

I liked the young lawyer and his wife because they often spoke at meetings on a personal level, about how they felt about things, while most of our people maintained a kind of cold objectivity, only discussing things external to themselves. It was this lack of "feeling" which brought the lawyer to say that Cold Mountain was certainly an apt name for the place. And his wife complained, not unjustly, that there was not enough making of music, not enough dancing, and she felt her joy was being stifled here.

We seemed to have reached an all-time low. We had passed the summer solstice. Our money was all but depleted. We could work at haying for local farmers, but $1 an hour wasn't a hell of a lot. Until now we seemed to have been subsisting mostly on enthusiasm. Now it was hot and even our enthusiasm was gone. There was a general feeling of emptiness. Times were very bad, but we tried to hold on until the times were more favorable.

We decided to limit ourselves to just a few staples (rice, oil, powdered milk, soy sauce, flour, salt, soybeans, brewer's yeast, molasses, grass—always purchased in huge quantities to save money) and whatever we could get from our environment at this time of year: dandelion greens, wintergreen, burdock root and, in a little while, fresh strawberries, rhubarb, and wild leeks. And we'd soon be getting edible weeds from the garden: milkweed, sorrel, lamb's-quarters. And then we would discover violet leaves, for salads. Still later, there would be mushrooms, raspberries, currants, and blackberries; wild mint, thyme, and oregano; green apples, pears and plums, and by then we would be getting at least zucchini, peas, and baby onions from the garden.

Then, one morning, someone took the shotgun and killed a groundhog. We'd been talking about hunting for a long time, but most of us were vegetarians and meat was a rare sight in these parts (the hunter himself hadn't eaten meat for the last two years!). But that night he cooked up a fine groundhog stew. Which he ate. And that big pot of stew sat on the stove and people thought about it and talked about it and went to bed without dinner. In the middle of the night a couple of us woke up and had a little. Next day some of us had some for lunch. Only four people remained staunch in their vegetarianism, and mostly they didn't condemn the rest. Each of us worked it out in our own way.

Still, the diet wasn't satisfying. Subsistence living was one thing, but we all felt damned hungry. We called a meeting and decided this had a great deal to do with the cooking, which, until then, had been just a matter of chance impulse, so that the task usually fell into the hands of the same people every day. Their boredom with cooking showed up in the quality of their meals. It seemed reasonable enough that if two different people were responsible for the kitchen each day there would be more interest and variety in cooking, the house would be kept neater and more organized, and it would leave the other people free to concentrate completely on the garden or whatever. At that time we had 14 adults, so it was pleasant enough to know you only had to cook and clean one day per week.

It's amazing how much this helped. We'd all begun to grow so discouraged with each other and the mess we were living in. We all felt like pigs and everyone blamed the next person. Our morale was sinking fast, the kids were screaming, and we were at each other's throats. Now suddenly the house was clean—spick and span, almost.

We felt we had been reborn. We'd stuck it out through hard times and now virtue had its reward.

At that time, four Puerto Rican friends from the city joined us. They emanated new energy and worked hard. And they had a certain Revolutionary spirit which none of us quite had. One would say, "Communism and capitalism they are both no good. But if I had something like this farm to fight for—why, I would give my life for it." At night you could hear the guitars and there were big fires, and dancing and singing. The hardest work was over. All we had to do now was weed and mulch. Now we had time to make music.

About this time, an article appeared about us in the East Village Other without our knowledge or consent claiming we needed people to help out on the farm (as if we hadn't had enough trouble discouraging people we knew from coming up!). And we were soon flooded with letters, and every two or three days a new visitor would arrive. It created terrible tensions to have to ask them to leave, to tell them it was all a mistake. And then a couple of people we did know arrived and announced their intention to move in. Some of us didn't want to live with these people, while others either wanted them to stay or felt we didn't have any right to ask them to leave. We had decided a long time ago that if this happened, each person in the community would just do as he felt best, and there would be no group decisions.

But how can you ask someone that you know to leave particularly when they've brought all their things and say they have no place else to go? I think this must be a dilemma suffered by all communities. Certainly my way of dealing with it (absolute frank honesty) was far from effective. They just stayed. And stayed. And gradually, for this reason and others, the warmth and trust and sharing between us began to die. Whatever tribal or family feelings we had had were gone.

We weren't ready to define who we were; we certainly weren't prepared to define who we weren't—it was still just a matter of intuition. We had come together for various reasons not overtly for a common idea or ideal, but primarily because there was land and there was supposed to be a "community." Even in the original community there were people who thought of themselves (and their reason for being here) as being primarily communitarians, or primarily farmers and back-to-the-soil revolutionaries, or primarily political revolutionaries (anarchists) or "tao-archists" for whom farming and community was just one integral part of the totality, or just plain hermits who wanted to live in the woods. All of these different people managed to work together side by side for a while, but the fact was that there was really no shared vision.

And then still more people arrived—people we had all been looking forward to seeing. And the house was very full. And there was a lot of confusion. And it was very difficult to cook for that many people. Again, tensions began to mount. There was so little money, and now there were three or four pregnant women here, and one or two nursing mothers. Their dietary needs were very specific and important, and the community was unable to fulfill them. They were forced to fall back on their own resources. In similar ways, one began to feel they couldn't trust the community to meet their needs, to take care of them in an emergency. There was a feeling of general malaise. The garden wasn't being weeded. The grass was growing higher and higher. Everyone felt as if everyone else was irresponsible.

In a community, things happen on such a large scale that you need the co-operation of other people in order to accomplish almost anything. But now one began to feel as if it was easier to do a thing by oneself. It was hot. Laziness had set in, very firmly. The word "failure" was being tossed around a lot. People began to just look after themselves and to talk as if the only reason they were here was the land. The City suddenly seemed to hold a great attraction, and whenever there was a car going in it would be filled to capacity. The young lawyer and his family finally left, quietly.

There was one ray of light in these somber times. A new couple arrived, to stay. Nobody knew them when they came, but everyone liked them at once. They brought new energies with them and they lifted our spirits. Slowly, all the stragglers had left—empty people who had come to fill themselves, sapping our energies, needing to be taken care of and giving nothing at all—and now there were only between four and six couples and a few single people left.

Winter Approaches

So we all lived together, peaceably enough, until one night it was very, very cold, and wet and windy, and we could smell the coming of autumn. Then it was time to begin thinking about what we'd be doing in the winter—staying here or moving on—and making plans accordingly. Mostly we had to consider the hardship of a very cold winter, no gas or electricity, a one-mile dirt road, which would probably be inaccessible because of heavy snow (even during the summer, only jeeps and four-wheel-drive cars and trucks could climb that road).

There were five couples, three of the women were pregnant, and a fourth was nursing. The babies were due in October, November, and February. The first two couples wanted to deliver their own but not take the chance of doing it here. A single girl was already building a small stone house for the winter. Another man intended to live in the big house for the winter. Almost all hoped to be here early next spring. By this time, two couples and a girl had moved entirely into their own shelters.

The communal garden was a monstrous failure. After the original enthusiasm of planting, hardly anyone cared enough to weed the rows. (Of course, the huge amount of rain this year retarded the growth of the crops and caused the weeds to grow like crazy! And six acres is a hell of a lot of land to weed by hand. If we try again next year, we'll certainly have to get a cultivator.) At least two acres of garden were lost, either because they weren't weeded adequately, or because they were planted too late and the growing season was too short, or because there wasn't enough sun and there was too much rain, or because of the aphids, or the potato blight....

We didn't become new people, we just became physically healthy people. We didn't find a way of sharing our visions (in fact, we didn't even have a conscious understanding of the need for such a thing), and we didn't have a shared vision to bring us and hold us together.

We had plowed and begun to plant the earth, but we had not pierced our own ego skins. Decay and stagnation had already set in. I went into the woods to meditate. The woods explained: it was high time we plowed the earth of this community. We must apply the blade to ourselves and cut back the outer skin to expose the pulsing flesh.

And then we must harrow and pulverize the outer skin and use our egos for compost. Then, in the new flesh, we must plant the seeds of the people we wish to become.

The few of us who remained at the farm were doing fairly well, enjoying the fruits of our labors in gobbling up the zucchini, baby onions, carrots and parsnips; savoring the apples, pears and plums; gathering myriad blackberries, chokecherries and gooseberries for preserves; eating delicious brown fertile eggs.

Sandy had been feeling unusually weak. He rested and fasted but only grew worse and Louise took him to the doctor and he was hospitalized with hepatitis. A few days later Sue Ellen and Dan complained of similar symptoms, Dan also going to the hospital.

The health inspector was obviously appalled by the way we lived, but was quieted down by our landlord (who has some monied influence in the area), who claimed we were just a summer camp.

Neighbors who had been our friends now avoided us. All their secret thoughts about how unclean we were could now be vindicated.

After a couple of weeks more on the farm, I too succumbed and took a bus back to New York. In the city our monstrous failure was greeted with "I told you so" and "I'm not surprised." Being a lone individual suddenly and having to live on concrete, in filth, almost no sunlight, trees, or earth I was completely shattered.

I was in bed with the flu when I first met Joyce. She and Elaine barged into my room, insisting on talking with me. Joyce was angry about the editing job; like most budding young authors, she didn't want one precious word deleted without her permission. Elaine disclaimed any responsibility for encouraging me to print the paper. And I, although the editing had been done by other staff members, reluctantly took the blame as publisher. In order to make amends I encouraged Joyce to write any additions or changes, which I would then publish in the next issue. She agreed and after editing and checking with her for approval, the following material appeared in the magazine (The Modern Utopian, vol. 3, no. 2, spring 1969).

The foregoing article on Cold Mountain was extremely condensed from a much longer article. It is impossible to give a truly fair description of community life in just a few pages. Consequently, the majority of space was devoted to the problems we suffered. Fortunately, our problems did not destroy us and many of the people who lived at Cold Mountain are still living together at a community in Vermont and elsewhere.

The community in (Southern) Vermont is a lot like Cold Mountain—particularly in how beautiful it is and how seldom its members ever see that beauty. Our heads are so full of our communities' shortcomings that we do not verbally express what our bodies show: the goodness of this way of life, sharing together, and being close to the land.

Now, while it is still fresh in my mind, is the time to express the beauty of our life. The way we all work and live together without any power or authority structure, simply following our own consciousness of what should be done each day. (Of course, some things have to be more structured than others—milking the cow, for example.) The way that children are cared for, with the men also caring for them. The way that tasks and chores are taken on by people, according to inclination rather than sex, men cooking, women chopping wood if that was what they wanted to do or what had to be done. And nudity, bodies of all shapes, readily accepted as part of nature. And almost no clash of egos.

And the way the kids play together sharing ecstatic joyful moments! Not that they don't fight or cry—but immediately on the surface and not repressed and distorted, so they love with as much confidence and fearless energy as they hate, they create as fiercely and passionately as they destroy, and they relax as magnificently and totally as they rebel.

And how seldom, with so many people living so close (about a dozen people in a 10-room house), anyone ever argues or bickers, except for real explosions of anger over real and immediate things—anger which clears the air and refreshens.

There seems to be less sexual uptightness here. You can touch anybody and speak intimately with them without feeling the force of tremendous psychic tensions from their spouse or anyone else.

This is a wealthy community. Woody provides the money for whatever is "necessary," though it is desirable that soon the community be self-supporting. The standard of living these people set for themselves is almost identical to Cold Mountain, except here are greater facilities for cleanliness (a toilet, warm running water, a tub) and sanitation (a refrigerator, big sinks for washing clothes and an old-fashioned wringer) and warmth (two huge wood-burning stoves, a chain saw). Also, there is electricity, although it's only used for two big lamps—one in the kitchen and one in the reading room.

It takes a little bit of humility to realize that, at least at first, no aspect of farming is likely to be easy for most people. We still have to establish certain rhythms with the seasons and the land. Once you're in a place you know that in the spring you'll plant, in the fall you'll harvest, and during the summer and winter you'll have time for yourself and friends. But if you're just moving into a new place, then everything must be done at once, and at least in the first year there is very little hope of having anything but chaos. If only we'd have expected that before we began, then it wouldn't have upset us so much.

Here there are also the same kinds of problems as at Cold Mountain, like the same small group doing all the work and taking care of the lazy transient people who only suck energy from the community and contribute almost nothing. At least here there is a constant small group of people who are truly committed and they know who they are and so does everyone else. At Cold Mountain, the conflict between city and country rendered even our consistent people unstable. Here the tree stands firm at the center though the leaves come and go. ■

STEPHEN GASKIN'S FARM

by Farm members, from a full-page advertisement in the local Tennessee newspaper

Monday Night Class

Stephen Gaskin gets people high by telling the truth. Through the question and answer dialogues of Monday Night Class, he illustrates how the universe works. He teaches that enlightenment is much like sanity and being a grownup, that you make changes in the world by making changes in yourself. Often the message of his teaching is simply to "straighten up." This is the "sudden school," which holds that everyone really knows where it's at all the time.

Monday Night Class builds bridges between people of all generations and religions and frames of mind. It's part of ongoing conversations about God, energy, organic psychedelics as an aid on the path, the function of a redeemer, marriage and the family, tantric yoga, the nature of the subconscious, telepathy, Zen, chanting AUM, and how to get it on.

The Farm

It's been over six months now since our arrival in southern middle Tennessee and it feels to us like it's time to introduce ourselves more completely. We like it here a lot and we're thankful to be so warmly received. We also realize that we're a large and rather unusual group and that there are many questions that we could answer. In order to answer some of those questions we have taken this page to inform you of our intentions and progress and to describe by Farm members the nature of our community.

Four hundred of us, including our children, live on The Farm.

One Sunday morning in San Francisco last February Stephen said, "Let's go to Tennessee," and we all thought it was a good idea. For five years before that Stephen had been teaching a weekly class to hold communion, and becoming a Church. Most of us had originally come to San Francisco from all parts of the country. Stephen's Monday Night Class and Sunday Morning Service were at the center of that spiritual awakening. A community evolved over the years, until we left San Francisco in a caravan of remodeled schoolbuses and trucks to follow Stephen on a tour of speaking engagements at colleges and churches around the country. After twelve thousand miles and four months on the road, we returned to California, only to decide after a week that all of us who had been living and traveling together wanted to go on living together on a farm, and Tennessee had been a place where we had felt welcomed by the people and the land.

Everyone who lives on The Farm follows Stephen as his personal spiritual teacher and values his counsel on how to change. Stephen believes that all men are capable of change, and he teaches them how to improve their lives by being peaceful and honest. Living with him requires a willingness to have not just your

43

outward actions but your innermost thoughts illuminated by the clear light of spiritual purity. It works out that The Farm is a non-denominational family monastery with Stephen as the head of the household.

There are 82 married couples living in the community. Our church is recognized by the State of Tennessee and Stephen performs the sacrament of holy matrimony. He has married 46 couples since June, with marriage licenses and certificates issued by Lewis County. "You can look in books on how to carpenter or old-fashioned books about how to weld by hand, and you can find a usage of the word marry, and it means to take two things and put them together so that they be one thing. It means union. Union is one." (Stephen—Sunday Morning Service, 6 June 1971.) Our marriages are lifetime commitments, and married couples are faithful to each other and raise their children together.

Good health is important to us at The Farm. From among our members we have evolved a medical staff that administers first aid and dispenses medical supplies. If a member of The Farm becomes ill or is injured he can go to the medical staff for immediate diagnosis and treatment. If necessary the patient is sent to town to see a doctor. We like to be self-sufficient but we also appreciate the cooperation of the County and State Health Department. Our nurse gives all of our children their childhood inoculations.

Farming: Although we'd been saying for a long time, "As you sow so shall you reap," we found out when we got our piece of dirt that none of us had ever really farmed before.

Our aim is to grow as much of the food we consume as we can. In the time from our arrival to now we have brought under cultivation nearly 100 acres. We've purchased two old tractors, rebuilt one, got a hold of a bush and bog, a two-row planter, a transplanter and cultivator. We're trying to build and improve our soil. Sorghum pumice is returned to the field in the form of sheet compost. Our late cane fields are covered with a winter legume.

We're working out a technology as we go along. None of us ever tried to build a town before. It's keeping us busy. If we decide we need something, the first thing we do is see if anybody might have one under their bed or somewhere. If not, we want to know if we can get it used or possibly make it. We've got a heavy-duty 1946 Diamond "T" that used to be a lumber truck. It cost a dollar. We've used it to haul from as far away as New Orleans. We cut a bus off to just below the windows and made a giant pickup truck out of it. Then there's the jeep, a big four-wheel drive International, that was used by a Hollywood studio in army movies. That's some of our motor pool.

When we first got into farming we thought we might like to try to do it all with horses and hoes. We soon found out that for a community of our size that would mean about a horse per family to do the job. So right now we've got two Belgian mares and two tractors and we're buying another tractor. We have electricity in the schoolhouse and office, and other places of work with kerosene lamps, and cook with propane. We still take our laundry to town but we're building a laundromat where we'll have electric wringer-type washers.

One of our seven houses is under construction. Foundations for eight more are started. The design we've chosen for houses is the Dutch Frame, with added dormers to make the designs more flexible for larger families. We're using local materials like stone and rough-cut oak and poplar. Some of our men are working at nearby sawmills in exchange for lumber. The rest of our lumber and hardware is purchased from local suppliers. The roof, wall and floor joists are pre-cut for each house by a crew using power tools and assembled at the site by a carpentry crew. The foundations consist of stone and unhewn logs or railroad ties set in concrete. Plywood and roll roofing form a structurally rigid weather seal, and a Nashville plastics firm gives us its rejects of styrofoam, which provides noble insulation. When we get caught up with our housing we'll build a church.

We have a spiritual agreement to keep peace with the animals, so we don't eat meat. "Somebody with a bachelor's in chemistry and a doctorate in biology is helping us work out our diet. We're complete vegetarians. No cattle, all we have is the horses to work. But we don't use any animal foods at all, even dairy products. Because we should be able to make it on our own life force. Like that cow can make it on alfalfa. We ought to be able to make it on vegetation too, not necessarily alfalfa either, a rich and a varied and a balanced diet." (Stephen—WGTV, Athens, Georgia, 15 November 1971.) A typical meal for us: black-eye peas and cornbread, collard greens, sweet potatoes, mint tea and sorghum cookies.

There are 75 kitchens on The Farm including our school cafeteria and the community kitchen, which feeds about 40 people three meals a day. Each of these kitchens gets all its food from our store. Much of our food is purchased in quantity from local wholesale grocers and farmers. Sometimes we send a truck out with some pickers. We worked for wheat in Kansas, picked apples in Michigan, pecans in Georgia, and peppers in Lewis County. We've also harvested several crops of vegetables from our own gardens. Some of our ladies have been canning and dehydrating fruits and vegetables for the winter store.

The rolling Southern countryside, tropically warm and damp in the summer, teems with life, and the Westerners and Northerners were taken a little by surprise. They had some trouble with an impure water supply in the springs and rivers that cross the farm, and several people fell sick before they learned to boil or chlorinate their drinking water. Then they were attacked by a swarm of chiggers. Staying stoned helped them to get along with the bugs, and also gives them a sixth sense about when a chigger is about to bite so it can be snatched away.

Having so much free land to live on has led the families into some heavy experiences with one another. Early in the spring they decided to end all the music being made on the farm because too many people were relating to it in old ego-attached ways. But eventually it was worked out, and now there is a lot of singing and playing once again. "Amazing Grace" is the family favorite, and a lot of down-home country music is creeping into the singing circles.

The camp has at least 30 children, with more arriving every month. They are being raised almost completely free from things like TV, cars, money, police, and all the rest—coming back to the city seemed like a shock to our friends. One of the little trips they have is that when someone absorbs some bad karma—say by scalding herself—she lets out a shout which is picked up by someone within earshot and passed along from person to person until it disappears over a hill.

Now that the crops are in, the family is getting down for winter. They have one adobe and wood house up already. Now they are hurrying to finish some more plywood, foam-insulated A-frames for the people still living in tents before the cold weather and snow sets in. The family is using some of its magic to hold back the snows long enough for them all to get set up.

Steve Gaskin himself has been convicted and sentenced to a three-year sentence for pot after a huge police raid on The Farm's three-acre marijuana patch. The family has been getting itself together to do without him for what may be an extended length of time. He has been speaking to them individually, helping each person as much as he can to be strong and wise for themselves. If the group can make it without him, it will be all the tribute he wants to the wisdom of his teachings. ■

VIRGINIA COMMUNES

by Virginia Communes, Jay Mathews
Washington Post

EXPERIMENTS IN RURAL COMMUNAL LIVING ARE HAVING A HARD
time making it in Virginia. Of 11 started up in the past three years, only six remain.

Membership turnover, ideological differences and local hostility pick away at
commune efforts. But the central disruptive force is the need for money and the
inability of many to earn enough to keep going.

By the end of the first year nearly every experimental community has faced a
similar distasteful choice: either continue to let members work where, when and
at what they choose, and risk bankruptcy and eviction, or require members to do
whatever is necessary to ensure survival.

So far, only those communities that have compromised enough to keep the
money coming in have survived. Even where survival is temporarily assured, the
restlessness of the young people who inhabit most communes has killed some experiments and forced others to accept high turnover rates. Seven of the rural communes started in the last three years have been located in a 30-mile strip between
Sperryville and Stanardsville on the eastern shoulder of the Blue Ridge Mountains,
an area well known for its peach and apple crops.

Four of those survive, but two of them, "The Center" near Criglersville and
a farm in the same area owned by a Washington yoga group, now serve more as
temporary quarters for visiting city groups than permanent communities.

Other efforts have succeeded, such as the Twin Oaks community near Louisa,
situated halfway between Charlottesville and Richmond. Twin Oaks is considered
a colossus of the national commune movement. It is the oldest experimental community in the mid-Atlantic states and is now helping organize an offshoot commune 25 miles south near Buckingham.

But Twin Oaks has to send many of its members into Richmond to find menial
jobs, and the commune now runs a thriving hammock factory. Other experimental communities have not learned those lessons.

On a mountaintop outside Stanardsville at the southern end of the Blue Ridge
area, two communes have found the going too rough to continue. The first, an
experimental school that has since moved to Maryland, left when a mysterious fire
(set by "local rednecks," the owner said) gutted the old Episcopal mission buildings on the site.

A second group of 12 people, calling themselves the Sunrise Commune, moved
onto the mountain soon after and lasted only three months. The owner of the property at the time, an Arlington architect sympathetic with the commune movement,

blames their leaving also on threats from the local community, but a Twin Oaks commune member who visited the place said the problem went much deeper.

"One half of the group was seriously interested in making the thing work, but the other half were lying on their backs and saying, 'hey, hand me a cigarette,'" Kathleen Griebe recalls from her visit in the fall of 1969. "The resentments within the group just got higher until they left."

In Berea, 40 miles east of the Blue Ridge area, a farm owned by a Falls Church woman has seen two experimental groups come and go.

The first, its nucleus a rock group called "Sea and the East Utopian Mission," weathered a threat from one local farmer to dynamite the place in its first week and stayed for a year.

Barbara Westebbe, the owner, says the commune, grown to 23 members, left after "they were doing ouija boards in the town cemetery and they had a vision that if they went to California they would make their fortune."

A small leatherworking commune rented the place next. After four months they left in a dispute over whether the farm needed a geodesic dome (Mrs. Westebbe told them it didn't).

Many similar makeshift groups have come and gone on the land of a 51-year-old farmer and former chauffeur in the Blue Ridge area. The man asks reporters not to reveal his name and the location of his farm for fear of too many visitors, so we shall call him Jethro Wilson.

He has held a year-round open house on part of his 600-acre Rappahannock County farm for the last 20 years, and he says he is not discouraged by the turnover.

With $1,000 saved from his job as a chauffeur in Washington 20 years ago, Wilson bought his property just down the road from the house where he was born. Since that time he has raised two sons on the farm, while leaving some land for anyone who cared to live on it.

Wilson says that until recently most visitors to the farm were hobos. But the lure of experimental communities, usually only loosely organized for short periods of time on Wilson's land, have brought in more and more professional people. One group, recently introduced by Wilson to a reporter, included two architects, a social worker and a professor of medical psychology from UCLA.

"You probably wouldn't call what we're doing a commune," Wilson says. "Some places everyone does the same thing, but we're interested in evolving."

The most recent visitors have included a religious meditation group that split up in early July after some members tired of their resident guru. In April about 10 young people set up a farming community to supply the Georgetown-based Food Co-op with vegetables. They were still on the land in early August.

The rapid turnover of guests, Wilson says, is a safety valve that keeps life on his farm from souring as it does for many communes that isolate themselves on their own land.

Instead, he says his farm occasionally serves as a seed bed for groups of individuals that later transplant themselves elsewhere in the area.

Carla Eugster, a 48-year-old mother of three girls, fell in love with the area after a brief stay at the Wilson farm. Pooling her savings with a retired Navy man and an ex-government poverty worker, she bought a 27-acre farm near Woodville and turned it into the Nethers Community School.

The school, made up of six adults and 10 students, operates as one large family. "Everything that happens here is school," Mrs. Eugster says, although students have the option to study regular programmed materials to prepare themselves for college.

Since they moved in last September, the six adults living on the farm have been paying $200 a month mortgage and food bills out of their own savings.

Their money is about gone, and the community hopes to survive on tuition from 10 students, at $2500 a year each, sought for the upcoming fall term.

So far, Mrs. Eugster says, the school has received 40 inquiries about the openings for students, but only one of those accepted has sent the required half-tuition deposit.

In the meantime, the community members spend their time building more living quarters, feeding the goats, chickens and horses, plowing the vegetable garden, and developing the curriculum for the school patterned in part after the freeform Summerhill school in England.

To some extent, Nethers' development has paralleled the beginning of the Twin Oaks commune. The Nethers members recently decided to impose set hours for various farm chores and some members have begun to look for odd jobs in the area to bring in more money.

In addition to providing an example of one way to solve a commune's financial problems, Twin Oaks members have also shown that rural Virginians will accept such experimental communities over the long haul.

Twin Oaks' neighbors, one member says, have either been friendly or ignored them. The sheriff has come out two or three times, says Kathleen Griebe, 40, who serves as one of the commune's three "planners." He asks about the group's philosophy and once he is told they stay clear of drugs and revolutionary violence, he goes back to his office to reassure neighbors who might have complained.

The local health inspector told the commune to put in a better septic tank, which they did with no further problems. "The FBI, a man from the Fredericksburg office I think, also comes by to make a regular check for fugitives," Kat Griebe says.

"We look at the pictures he shows us and tell him we haven't seen them. And the last time I think he bought a hammock from us." —*Washington Post*, August 18, 1971 ∎

THE WEAVERS OF MAINE

by Gloria Hutchinson, Maine Times, *2/20/70*

TO A GROWING NUMBER OF YOUNG PEOPLE IN THE EASTERN cities, Maine is a mecca of land and trees and open spaces, a frontier where the air invigorates rather than suffocates. Turned off by industrial pollution and overcrowded cities, some have come to Maine to carve out another kind of life for themselves.

A few small groups are already making it. They are learning to live off the land, learning to survive without the accoutrements that seem essential in a product-saturated society. They have traded the advantages of comparative affluence for the labors of subsistence living.

Economically, they can be classified with America's 14,000,000 rural poor. One group, now in its second winter here, makes less money than Maine's poorest wage earners. But they cannot be categorized with Michael Harrington's "invisible poor." In Harrington's definition, the contemporary poor are "those who cannot help themselves." And helping themselves is at the heart of the matter for these young refugees from the cities.

As John, a thin, dark-haired member of one Maine commune, put it, "We've discovered that we can care for ourselves. We don't need a whole big mechanism to do that for us." He adds that most people haven't made the discovery because they have not yet broken out of the environment of dependence in which they have always lived.

John and his companions don't particularly like the term "commune," perhaps because it suggests inaccurate and unfavorable connotations to many. But if "commune" is understood to mean a community of people seeking mutual love, meaningful work, and spiritual development, the term would accurately describe this Maine group of five adults and one child. They ask that their names and location be unidentified because they have experienced the crowds of curious who come not to share or to learn, but merely to look.

Their work is the basis of their existence and a continuing flow of visitors can become what Paul describes as "a way of life in itself." Last summer a few hundred people came to the commune to ask questions about acquiring land, discuss the problems of group living, stay a while or share a meal. Luckily, many of them were friends who thought to bring something along in exchange for room or board.

Most often, the group is asked about how they got started in Maine. If it's a dreary, rain-drenched day, the five will take time to narrate their coming together from the beginning. Living separately in New York City (one was then in Chicago), they had grown "extremely tired" of the pollution, the noise, and the crowds. They took frequent camping trips out into the country sometimes for weeks at a time.

John remembers the smokestacks of Con Edison and the great clouds of soot and ashes that drifted down into his garden. Paul, his waving blonde hair parted in the middle, nods and says there was "an absence of anything natural." He recalls seeing derelicts lying in the city streets and realizing that they were dead.

A third member of the group, Tom, says that their ideas about government, politics, and social causes were changing. "There was no reason to stay in the city once we'd found what we wanted to do," he comments. They weren't a part of any movement. Rather it was a natural progression of leaving college, dropping out of jobs, reaching a dead end in the city, and leaving it altogether.

They made their first attempt in a large old house in Rhode Island where they planted a garden and set up a pottery shop. John had taken lessons from a potter in the city; he taught the craft to others in the group. Sarah acquired a loom and began teaching herself to weave. "We taught some little old ladies from the neighborhood in the evening. It was funny to hear them giggling together," she recalls. Sarah is soft-voiced and shy. Mainly, she lets the men carry the conversation.

During the Rhode Island experiment, the group was not yet into the life they envisioned for themselves. The house was equipped with a telephone and electricity; it was located in a residential area. They were still shopping at a supermarket although they had started buying bags of barley, rice, and wheat. The group was larger then and they were split by differing ideas about the direction the commune should take.

There was also a bad scene with a local gang of hoods who threatened to demolish the pottery shop with their chains and other weaponry. "We convinced them that we weren't against them and were probably closer to them than their parents. After a while, they liked us and even offered to protect us," smiles Paul. He adds that every member of the group was picked up by the police at one time or another. Not on any specific charges. Just curiosity. "We used to send the police invitations to our pottery sales," Paul remembers.

After about a year, the owner of the Rhode Island house decided to marry and five members of the group headed for Maine where, they had heard, there was lots of land and no congestion. They wanted to buy some land and build several small cabins. Everyone expected a more rigorous life that would demand independence of each member of the group. They first set up a camp on several acres owned by a Maine family who planned to sell some of the land to the group. "But the reality of our being there was too much for them. They felt responsible for us and our presence made them nervous." Having heard about an abandoned house in a rural area near the coast, the group packed all of its possessions into an aging black panel truck and headed south.

The house had been uninhabited for 30 years, was encumbered with wild rose bushes and sprawling sumac. A well-fed porcupine resided in the cellar. The group located the owner through a local tax collector. They offered to restore and maintain the house in exchange for the opportunity to live in it, rent-free. The owner thought they were "crazy" but told them to go ahead. He was surprised, on his first visit to the house, to find that his floors no longer sagged, broken windows had been replaced, insulation had been installed, and a wood shed had been constructed.

There have been two confrontations with the owner during the two years that the group has lived in Maine. He wanted to paint the house, but was convinced by the young people that it looked more natural and attractive the way it was. He wanted to cut down several trees on the land surrounding the house, but was convinced by a letter from Paul that his tenants "felt a connection with the land" and the trees represented something more than money to them. On his next visit, the owner brought a rosebush for his unusual friends.

Convinced that they won't be able to make it alone as they grow older, the owner worries about the group. "He's really into security," Paul explains. Their neighbors, from whom they are separated by an almost unpassable dirt road, are bothered by the group's unemployment. The young people don't get up early and rush off to a job every morning. Men and women live together in the group, and some of the neighbors don't approve of that either.

However, it isn't the censure of outsiders, the physical labor, nor the deprivation of luxuries (like electricity, a phone, or a shower) that create problems for the commune. Unlike many others who have attempted to live off the land and been defeated their first winter, the Maine group armed itself with practical knowledge about planting, cultivating, and harvesting. They knew how to preserve foods, bake breads, and create nutritional meals from organically grown substances.

The problems lie instead within the group itself: the internal pressures originating when six people of varying energies, talents, and ideas interact in a close, community setting. Chores have to be shared. Each member of the group has to carry his own weight. Things have to be worked out together.

"Everyone has to give up his ego or idea of himself. You have to let go of your own wants and consider those of others," Paul says. John agrees and expands on the idea. "You come to the point where you have to be able to accept a situation rather than continuing to resist because you don't like it." This resiliency, inspired by unselfishness, is hard to come by, he admits.

The group hasn't given up the original idea of separate cabins a little distance apart. That's something they are working toward. As Tom sees it, they must learn through their present experience first. Then, when the time comes for the cabins, it will be a natural and positive step. "It won't be a reaction against others we find hard to get along with. That would be the wrong spirit," he says. They left the cities three years ago with a romantic ideal which they are gradually "paring down" to a realistic experience, John adds.

United in their desire to "weed out all foods that don't help you in any way," the group is actively concerned about its diet. Meals are based on grains (millet, oats, wheat, barley, and rye) and several varieties of beans. No one eats meat, although there isn't any regulation prohibiting it. Egg dishes are common fare (the group keeps several chickens) as are vegetable stews and soups.

Paul, who with Emily does most of the cooking, recently discovered a squash soup that he describes as "bright orange and delicious." He sautés onions and cut-up squash in oil, adds a half-cup of water and salt, and pressure-cooks for 20 minutes. He then makes a purée of the ingredients, adding more water and possibly some Tamari soy sauce to taste.

Many of the group's recipes are taken from a book of Zen cookery. Cakes are made without baking soda or baking powder, and beverages are not served with meals because they "dilute the digestive juices." Paul admits that some of the things the group eats take a little getting used to. The tastes are more subtle: the taste buds have to grow accustomed to them.

A trip to the supermarket is now a rarity. John compares the experience to going to a museum and seeing "all those carts filled with incredible packages." Although he doesn't say it, the thought is, "How many of those people actually know what is in those packages?" No one in the group would think of buying a mix or a convenience food or a loaf of commercial bread.

During the winter, with the gardening, food processing, and wood gathering behind them, the group spends most of its time at the looms or in the pottery room (a converted woodshed). Each of the four bedrooms is furnished with at least one loom, and each weaver has developed a particular style which distinguishes his works. John weaves primarily in muted earth colors, greys and browns. Emily is partial to blues and greens, while Paul's works are accented by clamorous reds, pinks, and oranges.

The weavers sell their scarves, tunics, pillows, handbags, and blankets to a few Maine shops like the Custom House in Wiscasset and to individuals who have discovered them via the grapevine. Much of their plenteous supply of wools and yarns has either been given to them or sold to them at drastically reduced rates by wholesalers who have become friends.

They have an idea that they might like to open a small shop for their weaving and pottery in a nearby town. It would not be primarily a commercial venture, but an outlet for their numerous creations and an opportunity to expose themselves to people who might have questions about their way of life. The shop, should it materialize, would be open only part-time. No one in the group likes the idea of balancing the books or getting too involved with money.

Besides, it's still just an idea, Tom reiterates. "It might be something we have to go through so we can leave it behind," he says.

Money isn't evil in itself, Tom goes on. It's just that too often money represents the distance between a man and his work. Too often it becomes an end in itself, rather than a tool to be put to good use. The group doesn't worry about money. There is no communal bank account, no savings, and no regular income. But neither are there any bills (rent, lights, phone, fuel).

"We haven't had any money for a couple of weeks now. But it doesn't matter. We have a life here that supports itself," Paul comments.

Having detached themselves, in good measure, from money, the people of the commune are also trying to detach themselves from material possessions. The fewer things you own, the freer you are. The weavers do not speak quite as openly of their spiritual lives. Spirituality, they feel, has to evolve "on its own" and cannot be imposed on from the outside. Paul describes their common involvement as "opening ourselves to the present moment, to all that's going on around us. We're learning to take care of ourselves. And to let each other be free. That's what is so hard," he smiles.

Somewhere in a wooded area near the Maine coast, five young adults and a pink-cheeked toddler are working it out together. They are trying to keep their lives poor and simple so they can appreciate the land, the trees, the open spaces, the unpolluted air. There are a few others like them here now, and there are more to come. Maine is their kind of place.

Part Two (Maine Sunday Telegram, November 28, 1971)

November's chill intrudes early into the wood-heated house. The drafty floors discourage even those bare feet that have weathered spring mud and autumn rain. Each day's threat of precipitate snow hastens the nailing of tar-paper and heavy plastic windows.

Facing their fourth winter in Maine, the weavers know the value of an insulated house and an ample woodpile. They appreciate the January returns on a fall investment of work-hours in the root cellar and the greenhouse. They know the wisdom of digging and mulching, of canning and drying.

The commune, of five adults and one child, lives in wooded seclusion on the coast of Maine. Their farm was innocent of telephone poles and power lines when they arrived and they have kept it that way. In the beginning, all their time was consumed in manual labor and working at the looms. The five had learned to weave and it was this craft that came to identify them as a group. Their woolen bags, shawls, and ponchos were soon familiar to the customers of a few coastal shops. But the Weavers themselves—and their location—remained a relative secret.

They wanted it that way for two reasons: a flow of visitors would postpone their work and impede on the more difficult task of building a livable relationship within the group itself.

Sharing the work holds inherent difficulties. More intense conflict is generated by the sharing of emotional and spiritual lives.

Says Ed, "The central question for us is still, 'can conflict among people come to an end?' Do you ever reach the point where, at the end of the day, people have no feeling of pain or conflict within the group?" He is slim and black-haired, reflective and, like the others, quietly spoken.

Ed is convinced that living off the land is "easy and joyful," while living intimately with five other individuals is a task that must constantly be worked at.

For Jackson, it's a question of energy. Do you waste your energy on rejection and worrying about who's responsible for what? Or, do you use it to help harmony come about? The experience of communal life, he says, leads to an awareness of the value of "relating to everyone—not just those you like and are comfortable with."

At times during the past four years, Jackson has left the group to travel and sail on a friend's boat in the Caribbean. More than the others, he feels that the commune has become "root-bound" to its present home. "The world is so much larger than this one place."

But he doesn't want to get caught up in organized activities that become social outlets. He worked with an environmental group until he found himself serving as an officer, attending cocktail parties and dinners. "I took notes and did things to prove that this hippie could really produce."

Until this year, Sylvia stayed primarily within the group, focusing on her child and her work. "It took me four years to meet our neighbors at the end of the road. But now that we've learned to relate to each other here, it's easier to relate to others outside." Her goals now include helping to alert Maine people to the uncertainties of nuclear power.

She and Jim have been active for several months with the Citizens for Safe Power, one of three organizations within the state that petitioned the Atomic Energy Commission for a hearing on the Maine Yankee Plant in Wiscasset.

When visiting dignitaries arrived at Maine Yankee's opening-day ceremonies last summer, they found a line of placard-carrying mothers and children. The impromptu march had been pulled together by a non-subscriber to Central Maine Power who, although she didn't have a telephone of her own, decided that New England Telephone's communication tool could be put to good use at a time like that.

Jim, the Weavers' mechanic and inventor, appears to be the central figure of the group. Ed and Jackson and Sarah are more contemplative, even philosophic. Sylvia, small, braided and slender, is just emerging from her isolation. Perhaps because he is a father, Jim is the one the others rely on to keep things going: the Volkswagen bus, the woodstove, the pump, the potter's wheel.

Ensconced in a clutter of handcrafted tools, cast-off hubcaps, assorted screwdrivers and spark plugs, Jim designs and repairs things in his shop over the woodshed. Wooden trucks for Aaron, a workbench with catchall drawers, a makeshift hammer, the plans for a greenhouse and a brick kiln have all emerged from the workshop. When Jim isn't there, he is in the pottery room near the kitchen, or at the loom, or off in the woods walking and taking photographs. (Sylvia uses a stick to leave a message for him in the dirt surface of the road: "Jim—Lunch.")

Aaron, at the age of two and a half, is a curious, trusting child who thrives on organic foods, fresh air, and the love of five adults. He likes tossing stones in the trees, eating apples, running down the road in his bare feet, and emptying his dirt-filled dump truck on the bedroom floor.

He calls his mother "Sylvie," and he takes his troubles, a scraped knee or a sliver, to the Weaver who happens to be nearest at the time. His blonde curls grow unrestrained by scissors, and he frets at the necessity of being fully dressed in freezing weather.

Although the Weavers can all be described as gentle people, the adjective sits easiest on Sarah's shoulders. She is good with children and adept at making squash pie with apple topping. Like Jackson, she has left the group for brief periods to travel, on a trust fund. She went to Norway to learn more about weaving and to Spain because she had never been there before.

In the summer, she spends warm evenings in a small, screened-in wooden house in the woods. (Aaron, with a slight mix-up of consonants, refers to it as "Sarah-Beara's chicken poop.") Furnished with a wooden bed, a miniature table and a few treasures—Japanese coins and a long white feather among them—the summer house is a place all children have seen in at least one dream.

The diversity of personalities among the Weavers is expressed in their work and in how they feel about the finished product. Ed favors muted earth colors, Jackson works with outspoken oranges and reds, and Sarah experiments with blues and greens. With the recent acquisition of a spinning wheel, the group was able to get away from some of the limitations of commercial yarns and come closer to the basic process of creating a fabric.

They began dyeing yarns this summer and fall with goldenrod, onion skins, elderberry, marigolds, mullein and sumac. They soaked, boiled and simmered various combinations of natural substances, producing a whole new range of colors for their looms. "Now the yarns we've purchased don't seem to be as real as our own," Ed comments. He feels that both the spinning—"Just a matter of learning to coordinate your hands, knowing when to hold and when to twist"—and dyeing are amazingly simple processes which the group should have attempted earlier.

The weaving itself, an ancient craft of threading weft yarns across warp yarns, has been varied this year by the addition of a four-harness floor loom borrowed from a friend in Boston. Treadle-operated, it gives the Weavers a chance to work larger fabrics: rugs, blankets, and afghans. Their table looms—in the living room and all the bedrooms—turn out placemats and potholders, scarves and bags, ponchos and shawls. Most are sold to or through friends. This income is crucial because the Weavers have no other continuing source of cash. But profit is not allowed to dictate to the group.

They have no communal bank account or savings. Some weeks, no one has any cash. But their life supports itself until someone sells another tote bag (lined for heavy duty with a rice sack) or a piece of pottery.

The commune has few recurring expenses other than the health foods that supplement the garden's produce. Grains, rice, beans and nuts are purchased in bulk quantities on monthly trips to Boston. Everyone shares in the work of preparing meals, but Jackson has a recognized talent for Oriental cookery. His rice and lentil dishes are laced with tarragon and Tamari soy sauce and sunflower seeds.

Dinner, on the day of our visit, included a thick soup of turnip, squash, parsley, and dried seaweed; a main dish of brown rice and beans; a dessert of mixed nuts and seeds warmed just before serving. Tea or Pero—a cereal-grain coffee substitute—are served between meals but not with dinner. All bowls and utensils are wooden, and the Weavers themselves use chopsticks.

The Weavers estimate their total annual cash income at something under $3,000. They get by on so little because they don't pay rent or buy fuel oil, they grow much of their own food and they avoid hard cash transactions as much as possible: they'd rather trade. Last week, for instance, they swapped 30 potholders for a sack of grain, which they grind to make their own bread, etc. Over four years they have built an extensive network of business relationships based on barter.

During their first few autumns in Maine, the Weavers spent long hard hours canning all their vegetables, apples and peaches. Someone finally brought them one of Scott Nearing's books about living off the land and they began to learn about storing cabbages, carrots and parsnips in leaves and sand in the root cellar.

That was the beginning of a more conscious effort to simplify the external tasks that consumed so much of their time. It was also part of their schooling in "taking care of ourselves away from the environment of dependence" in which most people spend their lives.

But where do the Weavers go from here?

Unexpectedly, at the end of the summer, the owner of their house came for an infrequent visit. He suggested that the group wasn't doing "enough work" around the property anymore and that it would be advertised "for sale." As they saw it, he was "enacting a role but not a need." Having gone along with them for four years, he was returning to the role of the real estate man who if he is not making money, is losing money.

At some uncertain point, the house will be sold and the Weavers will be out of a home. They are neither anxious nor angry.

"We came here freely and we'll leave here freely. We're open to whatever happens," says Ed.

"We've all changed here. The stability of staying in this one place has allowed us to grow. We're not anticipating the sale of the house. But we aren't worried by the possibility, either."

"I feel that my life is much larger now. When we came here, we had to have the organic garden and the looms and do without electricity and things like that. Now I'm not compelled to do any of these things. I would miss this place, but I'm not attached to it."

Their future is uncharted.

They may not even stay together.

But those separate cabins in the Maine woods are still part of the Weavers' dream. And they believe, as The Last Whole Earth Catalog teaches, "If you want to try a new way, you've got to build something." ■

SCHOOL OF LIVING
by Richard Fairfield

RALPH BORSODI, AN ECONOMIST AND NEW YORK CITY ADVERtising and marketing consultant, wrote several books in the '20s and '30s, chief of which were National Advertising vs. Prosperity and This Ugly Civilization. After moving to upstate New York in 1921, Borsodi experimented with developing a self-sufficient homestead. He and his family cultivated a garden, began a small orchard, raised chickens, pigs and goats and constructed a big stone house of native rock with a pool. He even constructed two small cottages for his sons when they married. In This Ugly Civilization (Harpers, 1928), Ralph Borsodi described his experiences with homesteading and tried to show how this approach was a constructive alternative and an antidote to modern technological civilization.

During the Depression, the government was desperate to help the unemployed find meaningful work. Borsodi was invited to Ohio to help establish the Dayton Homesteading Experiment. A million dollars was earmarked for this project with the provision that the federal government exercise overall control. Borsodi was opposed to governmental intrusion and refused to accept such supervision. He left the project and it soon lost most of its direction and momentum.

Borsodi decided to develop the homesteading movement on his own, independent of government subsidy and control. He moved back to Suffern, New York, and founded the School of Living in 1936. He and friends bought 32 acres of land and named their community Bayard Lane. They also established the Independence Foundation with a low-interest credit plan and a group-landholding plan to make it easy for people to become members of the homestead community. Sixteen families built homes there. The School of Living held many seminars and informal lectures centering around the ideas of Ralph Borsodi.

His assistant, Mildred Loomis, formerly a teacher and social worker, became totally convinced that this approach was a way out of the increasing urban rat race in American society. When the School of Living closed at Bayard Lane during World War II, Mildred and John Loomis moved to Brookville, Ohio and developed Lane's End Homestead. At Lane's End they lived entirely off the land, keeping their income below taxable level, producing up to 95% of their own food supply, all of their meat, grain, vegetables, fruit, honey, dairy products.

Since 1950, Mildred Loomis has carried out the educational function of the School of Living. She has published a monthly newspaper, The Green Revolution, and distributed it to all parts of the country. Also with the help of friends, she published a more scholarly journal, A Way Out (originally titled Balanced Living).

The homestead grew and soon it was necessary to add a second building. In addition to accommodating assistants and apprentices, the structure was utilized as a meeting place and library. Over the years Mildred Loomis has built a committed following of many hundred readers and some of these have become active supporters. In 1966 a 40-acre plot of land and five buildings, including a large 150-year-old stone mill, became available in rural Maryland. Mildred and friends at Lane's End wanted to expand the School of Living and develop a full-blown community. Financial support came in the form of $1000 investment shares and the property was purchased.

Frequent work bees were held to renovate the mill building and make the six-room wing habitable. By August 1966, the property was ready for its first annual workshop on major problems of living. Since then, under Mildred's direction, at least one family has lived in the mill building year-round supervising the activities of the center from April through September, when monthly weekend seminars are held. Because of Mildred's searching mind the School of Living at Heathcote has not stagnated or become irrelevant as have most of the ideas and activities of the Old Left.

Mildred, although still dogmatically enamored of Ralph Borsodi and his "17 Major Problems of Living," has been sensitive to the new community movement emerging in the '60s. She has been sympathetic and encouraging to the young dropouts and hippies, seeing in the young the only hope for a rural revival toward which she has so fervently worked all her life.

At the end of the first year of The Modern Utopian, I moved to California. Before leaving I went to Heathcote to talk with Mildred.

Mildred was much older than I had expected. Pictures of her were 20 years out of date. Though in her 70s, she was still an attractive woman, vital and alive. She seemed extremely fair and open in her approach to life and willing to listen to opposing points of view. She was not dogmatic about most things, though somewhat confused in her search for meaning. The old ways were crumbling and she was trying hard to adapt to new approaches to homesteading and community without losing her grasp on the views that had sustained her own approach for over 25 years, an approach nurtured by Borsodi's Problems of Living and Georgian economics (free land and no land tax). She had been the leftest of the leftists in the '30s. Now, with the open land movement espoused by Lou Gottlieb at Morning Star in California, the idea of land trusts and other organized cooperative land-holding plans was becoming immensely conservative. Mildred tried to understand the conditions around her. It was not easy. Most of all she wished to communicate her own ideas, à la Borsodi, George and others, to as many young people as possible. She was unhappy that too many of them did not grasp the evils of the land and banking monopoly in the capitalist system. She was unhappy that youth did not give more attention to economic problems in their return to the land and intentional community. She saw The Modern Utopian as a vehicle to communicate her point of view.

At Heathcote Mildred was leading the annual weekend seminar on Homesteading Problems. Pat Herron, who lived on a ranch in northern California, led a few sensory awareness sessions, a new group phenomenon which was just beginning to emerge on the East Coast.

I left Heathcote much impressed with Mildred Loomis. We had established a comfortable rapport and we have retained that rapport even today. In the fall of 1969 Mildred wrote,

Yes, times (meaning people) have changed. The group here are part of the new people—little concerned in the old work, luxury and success patterns, and definitely concerned in simple living, direct experience, honest and open and warm relationships. The spend time together; they play a lot; they eat at their own convenience, which means the kitchen is almost always in use and in disarray; they are not careful or tidy in this pattern, so unless someone values tidiness and does a lot of sweeping and "putting things away" the place can be quite disorderly. This can bother and upset older people—though we have not had any real hassles to date. Even so, a good deal gets done around here, on a very do-it-yourself basis. Two wonderful and huge gardens are producing most of the food for 15 to 30 persons daily; some people are digging a root cellar for storing carrots, potatoes, squash, cabbage, etc. The building is better organized and new office space has been developed. Love, Mildred.

To think and write of Mildred Loomis makes me feel warm and joyous. Would that all elderly ladies were as young and vital and gentle of soul as she. She could accept the lifestyles of others and be open to their values though she herself might prefer a different style. As cold weather approached and the wind swept through old walls at Heathcote, Mildred began to look for another home, warmer and more peaceful than with the anarchists in Maryland. I received a note saying she'd be at Pat Herron's Northern California ranch for the winter, and then back to Ohio in the spring and summer to build a community at her deceased husband, John's, and her old homestead, Lane's End.
—Richard Fairfield

∎

TOLSTOY FARM
by Richard Fairfield

LATE IN 1968 I RECEIVED A COMMUNICATION FROM HUW WIL-
liams in Washington State. I published it in The Modern Utopian.

My wife and I have 80 acres which we would like to use as the basis for a
community of homesteading families and a cooperative free-learning school. We
can also rent more land nearby to use for a co-operative cattle business. We have
homesteaded on this land for three years and supply our monetary needs through
farmwork and a small leather business, making moccasins, sandals, papoose car-
riers and saddles. Our current desire is to get in contact with other families who
need land and want to homestead and participate in a cooperative school, cattle
business, and/or handicrafts business.

Later, when I reread the old community news digest in back issues of The
Modern Utopian, I realized that the 80-acre tract of land Huw was talking about
was none other than a portion of a commune called Tolstoy Farm. I had already
heard from and about Tolstoy Farm earlier that year, having received a letter from
someone there. That letter, too, had been published in The Modern Utopian, although as an anonymous piece:

I am writing to request a favor. We would really appreciate it if you would absolutely not print ANYTHING about us in your magazine. Nothing against The
Modern Utopian. We read it with interest and pleasure. But we have a serious (for
us) population and transient problem and we don't want any publicity at all... for
us it is a matter of being able to survive here.

This is a problem I am continually running into—first a group wants publicity in order to attract new members, then they holler, "We can't handle all the
visitors." In time I got to learn more about Huw Williams and Tolstoy Farm. I
discovered that Huw's parents and grandparents had owned over 800 acres of
land in the state of Washington. And it was Huw's mother who had given him 80
acres of the land after he dropped out of the University of Washington and started
a nonviolent training center. Huw rented a building, near his land, called Heart
House, for the center. More than 50 people passed through the center during its
first summer of operation. Huw married one of those visitors, Sylvia, and the two
of them decided to form an intentional community based on the anarchist principle of voluntary cooperation: no rules, no structure, people helping each other
because they saw a need and wanted to be of service. The community would be
open to anyone and no one would be asked to leave.

Heart House became the center of and living space for this communal experiment. But without any rules or structure, so many people living in such close quarters were doomed to chaos. Constant interpersonal frictions rubbed people raw, as could be expected.

People who are new to each other and refuse to develop any sort of structure, group consensus, or methods of dealing with problems inevitably become enemies rather than friends. The larger the size of the group, the worse the problem, and the greater the need for structure. If they are reasonably compatible, two people may be able to live together well without structure. But five or 10 or more people will need some sort of framework for dealing with the inevitable variety of problems that will arise. Three basic rules of thumb for new communes organizing are: (1) the more people, the more structure; (2) the less thoroughly members know and understand each other, the more structure; and (3) the less time members spend together, the more structure.

In 1967 there was a mass upsurge of nationwide interest in rural living in the hippie subculture. Tolstoy Farm was among the places invaded by wandering nomads from psychedelia. As publicity grew, there were runaways, speed freaks, and all varieties of teenyboppers looking for a home on the land, where they could "do their thing" without being hassled by parents and authorities. These transients wanted to be free of responsibilities that were forced on them at home, yet they still wanted to be fed and clothed by "mommy" and "daddy." At Heart House, the permanent residents were forced into the role of parents. And because their resources were limited, the transients considered them uptight and stingy. Dissatisfaction grew so intense that permanent members of the group pooled their resources and bought 120 acres of land located at the far end of the same canyon, some two miles away. These people, including Huw and Sylvia, then moved out of Heart House and built separate living quarters on the newly acquired land. (It was around this time that I received the plea to stop publishing their address; they had really had it up to here with "guests.")

There was a lot of talk about burning Heart House down. This mood must have been strong for the house was mysteriously destroyed by fire in the spring of 1968. It seems that most of the serious-minded folk at Tolstoy were prepared or nearly prepared for the fire. They completed their separate housing, while those transients who were not really serious about the community soon left. A few lean-tos or makeshift structures were also built for temporary shelter during the warmer months which followed.

Since mid-1968 Tolstoy has settled into the individualistic community pattern. It is open "land access to which is denied no one." Huw's North 80 and the South 120 are now cooperatively owned by the Mill Canyon Society. Each family unit establishes its own household by building its own dwelling, tending its own garden, and furnishing its own supplies. Each family usually owns at least two vehicles—a car or motorcycle plus a truck or tractor. Families who live near each other work out cooperative arrangements regarding babysitting, household and farm chores, and, on occasion, the sharing of a meal together.

On the North 80, residents gather in the evening at the cowshed. The two dairy cows give nine gallons of milk a day. Any food produced for communal use is stored here. Mail is delivered to this location for distribution. The cowshed is, in fact, the gathering spot for people living at this end of the canyon.

There are no modern conveniences at Tolstoy Farm: no electricity, no flush toilets, no gas heaters, no clocks (and therefore no regimentation of time and dates). The people tend a communal garden, as well as their many individual ones. Many of the residents get food stamps and unemployment compensation or welfare. A few of the permanent people take part-time jobs to earn extra cash to support their families. Huw makes and sells leather goods; some residents make wall hangings, pottery and jewelry, and other craft products.

During the warmer months of the year, 50 or more adults live at Tolstoy. There are at least two dozen year-round residents and almost as many children. Besides Thanksgiving, which all families celebrate at the schoolhouse, there is a communal celebration on the first full moon of May. This is a corn dance festival, adapted from the ceremonies of the Hopi Indians, during which the families have a huge feast. They dance, sing, get stoned, and take turns beating on a homemade drum. It is a nightlong event that lasts until dawn, when everyone falls asleep in exhaustion.

Like most homestead-oriented, individual family-unit communities, Tolstoy retains traditional sex roles: men do the heavy work—haul that barge, tote that bale (of hay); women do household chores—cooking, cleaning, sewing, child tending. The roles are more clearly defined here than in contemporary suburbia. For those who can accept these traditional roles there is a great deal of satisfaction. This seems to be the case for most of the men and women who live at Tolstoy, as well as for the people at other open-land communities and hippie-style communes.

By 1969, a total of 13 homes had been built at Tolstoy Farm, many of them with livestock and outbuildings. At present, Huw is trying to develop a free school for the children at the farm as well as for outside children who would like to attend. As Huw envisions it, the school would be a place where the students are "free to choose their own projects and pursue their particular interests at their own speed."

The community already has the facilities, having built an 18-sided (nearly round) schoolhouse made of pumice block, concrete, wood, and glass. It is designed to support a geodesic dome as a second story. The cost to date has been approximately $1,300.

Huw and the other members emphasize that the entire farm can be the educational environment not only for the children but for the adults as well. They hope to cooperate more and more in the future to provide everyone with a wide range of cultural activities, drawing on the resources and talents of all the members.

There are several different points of view at Tolstoy about what the ideal community should be. Huw still holds firmly to his anarchist philosophy. He'd rather do all the work himself and not impose any rules upon others (the good old American pioneering spirit). Others feel that there needs to be some authority and organization in any situation where people live together. And a few others feel they would like a much more intimate community, forming a group marriage with six or more adults. As a result of these differing viewpoints, a certain amount of unrelieved tension is generated among these people when they come together. Fortunately, there are 200 acres at Tolstoy. Perhaps as each group comes closer to its own ideal or mellows in its position, the tension will diminish. ■

CHAPTER 2

open land communes

THE MODERN UTOPIAN
P. O. BOX 1264
BERKELEY, CA 94701

The MANDALA of GREAT NATURE

POLE ☼ STAR

PRAISE THE NYMPH EVOE

PREDATOR and EROSION CONTROL)

CALIFIA comes... AWEEYAAAA

RAIN WATER COLLECTION
STAR OBSERVATION
PYRAMIDS
WINTER DWELLINGS
MAGICAL RETIREMENT
TOWERS
MEDITATION
GREAT HEARTHS
FAERIE PALACES

CAVE TEMPLES
EMPIRE OF MILLENIAL
AGE and CHILDHOOD

(FOOD, FIBER, WEATHER,
NATIVE PLANTS
COMPOST HEAPS
HERBAL CONCOCTIONS
TUNNEL

HARVEST HOME 22 min.

ECONOMIC

AVAL CELLARS FOR
FRUIT STORAGE
DECIDUOUS GROVES
FUNERAL PYRES

SEPT. 23
DIVERSIFIED

FEASTING
ISLAND FOR YOGA and
MAGICAL STUDY
LAKE WITH
UNDERGROUND
SEED SILOS
ECOLOGY CENTER
and EROSION CONTROL
MAIN MAZE
GROVE FOR WINDING UP
MAENADIC RACES
and SEEK
PSYCHICAL PERFECTION

HARVEST HOME West

HARVEST HOME
(SEARCH FOR THE

EVOE

PANEROTIC PRIMATE
FREE PLAY GROUNDS:
CLIMBING, SWINGING,
and SWIMMING WORKS
HONEYMOON HIDEOUTS
POETRY TRACKING
LANDSCAPES
FEERIE DES BOIS
FOOD TREE
GROVES and
ORCHARDS

LUGNASAD S.W.

Appropriate
monuments in each
realm for its Seasonal
Feast. (SAVE NATURE FROM MAN)

MIDSUMMER
South
FRUIT DRYING
EMPIRE OF
MATURITY
OPEN SUMMER
DWELLINGS
GROUP COVEN
MARRIAGE ALTARS
LOVE and LOUNGING NOOKS
SENSUALITY DENS
FRUIT IMMERSION PITS and
PILLOW MOUNTAINS
MAGIC MAIDEN ...SO SHE MAY FIND YOU.

SAMHAIN
INITIATION
AVENUES OF
VISIONARY
MONUMENTS
North
YULE
UNDERGROUND
PASSAGE

H E N G E

OLMELC

ARTS, CRAFTS,
WORKSHOPS
ALCHEMY ARCHIVES
BURNING PLACES
FOR NITROGEN
FIRE FUEL
PRUNING
CATHARSIS
BLENDING INTO WILDERNESS

BOTANICAL
NURSERIES

OSTARA East
EMPIRE OF
CHILDHOOD
GARDENS
HERBARIUM

UNDERGROUND
FOUNTAIN
of FIRE
and WATER
ELEUSIS
MARRIAGE CHAMBER
REPOSE

S W A M P S
and
P L A Z A

BIG OPEN FIELD
PLAYGROUNDS
BELTANE S.E.
EMPIRE OF
ADOLESCENCE
HEDGE MAZES
PHYSICAL PERFECTION
GROUP SEVEN
ENGAGEMENT
ALTARS

THE MAGIA MAIDEN MARRIES ALL.)
AUTUMN LENDS THE LOVERS
HOME. FRUITS GARNERED,
NECTARS PRESSED.
LEAF GOLD GIVEN
ANTUMCAL
ATION.

KORE!

Outer henge
on each menhir
Ray in appropriate
biome.

(SAVE MAN FOR NATURE)

First great 🍎
PARADISAL SANCTUARY
in all history, realizing
age-old Paradisal
Dream of all peoples,
uniting MAN and
all LIFE.

Path leading out 🍃
from each menhir into
associated Seasonal realm,
which overlaps others.
Visionary Nature shrines
throughout

Feraferia INC.

General scheme for
KORYTHALIA HESPERIDES,
a Faereland Sanctuary
uniting cult, culture, and
cultivation for wholehearted
dedication to WILDERNESS
centered on
Wilderhenge Circle.

P.O. Box 691 Altadena, CALIFORNIA 91001

Chinigchinich, come back to Yang-Na !!!

GORDA MOUNTAIN, THE FIRST OPEN-LAND COMMUNE

by Richard Fairfield

TO THE BEST OF MY KNOWLEDGE, THE FIRST OPEN-LAND COM-
mune was Gorda Mountain, on the Big Sur coast of California. In 1962 Amelia Newell decided to make her land there available to anyone who wished
to come and live on it. As the U.S. hippie movement grew, so also did the
population of Gorda.

At the peak of the 1967 summer there were over 200 young hippies living on
Amelia's land. Local residents became quite hostile about this influx of strange,
long-haired, dirty, drug-crazed deviants (to use some of the phrases most favored
by the press in describing hippies). One local gas station owner took to wearing a
revolver and refusing to service cars and trucks from the Newell community. Other
local businessmen placed signs in their windows: "POSITIVELY NO SERVICE
TO HIPPIES (Except the use of the public telephone) ON THESE PREMISES."
The health department was the willing tool of the county politicians who decided
that Gorda Mountain was a menace to their political positions given the opposition of older residents and businessmen. The politicians therefore determined that
Gorda Mountain should be closed down—an objective in which local vigilantes
aided the county authorities. Gorda died in 1968. ■

MORNING STAR RANCH

by Richard Fairfield

MORNING STAR RANCH IS AN OPEN-LAND COMMUNITY IN SOnoma County, California. And it is based on the fundamental principle that all land should be available to those who wish to use it—a principle known acronymically as LATWIDN (Land Access To Which Is Denied No One).

"Open land means simply that God is the sole owner of the land and that we, as His children, are not meant to fight, quarrel, and kill over the land, but rather to share this natural resource to each according to his needs." At Morning Star there are no rules, no regulations, no organization. The land itself selects the people. Those who do not work hard to build shelter and provide for their basic needs do not survive on the land. If the land gets overcrowded, people leave or spread out. The ideal is "voluntary primitivism," a term used by Ramon Sender to mean "the reunion of man with his greater self—God's nature"; that is, living in harmony with the four elements—earth, air, fire, and water. In practice this means building your own biodegradable home out of mud and twigs and dead branches and old lumber. It means giving up electricity, gas, running water, and the telephone, as well as other modern conveniences. Living on the land also means conditioning your body to withstand cold and damp weather, carrying your own water for drinking and your own wood for cooking. It means planting and harvesting your crops by using muscles and not machinery.

In the Beginning, and a Year Later

Originally purchased in 1962, Morning Star was initially the private retreat of Lou Gottlieb, a singer with the pop-folk group called The Limelighters.

In 1966 Lou and Ramon Sender, a friend, decided to open the land to anyone who wanted to live there. The property consisted of approximately 32 acres of land. Forest, meadow, and orchard made up about half of the area; banks and inclines too steep for use composed the rest. The topsoil was not fertile, being generally a clay mixture that possessed only marginal potential for crop-growing purposes. There were two wells, both of them usable throughout the year. Buildings on the property included a small, light-framed house (about 900 feet square), a barn, and a prefabricated chicken coop and shed. Morning Star took on the appearance of an ashram. It began with a half-dozen permanent residents and gradually increased its population to over 35. A college student in Maryland named Michael Howden visited Morning Star late in December 1966, when the commune was still less than one year old. In writing about his experiences at Morning Star, he reported:

When I arrived it was chilly out, but people were working and it seemed very natural to work with them, hauling firewood to the lower house. There was no pressure to work, nor was I trying to impress anyone. It was just what was happening and it seemed natural to partake of it. Dinner, as with all the meals there, was a communal affair. Each day, different people cooked breakfast and/or dinner; others washed the dishes. Before the meal we all held hands in silence. Some very nice things happened through this, a very warm feeling, becoming part. The meal was macrobiotic, zucchini tempura, rice and greens, though there was milk as well as tea.

If the ashram had centrality, it was about Lou Gottlieb. He is free from pressures, direct, outspoken. The land is his, but no one was really conscious of this; all were part of the community. Whom the land in fact belonged to didn't matter. Lou made this possible; he was never overbearing, demanding. Yet things happened; they happened because of Lou's non-possessiveness, his tolerance, which created the sense of all belonging equally, which made sharing and work not only possible but enjoyable.

I went back in late January or early February of 1967. The currents had matured. Some people had gone, but there were still about 14 to 18 people around. The atmosphere was calm and free. Chicken coop areas had been cleared away for an organic garden. Scrap that had lain around for months was being cleared. Trips were made to the ocean for shellfish. The weather, too, was better, better, more sun and a warm wind.

As spring arrived, more and more people heard about Morning Star. A few moved in to become permanent residents. By late summer there were at least as many semi-residents as permanent ones, semi-residents being people who divided their time between the ashram and San Francisco.

As the word got out that Morning Star was an "open" commune, more and more people split from the city, especially from the Haight-Ashbury. These transient hippie types would visit for a weekend, or sometimes for a week or two, and then leave. By June 1967, they constituted over half the total population; on weekends they made up an even larger proportion. During June and July an average of 90 people per day ate the communal dinner; on weekends this number doubled. One Saturday in late July over 300 were fed (a figure that does not include the ever-increasing numbers of people who elected to eat separately).

Problems

The commune was changing, but not necessarily for the better. Mike Howden noted, "Morning Star was no longer an ashram, but an open community. Many people came and went. The food supplies and general quality of the meals fell off...." But it was not only the quantity and quality of food that worsened; the composition of people on the farm became increasingly urban in outlook as well as origin. As publicity mounted, tourists flooded the place, particularly on weekends. At the peak influx, over 2,000 tourists visited the farm. Few of them, though, stayed overnight or ate the common meal, but they still needed other facilities.

Chuck Herrick, one of the residents, noted that "With the greater number of people on the land, the two inadequate toilets are literally inundated by a river of shit. The situation was made worse by the interruption of services because of frequent stoppages. At one period, neither toilet functioned for over a week."

The commune's problems multiplied as its population increased. One of these problems was that, owing to the lack of toilet facilities, most people used the woods. Many were careless and did not bury their feces and paper adequately. Thus, this lack of sanitation constituted a serious health hazard.

Another serious problem had to do with the limited availability of living quarters. Buildings on the property, including the barn and sheds, provided only 14 small but habitable rooms. Some of these rooms were claimed by permanent residents as "private space" and this space was seldom disturbed. The newest transients crammed into the two small houses. As a result, both houses deteriorated rapidly and their bathrooms, kitchens, and floor surfaces required major repairs. Such crowding increased the danger of disease as well as of social stress.

Then, as Chuck Herrick noted, "The reaction to this stress was rapid construction of individual shelters ranging from carefully designed and environmentally integrated dwellings to tin shanties. None were blessed by the county building department. About two dozen structures were built. Tents also became common."

The scattered locations of all these structures caused still more problems, such as the fact that the tourists began roaming through the woods in search of more real live hippies, thus trampling the vegetation. Three other problems resulting from the influx of all these transients and tourists were that: (1) a considerable number of trees were cut down before community consensus stopped it, (2) the clearing of ground litter and the leveling of campsites broke natural drainage and water-absorption patterns, and (3) the fire danger from so many transient campers became acute by late summer.

Coping

As the number of people and the problems increased, a weekly meeting was instituted. It was the only formal and structured arrangement of the community (although informal groups were created around specific interests).

In the meeting, members attempted to reach some agreement about methods of dealing with these problems, as well as about soliciting volunteers for the work involved. Over half of the community weekday population attended.

Chuck thought that these meetings were remarkably helpful in dealing with the problems, in view of the fact that Morning Star had no mechanisms for interim decision-making, no prohibitions on any specific acts, and no organizations for such complex long-range projects as building communal facilities.

Collective concern and coordinated action deriving from these meetings produced a number of successful problem-solving activities. Among these projects were:

1. The regular removal of great amounts of trash and litter; this became especially necessary because of the transient population.
2. Restricting the use of automobiles on the property.
3. The implementation of fire-control programs.
4. The prevention of indiscriminate cutting of trees.
5. Use of composted vegetable waste for soil replenishment. In connection with this project, one man who joined the commune in the spring was particularly influential in developing an organic garden and teaching all who were interested. Overpopulation drove him off the land before the end of summer. An ecology class was also organized and taught by Chuck Herrick, co-founder of Ecology Action and a leader of the Peace and Freedom Party's ecology caucus. However, the class was discontinued because the pressure of existing problems was so acute that they had to be dealt with through action rather than just talk.

The Land Selects the People—Or Does It?

To Chuck, the lack of both population planning and control for an ecological balanced community was the major cause for the problems at Morning Star. On the other hand, to Lou and Ramon, control and regulation of the land and people were undesirable and unnecessary. "The land selects the people." When things get bad enough, according to this view, people will leave and the land will be adequate for those who remain. Thus it is apparent that Chuck, Lou and Ramon, between them, represented and espoused two opposing views.

One view is: regulate nothing. Let nature take its course. Nature knows best. Balance will be restored if only man will stop trying to "fix things." It is only man who persists in trying to foul up nature.

The other view is: there has to be an ecological understanding of nature—that is, the dynamics of how each aspect of nature relates. Then we must institute certain controls to keep us from indiscriminately destroying nature and eventually ourselves.

County, health, and sanitation authorities, as well as fire and building inspectors, descended on Morning Star and required major changes in toilet facilities, building improvements, etc. So much needed to be done. The county had no patience. Finally, the authorities required Lou to clear the land of all persons or pay

$500 per day in fines. Lou made one attempt to comply with the clearance order, but when the county made additional demands about cleaning up the property, Lou balked. That fall and winter found Lou in and out of court on charges of contempt, facing fines of over $14,000, which were eventually garnished from his bank account.

Chuck Herrick and Betty Swimmer left Morning Star and worked on The Modern Utopian. Later Ramon also came to Berkeley to work with us as an editor.

Lou at Santa Rosa and Sebastopol

In the spring of 1969 I became minister of the Unitarian-Universalist Fellowship in the city of Santa Rosa, not too far from Morning Star. Lou came to speak to my congregation. Was I impressed. As a guest, he could tell it like it is and that is exactly what he did, turning on the audience that had packed the hall in order to see and hear this controversial local figure.

What a showman. There he was, a huge hulk of a man, tall, with a broad satirical grin and bushy beard. In his worn work clothes and hip rubber boots he looked like the Paul Bunyan of the commune movement. He spoke of avatars and religious practices, sex and dope:

Everyone thinks that if we discovered that opium was good, mankind would then become a group of angleworms, just copulating and ohhhh, God, it would be terrible! That is the kind of fear we have of the poppy. But it's the only way to fly! I'm serious. I'm serious. A quarter grain—nay, an eighth grain of morphine when you got on the airplane, and you would arrive in New York with your face a mask of composure. It's a fact! But it's illegal. A little ball of opium is also excellent for Hong Kong flu. . . . That's all they give you anyway, if you've ever eaten codeine, but that's a false opium. Opium is a little sap which has a bitter taste; it will keep you from taking more than you need. It's good, though.

Now, in India, it is generally considered poor form for anyone to turn on prior to the age of 40. I mean, up until 40 you have this world to deal with, children to rear, a business to get into; but after that, then you must try to free yourself from as many attachments to this world as you can. And if the divine has placed some substance here which, if taken as a diet supplement, helps you to do the trick, you're a fool to not make use of it. Anyone who has prayed seriously in his life, both under the influence of the poppy or the hemp, who will tell me that these substances hinder the progress of prayer, I know he is crazy. They were made to pray with, and that is why the devout Shiva worshippers use these substances in a sacramental manner....

You see, all men are not created equal. All men are created to reflect a facet of His great glory. And the discovery of what your facet is, or as the Gita says, "your own thing," but really your own thing, is the principal job of every human being. It may take a lifetime....

During 1969–1970 I lived in Sebastopol, near Morning Star, and Lou and Rena (his "old lady") and Ramon (who was then living at Sheep Ridge Ranch) would drop in at my place, where we would chat briefly about the magazine, the open-land movement, and the commune movement in general.

While we were talking about communes, Lou blurted out in an authoritative manner, enthusiastically raising himself up on his toes in order to punctuate his remark:

"Morning Star is a training replacement center, or rest and recuperation area, for the army of occupation in the war against the exclusive ownership of land."

"Wow," I replied. "Say that again. I must write that one down."

Lou was pleased. "Here, give me paper and pencil and I'll write it down for you." And he did.

Deeding the Land to God

The county had bulldozed all the Morning Star buildings save one in order to prevent them from being occupied. But people still lived on the property. They slept in tents and bedrolls and sleeping bags; they continued to build temporary shelters. Lou never turned anyone away.

There was little publicity for there were now many more communes around the country than there had been in 1967; the hippie exodus from the cities had already taken place, and only a small number of people lived at Morning Star at any one time. Morning Star was not an ashram, not a commune really, but simply and still emphatically "open land." People came and stayed mainly in warm weather and remained transient.

Lou was still going to court. Now, though, in order to solidify his belief in LATWIDN, Lou decided it would be best to relinquish his legal title to the land and turn it over to a more universal figure, one whom he believed would not be possessive and greedy and restrictive about 32 acres of marginal farm land. So, in the spring of 1969, Lou deeded his land to God.

A short time later God became involved in yet another case in the California courts. In June one Betty Penrose of Oakland sued God for the Morning Star property, claiming that God "so maintained and controlled the weather . . . in such a careless and negligent manner as to cause lightning to strike [her house], setting it on fire and startling, frightening and shocking [her]." At the same time, Paul Yerkes Bechtel, of Tarnal, claimed to be God and became the defendant in the case.

County authorities took Lou to court with evidence that people were still residing on the property in spite of the injunction against him. Lou, standing before the judge in his own defense, stated, "Your honor, you have the wrong person before you. I no longer own the property and therefore am not responsible for anything that goes on there." Lou told the judge that he, the judge, would have to make a decision that would set a precedent, as there had been no similar case in the history of jurisprudence. The assistant district attorney argued that there was a precedent, to which the judge good-humoredly replied that the case would have to be investigated further. And, with a twinkle in his eye to match Lou's, he admitted that this might just be a matter for the appellate court. The judge, it seems, was in good spirits. He was the same judge who had ordered the county to bulldoze the Morning Star buildings.

Eventually, the judge, Judge Kenneth Eiman, ruled that God, not being a "natural or artificial person," could not legally own Gottlieb's property; thus Lou was still the owner and would have to comply with the court's injunction—that was, no one but Lou could live on Lou's property.

Lou then spent several days in legal research and then prepared and submitted a seven-page brief entitled "Memorandum of Points and Authorities" in support of his contention that God could own Morning Star Ranch and that he, Lou, could deed the land to God as free exercise of his religious beliefs as guaranteed under the First Amendment of the U.S. Constitution.

As of this writing (February 1971), the case continues in the courts.

Lou: You know Sun Bear? He's a wonderful man. He told me that among certain Plains Indian tribes they have a custom which is that the minute a chief ceases to serve the interests of his people he awakens one morning to find that his is the only tepee on the campground. The rest of the people have just left—voted with their feet. Many people are doing that in spirit nowadays. I mean they do not wish to be informed of Washington's latest step in the direction of inevitable cataclysm. I don't need that. I don't want to be posted on the minute-to-minute basis of the latest count of catastrophic maneuvers.

Dick: It's a real downer.

Lou: Complete. And anyway, the more I view the situation, the only hope I can see for the future is open land. The only hope ecologically. The only hope sociologically. The only hope in any number of areas. Why? Because on open land you have a juxtaposition of people that is devised by the divine. God is the casting director. God is the personnel manager. And it is the people with whom you live that constitutes the most critical factor in your environment.

Dick: Wouldn't that result in a necessary decrease in population? Because there's only so much space people can live on, otherwise they either kill each other, die of disease or have to move, and there's only so many places where people can live—like people can't live in the middle of a desert or on a barren mountainside.

Lou: Well, you see, first of all it's not so much how many people there are. It's who has put them together and what reason have they been put together, you see. If they have been put together to maximize the rent that can be extracted from a given area, it will be a very sad situation.

Dick: High-rise apartments.

Lou: Yes, that's very bad. And particularly as people rise in the life of the spirit. The minute that consciousness expands at all, you become highly sensitive to what's going on on the other side of this wall. It may be somebody having a terrific hassle with his old lady, whom you've never seen before, and the wall is only four inches thick, and you begin to get these terrifically bad vibes, and you don't understand what's happening, you know. That's one of the things that's wrong with living in the city. All cities are obsolete. They must be evacuated, not as London was evacuated during World War II, but the people who are desperate must be tempted out. How? Not by preaching, certainly. But by an ongoing pilot study of an alternate lifestyle which can be visited. Now the only thing wrong with open land, as far as I can see so far, is there's not enough of it. I have a kind of mystical conviction that there is a proper set of coordinates on the earth's surface for every consciousness. You know, the right place for you to be. The right latitude and longitude for everybody.

Dick: Like in the Teaching of Don Juan. There's one spot on this floor that's your spot.

Lou: Yeah, and it's true on the earth too. Just because we're born in Bengal doesn't mean that's where we're supposed to be. I feel that doing away with no trespassing signs is a step in the right direction. After that come state and national boundaries. I really feel they are tremendously artificial and they are lethal in our time, because they perpetuate this horrible old obsolete territorial imperative that's just turned murderous on us now. The territorial imperative on open land has the tendency to transform into its opposite, which is an instinctive recognition of the privacy and companionship needs of everyone else on the earth. That is the territorial imperative turned into its divine essence. Or, as Walt Whitman says, "The real toward the ideal tending." Did you ever read The Song of The Universe? It's the Gita of the Western Hemisphere. It starts out, "Come, said the Muse, sing me a song no poet yet has chanted. Sing me the Universal." And, you know, it goes up from there.

Conversation with Rena Morning Star

I also had the opportunity in February 1971 to talk with Lou's "old lady" who goes by the name of Rena Morning Star. This is what we talked about (with Lou also joining in later):

Rena: My best rap is about childbirth. You want to know about having a baby on the land? It's all right? Having Vishnu [her son] at Morning Star—and it's important that it's open land, because I believe the policy is "open land, open cervix"—made childbirth much easier. We started out with a good fuck during labor. I highly recommend it! A good fuck sets the stage for a beautiful sexual orgasm. And that's what his birth was. During contractions we chanted "om," which was really really fine. I just put my head in the right place and kept my body relaxed. I was on my knees when he was born, like this, I was leaning on the back of a chair. Lou was massaging me and caressing me, and he just jumped out, I didn't have to push. He just came diving out. It was incredible. Afterwards I ate the placenta. I ate one bite raw, and the rest of it steamed. A few other people shared the sacrament. Many animals eat the placenta, and I tried it and it was really right, it was perfect nourishment. I was totally vegetarian completely, no eggs, no fish, no cheese, but I really put away that placenta. Within hours I was running down to the stream, fetching water, doing Yoga, standing on my head. It was really the biggest orgasm of my life. Incredible! I also stood on my head when I was in labor and did some other Yoga postures.

Dick: How were the labor pains?

Rena: It was all bliss, it really was. It was just a sexual experience, the height of which I've never seen before. It was just really fine.

Dick: I can't believe that now; you're putting me on.

Rena: No! It was really bliss. It was really, really comfortable. I was in shape; I mean, I walked. About 20 miles a week all during pregnancy, plus lots of Yoga every day. Eating right, too.

Dick: Did you do any preparation exercises for labor?

Rena: Just walking and Yoga. Living on the land, I just wanted to tune in to the land and let the trees and the sky and the sunshine teach me how. I've sunbathed naked a lot, maybe that helped. I didn't know I was in labor until 20 minutes before he came out.

Dick: That's far out, I have to say.

Rena: Also, as far as acid babies go, Vishnu was conceived on acid. I had a lot of acid while I was pregnant.

Dick: He seems pretty healthy.

Rena: Oh, he's perfect, he's really perfect. And he likes acid. When I take it now he gets high through my milk, and he's really really beautiful on it. I haven't given him any straight—just what he gets from my milk.

Dick: Babies don't need acid, do they? I mean, they already are high most of the time.

Rena: Oh yes, they're really happy. But he is different; when I take acid he tends to laugh a lot more and sleep a lot deeper. He just starts giggling, and then it's just a total pleasure. A very conscious baby… A critical thing is volitional conception. Vishnu was consciously conceived. Another aspect is eating right. If you don't eat sugar you won't get morning sickness. I was totally macrobiotic: no sugar, no honey, no meat of any kind. I never felt so healthy in my life as when I was pregnant. Also, when you eat sugar you get an artificial sense of nourishment. Most pregnant chicks will crave ice cream cones or Hershey bars. I would crave things like artichokes and spinach. . .

■ ■ ■

Dick: It seems that the open-land thing is a very male-dominated program. What about women's liberation?

Lou: I'll tell you why women like open land. It gives them the liberty to live like slobs. That's right. Women are absolutely slaves to the ridiculous dwellings in which they live. Dwellings that have to be kept neat—the neatness of the parade ground. Women want to live like slobs, without being criticized for it. And that's what you can do on open land. A lot of houses on open land really aren't very neat.

Rena: All I know is that living on the land has given me what I wanted to be when I grew up. My demonstration is in my lifestyle, seeing how much bliss I can tolerate, how much nothing I can do... Inaction in action. I guess Vishnu helps, though. Having a baby, having a family, living with God in the country. Just being free to trip as I want to. That's what Morning Star gives me. That's really fine. On open land you can just about make any scene you want. God takes care of all your needs. All you have to do is will it.

Dick: That's a very good combination. God takes care of all your needs—all you have to do is will it. Which is a combination of: you've got to do it, even though God takes care of it. The willing is something that you do, right?

Rena: Sometimes consciously. But it's all part of a divine plan.... ■

psychedelic
and art
communities

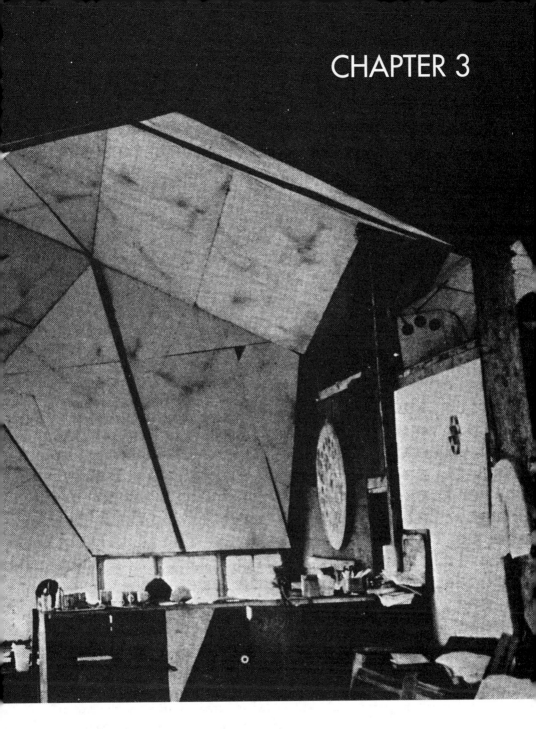

CHAPTER 3

SHEEP RIDGE RANCH (WHEELER'S)
by Richard Fairfield

IN THE WINTER OF 1967, AFTER SONOMA COUNTY OFFICIALS began bulldozing the buildings at Morning Star, a 28-year-old neighbor decided to open his land. Four years earlier, using money inherited from his father, Bill Wheeler had bought 320 acres of land in Occidental, California. He had built his own house out of hewn timbers and had made provisions for plenty of glass windows to let the sun shine in. He did all this because he wanted a place where he could paint and live quietly with his young wife and their infant son.

When he opened his land, the county authorities were quick to move in and condemn his home as not being up to code standards. They wanted to discourage another Morning Star.

After his home was condemned, Bill and family moved into a tent and an adjacent, 12-foot-square shed with old windows as sides. The home became his studio for painting and for building natural furniture; it also became a convenient place to hold community meetings.

So it was that Sheep Ridge Ranch (commonly known as Wheeler's Ranch) became an open-land community. People began to arrive, among them some refugees from Morning Star. Tree houses, shacks, tepees, domes—shelters of all sorts were built at the edge of the woods, on the hillside, and deep into the woods. A few residents acutely aware of the vogue for county harassment took great pains to conceal their homes.

At the present time, most of the dwellings at Sheep Ridge Ranch are small and airy structures made nearly entirely of used materials, such as old lumber, doors, and windows, which are employed for walls. Twigs, branches, and mud covered over by plastic sheeting are used for ceilings. The floor is typically a dirt floor, although a few of the better shelters have wooden ones. There is, of course, no water, no phone or mail service, no electricity. A few shelters have stoves. The climate is mild, sunny, and dry in the summer, but it tends to be damp and rainy in the winter.

It is a two-mile hike from the center of Sheep Ridge Ranch to the county road, then another five or six miles to the nearest small town. The last half of the trail into the Ranch, or The Ridge, as residents call it, is so rutted that only four-wheel-drive vehicles (and hikers) can make it to the parking area without danger. Still, there are always several vehicles and an occasional trailer on the property. Bill Wheeler, like Lou Gottlieb, preaches against the evils of the automobile and mechanized equipment but such opinions have not prevented him—until recently—from owning several vehicles, including a tractor used in the community garden. Cars are always available to take residents to town for shopping, to the city on business, or to court. Cars are among the harsh realities of modern life, even if one practices "voluntary primitivism."

Like Morning Star and other open-land communities, Sheep Ridge Ranch places its emphasis on people's relation to the land rather than their relation to each other. As a rule, there is little departure from traditional standards on the interpersonal level. Women retain their subordinate roles as homemakers, child-bearers, cooks, and bottle washers. Men roam the land in search of food, dope, and occasionally other women. The double standard, monogamous family units, separate housing and cooking, private property (except for land) prevail. Following the territorial imperative, each family unit usually stakes out its own space. Others are welcome to visit that space but not to occupy it.

No doubt, the concept of "Land Access To Which Is Denied No One" requires this separation of units on the land in order to avoid overcrowding in any one space and to maximize individual freedom. It supports and encourages the do-your-own-thing hippie ethic, which is very closely tied to the good old American tradition of rugged individualism, although the hippie way is in fact a rugged cooperative individualism rather than competitive. The ideal is for people to relate to each other as they feel the need. The problem is that individuals come together on the land with most of the hang-ups they acquired from the society they left. Little improvement in the depth and quality of human relationships can occur under these conditions, as the need for individual freedom takes precedence over the need for community. "Community" means working problems out with others, not just doing what you want to do. It means having to compromise and to do some things that may be disagreeable. Open-land people, like Bill, Ramon, and Lou, are highly individualistic, preferring to spend a lot of their time working on the land, reading, meditating, and tripping. Although they espouse personal change and personal enlightenment, they see this coming about in man's relationship to the land more than in his relationship to people.

Those on The Ridge who feel a greater need for community form loose-knit bonds with other residents and share a number of resources; also they occasionally eat together.

Residents, as well as transients and visitors, convene each Sunday for a communal feast and sauna bath. Wood is chopped in the morning and a fire is made to heat rocks for the bath. By noon, naked bodies are running into the plastic sauna tent, which is sealed off on all sides. Old wine jugs filled with water are poured on the red-hot rocks inside the tent and the steam permeates the enclosure. After a few minutes of sweating on the mud floor, naked bodies dart out to a cold shower.

This was the scene when Consuelo and I arrived at The Ranch in the spring of 1970. I was impressed with the fact that Bill had installed six chemical toilets and that they were all in good working order.

We sat down on the outer edge of the larger circle that was gathering near the outdoor communal kitchen. Big steel pots of food were being prepared. A gong sounded several times. Presently everyone stood up, joined arms, and began to chant and sway in thanksgiving for the food that was about to be served. Then lines formed and the food was passed out on paper plates. It was a tasty macrobiotic meal of rice and vegetables. Most of the residents adhere with varying degrees of fanaticism to a macrobiotic or vegetarian diet.

I had never met Bill Wheeler, but I quickly spotted him in the crowd, because I had published his picture (taken by a friend and professional photographer, Bob Fitch) in The Modern Utopian. Bill is a very young-looking man, and very Anglo-Saxon—blue eyes, light blond hair and beard. He talks with vibrant enthusiasm. He is not shy and seems glad to answer all inquiries and share his opinion on whatever subject is being discussed.

The subject we discussed most that day was his forthcoming trip to court. He had two or three cases pending. One was an assault charge, another had to do with the rights of way on the road, and the third was the usual harassment by county health and sanitation authorities.

Actually Bill and the other residents are quite conscious of sanitation: food scraps are buried for compost, paper and trash is collected and burned periodically. Yet it is easy for officials to find fault if they want to do so.

Early in the morning on October 31, 1969, a 25-man army of policemen, narcotics agents, juvenile officers, FBI agents, et al., had descended on Sheep Ridge Ranch without benefit of either invitation or search warrant. They said they were looking for juvenile runaways and Army deserters. When they arrested one of the female residents, Bill objected. Without warning, an officer swung around with handcuffs in hand and gashed Bill's forehead with them. This led to a melee of hitting, shoving, and pushing, and the subsequent arrest of Bill and four others on felony charges of assaulting an officer.

When the testimony was all in at the trial, Bill and friends were found not guilty on three counts. The jury could not agree on four other counts, so the judge declared a mistrial.

Bill Wheeler Bathes for an Interview

Going to court is a regularly scheduled event for Bill, which is why every time I see him he's either on his way to court or just finished with it. One such time was in February 1971, after I had moved to San Francisco. Bill came in to visit and be interviewed while taking a bath in my tub. We talked of many things:

Dick: What's happened in the last six months? I haven't been on The Ranch since last July.

Bill: Well, physically the place is growing, there are more and more people coming on. It seems to be the general consensus of opinion that the place is higher than ever, and there are just some really wonderful people there. It's also the general consensus that we're more together than we ever have been. The sort of organic evolutionary process that we're founded on is bearing fruit now, in terms of a real group head and a feeling of a real group purpose. We're all in a learning process and experimenting and trying to find out what will work, trying to find out in our own heads how we really fit in. I find I become more and more enthusiastic as time goes on.

Dick: That's good. Especially with the open-land concept. Because that's a pretty heavy trip on a person, to have people come in without kicking them off. Do you have any provisions for eliminating people if they get too troublesome?

Bill: Well, in the first year or two I had to kick off one or two people in a very—I didn't really kick them off—I merely said to them, "Look, we have a real personality problem here. The planet earth is a very large place. And we're not supposed to be in the same place." In the last two years, now, there's been no problem. With one exception—one kid who came up here whose mind was completely blown, I guess on speed or something, and was totally psychotic and was a case ideally suited for Marat-Sade. You see, there's sort of a fine balance on the land between private property and communal property, and people soon learn when they come on the land that just because it's open land doesn't necessarily mean that you have the right to go into anybody's place. A person's home is private and this boy couldn't comprehend that. He went in and tore places apart, and started getting automobiles and tearing them apart. At first the more devoted maniacs for open land would say, "Oh, he's all right," and then after a while said, "Something's gotta be done about that kid."

Dick: And you had to be the one to do the something about it, no?

Bill: Well, it got to the point where it was more than me. It wasn't a personal thing. . . But in general we've had a very beautiful sort of people, and I really see that the open-land concept—you know, all of Lou's theories of the divine casting—is true. When there's a need and when something has to be done, if you've got open land, that person appears and the job gets done. I've seen it happen time and time again. . . As time has gone on there have been people who have settled there, who have adjusted to the open-land concept and have become dedicated to it. They've also found their own niche, for what they do on The Ranch. We have one person who takes care of the water. We have one person who will do a community run of some kind or other, and we have another person who takes care of the livestock. Each person seems to have found a thing. It's really an incredible thing just to watch it happen, sort of unfold before your eyes. We've been very fortunate that the legal problems, although they're still very critical against us, have been somewhat resolved.

Dick: There was a time when you were worried that the road access to the property would be cut off.

Bill: Yes, absolutely. See, we've had a real hard time legally. We've probably had as hard a time as any commune could possibly have. The county is trying to close us down, the access is being denied to us by a neighbor: two major lawsuits. That's a pretty heavy thing to fight.

Dick: Why do you think that the county has been so opposed to this open-land thing?

Bill: There are many reasons. But I would say one of the primary ones is economic. Naturally, there are elements of politics involved. "The hippies are living off welfare, living off the fat of the land. Why are they having such a good time while us people have to slave in factories eight hours a day?" That's part of it. Another part is that we depress land values in the area.

Dick: People don't want to buy land next to a hippie commune.

Bill: Sure, unless they're hippies themselves. Also, the access road is through the property of a man who is very influential politically, and has, you know, made a major contribution to the DA's election fund. So, he's able to bring force against us.

Dick: I have theorized that maybe some of the local, rural teenage girls come out there. Then their parents get uptight because there might be a bad influence on them and so they go to the DA to try to get rid of you. Is that a valid reason?

Bill: No, not really. The high school was coming there. A couple of them, maybe five or six, were up there sitting around. Actually I was very nervous about it. But, our thing, our ace in the hole so to speak, is the access road, which is such a miserable road. It's the old Marshall McLuhan thing, the 20th century is communication. Well, we are living in the 19th century: that road buffers us. Primarily because of automobiles. People do not want to leave their cars. This is slightly off the subject, but speaking of automobiles, it's been a problem which has bothered me for a long time. . . the whole problem of exclusive transportation. My vision had been that The Ranch would have strictly communal automobiles, no private cars. As it's worked out, The Ranch is so large and there are so many people, it's really hard to have a policy like that. But we have gotten a school bus on the land, a 32-passenger 1950 International school bus, and we squeeze in about 50 guys. And we've got a ton-and-a-half flatbed truck. I've sworn myself never to own another automobile as long as I live.

Dick: That's a hard thing to do.

Bill: Yeah, well, it's where it's at, though. Because the air's becoming unbreathable. With the bus, we pollute much less. Like 1/32nd of a pollution per person. Less than that actually 'cause we often have 50 or 60 people riding in the bus at a time. The whole point of The Ranch up there, or a lot of it, is that we are learning new lifestyles. Part of that alternative lifestyle is a low-consuming way of life. So private transportation, which means more pollution, is out. We combine forces for communal transportation, otherwise just hitchhike. It's amazing what a wonderful way of getting around hitchhiking is.

Lou has found it out. He says he loves it. I told him last year, "Get rid of your car, Lou, like, you gotta hitchhike."

Dick: Has he gotten rid of his car?

Bill: Oh yeah. He doesn't own a car any more.

Dick: How does he get to court?

Bill: He hitchhikes.

Dick: Isn't that a problem? Hitchhiking is not a time-oriented thing and if you've got a time when you have to be there....

Bill: You'd be amazed at how easy it is to get rides. Incidentally, we now have our own food conspiracy on The Ranch—we order food in bulk about two weeks before we're going to buy it. We send out a list of available stuff and people order what they want. My wife adds it up, and then someone goes into San Francisco. We try to get about $50 worth extra for the free store, so that that people on the land who don't have any money can get free food. We do this once every month. People are very excited about it; it's a real getting away from health food stores and getting real participation in the commune. So that's been a really nice thing. We've also set up a church, the Ahimsa Church, which is tax-exempt for California, and we hope to get federal exemption soon. The ownership of the land will be in the church and the ownership of the bus and truck will be in the church.

Dick: You're not going to deed the land to God?

Bill: No, the land is going to be in the Ahimsa Church. It's written in the deed that it's "land access to which is denied no one." The land cannot be sold, nor can it be used for exploitative purposes. There always has been a funny dichotomy between Morning Star and The Ridge, in that, well, you know, we love Morning Star, it's our spiritual home, it's our Mecca so to speak. But we also see that we're in a New Age and we've got to get together. A lot of it has to do with the nature of the land, a lot of it has to do with who's there who originated it and stuff, and we've fought hard for our alternative kind of status. The reason we've been as successful as we have is because we're isolated. Appropriately isolated from straight society. Whereas Morning Star is so close and so exposed, it's like a raw nerve. This is one of the reasons why they've had such a hard time. Tourists in general are very debilitating to a community. I think most places have found this and it's really a drag. People coming in with cameras and people getting uptight. The reason we don't have to get uptight is because we're isolated enough that anyone who cares enough to walk in that far is cool. Also, if a person is uncool, there's enough of us and so few of them that we're protected. And they know it. There are a lot of people down there. Very rarely do we ever get any really bad trouble, in terms of drunks coming in and stuff like that. We had one scary thing happen up on The Ridge. One guy just opened up one day with a rifle. It scared the shit out of everybody. Some drunk came roaring in, you know. But this could happen anywhere. It could happen in San Francisco, walking up Haight Street. I'll say this, that The

Ridge is maintaining its record of lots of babies and no deaths. And no major injuries actually. We've had a few illnesses but....

Dick: A young person living on the land like that might be able to stand it better than someone who's older. But when he himself gets older, if he's there long enough, it might take effect on him—rheumatism, that kind of thing. I was wondering if there is an awareness of the possible ill effects of this. Obviously there are good things about living really close to the land, but most of us are not geared to that kind of thing.

Bill: I suppose this is one of the ways that open land has a built-in population control.

Dick: You either build a suitable place or you leave.

Bill: Yeah, it's not all a bed of roses. You see thousands and millions and millions of people in the city and you say to yourself: why aren't they all up on The Ranch, free land and all? But it's hard. And, I don't know, it's kind of a mystical thing. The thing about it is we are the avant-garde, we are the, if you will, the future. We are learning new ways of living. I was just reading—it's a ridiculous book but—Leon Uris' Exodus, the Israeli thing. Like, I'd never really read too much about Zionism and all the things they went through in Israel. But I see real parallels between what happened there and the young people who are moving from the cities and on to the land here. The parallels are alike in a lot of different ways. For example, much of the early experiments of the Israelis were very disappointing and they needed support from the world Jews to keep them going. They couldn't support themselves. In this sense I feel that the welfare trip which goes on at The Ranch is really just a subsidy from the government to help us get going. Because agriculture things take years and years and years to get going. Home industries take a long time to get going to support themselves. Most people want to support themselves. I don't think there's really anybody on welfare who doesn't want to support himself. But it's going to take time for us young people to find out where we're at, to know exactly what we want to do. The energies are there. There's no doubt in my mind about that. The imagination is there—no doubt about that. What I've seen of what can be done, it's incredible. But it's going to take time. The real insight which I had on this was the Bolinas thing—the Standard Oil disaster in the Bay. I was out in Bolinas, and just to see thousands and thousands of young people out—most of them longhairs—doing a really beautiful thing cleaning up.

Dick: Yes, and the older people there were Standard Oil employees. They were getting paid for the work, and the longhairs weren't.

Bill: Right. Therefore the experiments, such as Morning Star and such as The Ranch, are of critical importance to this country. We are finding ways—ecological ways—to live in harmony with the earth. It's not easy. Time's gone on and a lot of communes have fallen by the wayside; others are still there—like Morning Star is still there—in spite of everything that's happened. The Ranch is better than ever, you know: it's going great guns. And the authorities know it.

Dick: Do they still come onto the property to check you out?

Bill: No, they haven't been on the property for, oh God, well, they came up maybe three or four months ago, to deliver a message—some girl whose mother was dying or something.

Dick: I've been getting the feeling that there's getting to be an awful lot more tolerance of longhairs at least in urban areas where people have had more exposure. It seems the media have picked up on the positive aspects as well as the negative ones lately.

Bill: It goes in cycles. There was a cycle like this about a year and a half ago, in which it looked like communes were the up-and-coming thing, you know. Life magazine had their beautiful article, all those pretty, you know, apple-pie photographs. And I mean, it's just yummy! It looked like: "Oh my God, we made it! They've accepted us. Wonderful!" Two weeks later what happened? Manson. And the honeymoon was over. My feeling is that it's very similar to the Army, like Manson was the My Lai of the hippie movement. The Manson thing has blown over; people really don't have much interest in that any more. ■

OLOMPALI RANCH

by Richard Fairfield

THE ONLY TIME I RECEIVED PROMOTIONAL LITERATURE FROM a commune was in June 1968, when Ralph Silver, then a public relations man and now a film producer, sent a news clipping about Olompali Ranch to The Modern Utopian.

I had already heard that a dropped-out millionaire had started a commune a few miles north of San Francisco, but I didn't have sufficient time or motivation to check it out. Nevertheless, Silver's clipping caught the attention of Betty and Ramon, then editors of the magazine; they had lived at Morning Star Ranch and were much closer to the hip commune scene experientially than I could ever begin to be.

After a two-day visit, Betty wrote a brief summary about Olompali and its founder, Don McCoy:

> *Don McCoy has what at first seems a resort for the wealthy. The 750-acre ranch includes an elegant historical mansion with tiled swimming pool and four color televisions. The kids are taught by Mrs. Garnett Brennan, an exciting Summerhillian, fired as principal in Nicasio for saying she had smoked marijuana for 18 years. Don has long hair and, as her public ally, says that drugs, if properly used, can be the most valuable experience of one's life. People go around naked in and around the pool. Homegrown vegetables are part of the diet. Twice a week 1,000 loaves of free bread for San Francisco communes are baked by nude members of the community and SF Free City people, moving in the hot sun between the outdoor bakery on an octagonal concrete slab and the pool. The driveway has a sign posted that says no visitors unless you feel like negotiating about this policy. The community grows from inside out mostly, having expanded from 25 to 44. (June 1968)*

Don McCoy, a big man in his 30s, inherited some money from his father and then, through shrewd investments in real estate, amassed a fortune of $500,000. But accumulating great wealth was not enough for Don; he was looking for something else. He found it in San Francisco, where he discovered the flower children in the then-beautiful Haight-Ashbury district, turned on, grew a beard, and dropped out. With him went several friends, including Sandy Barton, a successful nightclub entertainer, and the children of Sergeant Sunshine, the pot-smoking San Francisco police officer.

Originally, Don McCoy leased only five acres of the ranch. But after patrons of a neighboring riding school complained about seeing nude sunbathers near the swimming pool, McCoy took over the lease on the entire property and evicted the riding school.

Most members found much to admire in Don, who had assumed the dual role of both leader and benefactor to the commune. However, there was clearly a streak of resentment in some members because of their leader/benefactor's paternalism and affluence.

Don spent his money freely and lavishly. During the first year, beginning November 1967 (when he and his friends first occupied the property), he spent half of his wealth on cars, motorcycles, color television sets, musical instruments and clothes. In addition, he set up an elaborate bakery, a recording studio, and arts and crafts workshops. As a result his father-in-law filed a lawsuit against him, contending that Don was squandering money that should be set aside to support his children and grandchildren.

After the lawsuit was filed, McCoy and two other members, including Sheyla McKendrick, flew to India to meditate with a holy man. Shelya's former husband, Robert McKendrick, then took over leadership of the commune. He had a background in business, plus unbounded optimism. He wanted the commune to become self-supporting, with income derived from the production of food and crafts. A leather shop and jewelry shop were set up; commercial plans were made for the bakery and organic garden.

Robert McKendrick's enthusiasm was not shared by most of the other family members. They did not wish to be regimented into a work schedule. Some of the people wanted only to look at trees—an activity that McKendrick had a tendency to interrupt with irritating and, to the watchers, incomprehensible, questions such as "What are you doing?" As a result, much friction was generated, but not much work. By the end of December 1968, McKendrick's leadership had declined almost to the point of disappearance. And in January he himself followed suit, leaving for parts unknown.

Meanwhile, on Christmas Eve, McCoy returned from India with an intense religious message for the members. Unfortunately, this neither averted nor alleviated the series of misfortunes that soon befell the commune:

—A visitor was accidentally killed while riding a motorcycle around the nearby village of Novato.
—There were two large-scale drug raids on the commune in mid-January.
—One of the ranch's horses wandered out onto Highway 101 and was hit by a motorist, with the result that the latter was killed.
—On February 2, the old wiring in the main house shorted out and the ensuing fire gutted the building.

—McCoy lost the lawsuit; his supply of money was cut to a bare minimum and he lost custody of his children.

He also spent some time in the Napa State Hospital and the Marin General Hospital, his ailment being described as a physical breakdown.

From February through July the remaining 20 or so commune members tried to pull things together. They wanted to create a working communal ranch with a school and spiritual center. But firm leadership was lacking. They could not decide which of their projects should be given top priority, nor how to go about implementing them.

Aside from difficulties about future projects, the commune had money problems right then, seriously aggravated by Don McCoy's decline in fortunes. The utility bills alone ran from $150 per month in the summer to $350 in the winter; the rent was between $600 and $900 a month. Getting this much money together was hard although donations, especially one for $2,200 and another for $500, eased the pressure somewhat. Nearly every day it was necessary to appeal for funds from visitors and residents just to get enough money together to buy dinner. There were continued purchases of musical instruments (including a piano), clothes, and other "necessities," yet everyone bummed cigarettes and there was no money to put the pool back in running order when warm weather arrived.

Like many other hippie communes, Olompali Ranch could not agree on how to deal with visitors. Many members wanted the commune to be closed with no outsiders allowed; others felt they should welcome everyone; no one, on either side, had the strength to actually turn visitors away. Guests might insist that they would vanish into the upper woods, but they all had a way of showing up in the kitchen at dinnertime.

The relationships between adults were often strained and abrasive. The pressures and diverse aims had taken their toll; disparaging remarks punctuated nearly every conversation. The most obvious interpersonal successes on the ranch were the relationships the children established with each other and with adults. The ranch's animal contingent—11 horses, a cow, and a vast number of cats and dogs—no doubt helped keep the children occupied.

But more than that, there was a near total absence of whining and bickering. Children were treated with the maturity they had earned. A 13-year-old could be treated as an adult on some matters and as a child on others. Breakfast was a free-lance affair, with the older children helping the younger ones.

Ironically, it was with the unfortunate deaths of two of the children in June that Olompali itself came to an end. Four-year-old Audrey and two-year-old Nika were pedaling a tricycle along the edge of the unfenced pool and fell in. By the time they were discovered it was too late to save them. The Establishment press sensationalized the accident, implying gross negligence on the part of the commune. County, health, and sanitation authorities descended on the ranch and produced a long list of code violations. The landlord ordered everyone off the property within 30 days. Within eight hours of these orders and after dinnertime, the 40 residents were reduced to 18—almost all the guests left; all the children were sent away before the impending visit of the probation officer. A few die-hard members remained at Olompali until they were forced to leave by the landlord's order.

So the commune at Olompali Ranch died in the summer of 1969, at the tender age of 20 months. ∎

THE HIPPIE TRIBE

by Jan Hammermeister, Morningstar Farm Tribe
Hundred Flowers, UPS Fall 1971

MY TRIBE IS MORNING STAR FARM NEAR TAOS, NEW MEXICO. I left Minneapolis last winter with some of the New Riverside Cafe Tribe to take a five-week vacation in California. While looking for the Hog Farm in Taos, we stumbled upon Morning Star.

After half a day there with mountains, a half-day's walk to the northeast and miles of plains edged by mountains to the distant southwest, I knew I would remain there. I could see sky from horizon to horizon as far as an eye at an altitude of 7200 feet can see.

This tribe had a rough beginning at the old Morning Star in Northern California. Having their houses bulldozed, some of them migrated to New Mexico. The land, mostly adobe mud, sand, cactus, sage, juniper and cedar, was declared unfarmable. Two years later, an Indian-Hippie-style adobe pueblo stands and in the fields, for the third summer, are growing roots and vegetables.

The tribe of 15 has grown to a tribe of 40 (50–60 in the summer). We remain open to everyone. There are lots of children, ranging in age from five months to 10 years. We have a healthy number of teenagers and the "elders" are from 27–31 in age. Because we are open to everyone, a lot of people pass through, most of them sightseers or "tourists" as we sometimes refer to them.

But many times people come through and dig it and have something to offer, settle and help improve the place. Like anywhere else in the world, the balance of energies is of prime concern. We are living at a very primitive level in that most of our time is spent on food, shelter, water, and in the winter, keeping warm.

We have no electricity. We cook on wood-burning stoves, use kerosene lamps for light and since our well went dry this summer, we have been hauling our water in 50-gallon drums on an old flatbed truck, up and down a hairpin switchback from our neighboring commune, New Buffalo.

We water our crops through irrigation with water from the mountains. We are the last people on the ditch and have to send a representative to ditch meetings twice a week to vie for our need of the water. We bathe at hot springs, swim in the Rio Grande or another small river near by.

There are no jobs to speak of near Taos, so many of us receive food stamps. Some of the men fight fires or lay pipeline for extra income. But a good portion of our food is donated by tourists. We sometimes refer to ourselves as Morning Star Consumption Company. We easily consume in one week 50 lbs. of onions, 100 lbs. of brown rice, 100 lbs. of pinto beans, 100 lbs. of whole wheat flour, four large tins of Bugler tobacco, five 5-lb. cans of coffee, etc.

Our winters get to 40 below and our summer gets to 100. The air is clean and dry. We can see the Milky Way every night, and with our little telescope we can see Jupiter and four of her moons.

We hauled the dogs to the pound not too long ago. They outnumbered the people. I love dogs, but dogs need to eat and we are sometimes concerned about where our next meal will come from. We have some cats, but they have learned to catch birds and mice.

We are gradually getting to know our neighbors better. There are many communes in the area. New Buffalo, the Lama Foundation, and the Hog Farm to mention a few. The city of Taos is more tolerant of us, too.

They realize that we increase their business. There is a free clinic and a dentist who works on teeth for exchange of labor (painting his office, etc.).

We have artists, musicians, architects, people into edible and medicinal herbs and plants and people with many other talents. We are becoming less and less a landing for burned-out hippies and more and more like a small town. We were an anarchy up until about two months ago when we started having meetings and now have a tribunal. The organization is sometimes hidden, and still loose, but is gradually coming together.

The Indians showed us how to make adobe bricks and how to build our pueblo. It has been rewarding to experience true friendships with Indians who have not strayed culturally. They teach us many things and are a true inspiration to our spirituality.

Some of the Indians call us the Hippie Tribe and treat us as their own sons and daughters, which of course, we are. ■

HIPPIES AND HASSLES IN TAOS

by Richard Fairfield

ALTHOUGH THEY DO SO FOR DIFFERENT REASONS, MANY people from both the straight and hip worlds descend on the Taos area each year. When Consuelo and I were there in 1970, we found the area swarming with hip people. Some of them were seeking out or setting up communes; many of the others, in pairs and small groups, were simply building homes for themselves wherever they could. Most of these people were too poor to afford good dope (marijuana, as well as acid and other psychedelics) and too wise to get into speed and amphetamines. But such distinctions were lost on the arbiters of morality and upholders of law among the citizenry. Consequently, it didn't take too many young hoods, alias transient hippies, alias teenyboppers, alias kick-kids (never the permanent residents) who were intent upon wrecking their minds and bodies in order to give all hip people a bad name.

One of the casualties of the Taos hippie-hassles was a nearby commune called Five Star. Situated in a resort town known for its hot springs, Five Star had consisted principally of a large building in which all the residents lived, a parking lot, and some hot springs. When hippies (from the outside, not the commune) began flooding into the town, the local authorities got very upset. After all, the hippies didn't have much if any money to spend and their presence scared off all the well-heeled citizens of America who were willing to pay well for their vacations amid the town's hot springs. So the authorities decided to harass the commune, and they continued to do so until they had forced it to close which happened shortly before we arrived in the area.

Meanwhile, not to be outdone in such matters concerning the public welfare, the authorities in nearby Taos called off that town's annual fiesta (an important source of income for local Indians and Chicano people) on the pretext that there would be too many hippies in the area and that such a gathering would constitute a health hazard. As a result, greater hostility was generated toward the newly arrived hippies.

Among the still-existing communes in the Taos area [as of 1971] is Morning Star East, which was founded by refugees from Lou Gottlieb's Morning Star Ranch in California. When started in April 1969, the 35-acre property had about 35 residents. Since then, however, the commune's population has varied considerably, because it is based on the same open-land principle as Morning Star Ranch, that is, no one is denied access to the commune's land. The residents at Morning Star East have been active in constructing a number of adobe houses and a communal kitchen. In fact, when much of the construction was being carried out, they were making close to 2,000 adobe bricks per month! However, because anyone can come and build a home at Morning Star East, the commune is, of necessity, loosely organized. This has resulted in some unfortunate occurrences. For example, when we were in the area in 1970, we heard that the community was attracting a lot of people who were interested only in getting high mainly on cheap wine and amphetamines. But we also got another report that was more positive and optimistic: a great celebration was being planned in which the residents would be getting together with the Indian members of the Native American Church for a peyote ceremony.

New Buffalo

We wanted to visit New Buffalo because it seemed to be the oldest and most developed of the hip communes in the Taos area. The sign near the gate indicated that visitors were not welcome, but we decided to go in anyhow.

We parked alongside several other vehicles in back of a long, low adobe building. This was a motel-like structure, with several private rooms connected to a large kitchen area and a high, oval living-recreation hall. Behind and nearly adjacent to this structure were two other motel-style adobe buildings. And farther back and off to one side was a community garage, with open car stalls in the front. We could see a mechanic busy cleaning and repairing some parts for a disabled truck. There were two tepees and a hogan or two situated a short distance from the main complex and two or three storage sheds somewhat nearer to it.

New Buffalo, we were told, had recently decided to reduce its population from 50 to 25. True, its population could drop as low as 10, as it had the previous winter, but the number quickly increased with warmer weather, reaching the intolerable level of 50. So it was determined that 25 was the maximum number of people that the land and buildings could support with comfort and good sense. Consequently, the 25 most recent members had been asked to leave by the older ones, for as in most communes, length of residence and age meant authority.

While at New Buffalo, we talked mostly with Bill, a serious-minded resident in his mid-30s. He was the one who seemed to hold most sway in the group. Bill was extremely critical of the transient hippies who were coming into the area and causing trouble for everyone, especially for anyone who stayed year-round.

Bill said that he and his wife and two kids were not going to stay. They had been there for several years and he now felt it was time to leave in search of a better environment in which to raise his kids. He was tired of all the hassles. He had, along with others, only recently learned to say "no." The open-armed philosophy of love that welcomed one and all had been beaten and flogged by every insensitive spoiled kid in the country. So it was now time to discriminate: time to take stock of ideals and decide how to live with the awareness that people are less than ideal; time to realize that love has two sides, positive and negative; and time to realize the ability to say, "No, I do not want to help you, I do not want to relate to you," which can be more loving and honest than saying "yes," and not really meaning it.

A list of projects that had to be accomplished was posted on a door in the kitchen. Most of this work related to farming, for New Buffalo was an agricultural commune. However, as Bill said, "This is awfully difficult land to grow crops on. People come here thinking it'll be so easy. It isn't. Then they leave, oftentimes taking much more than they give. Those who remain are the ones who get hurt. Now we have a rule that visitors can stay one night only."

"The sign by the road asked visitors to stay away altogether, didn't it?" I asked. "Yes, but who pays any attention to signs? Did you?" he retorted. "You see, people will come anyway if they want to. There is no way to stop them. We appreciated receiving your letter but we never answer our mail. If you want to come, you will, whether we invite you or not."

"Well, you can lock your gate and put up a sign: 'Trespassers will be shot.' And you can write back to inquiries saying, 'Take this paper and shove it up your asshole.' Or you can set up your own tourist bureau and charge admission for a guided excursion of a genuine hippie commune."

"Yeah, but we don't want to do that sort of thing."

"Perhaps the overnight rule will be adequate for you?"

"I don't know. I'm planning to leave this place in any event."

I felt pained that another idealistic youth had apparently blossomed into manhood at the cost of his ideals. These ideals are not so bad. Great religious leaders, from Buddha to Jesus to those of the present time, have preached them, and organized religions continue to pay hypocritical lip service to them.

It is always the problem of how to change an ideal into reality that gets in the way of both the leaders and the people. A thought is not a deed and never will be.

Consuelo and I gave one of the New Buffalo members a ride to a nearby general store. He had saved a little money and was going to buy some chocolate candy. He told us he was lucky to have been able to stay on at New Buffalo. Before they had taken him in that in that spring, he and his buddy had bummed around the area and lived at Morning Star East awhile. They got drunk all the time, shot speed, and went to town to have fun. Now he was off all that bad stuff. New Buffalo was home. He beamed and all 18 years of his life lit up. As he got out of the car he said, "I'm taking a lot of acid these days. It's a much better high and no hangover. Bye." ■

THE HOG FARM
by Richard Fairfield

YET ANOTHER COMMUNE IN THE TAOS AREA IS THE HOG FARM which gained national publicity in 1969 when members appeared at the Woodstock music festival in New York and ended up distributing free food to and caring for the hundreds of young people freaked out on impure drugs.

Driving in the Taos area is not particularly difficult, but unfortunately the directions on how to get to the Hog Farm were rather sketchy. We ended up atop a hill, driving along a road in which the rocks and ruts got increasingly larger until finally we lost the muffler. After finding the way back to the main highway, I drove to a garage. While waiting for the car to be repaired, Consuelo and I contented ourselves with reading about the Hog Farmers in the latest issue of The Fountain of Light, at that time the local hip newspaper, but now defunct.

We never did get to Hog Farm, but here's part of what that article said:

"The Hog Farm is about 75 people living on 14 acres of land in New Mexico, all taking care of each other and this one hog and her friend."

I started laughing. "All those people taking care of just one hog?"

"And each other. And 15 chickens that lay 10 eggs a day on methedrine."

"Hmmm…. Now let me see if I've got this straight: 75 people living on 14 acres of land, all taking care of one hog and 15 chickens laying 10 eggs a day, and each other?"

"From Woodstock the Hog Farm was hired to police a pop festival in Dallas. Again, they set up a free kitchen, first-aid and freak-out tents, ran a light show on the free stage, and gave both physical and spiritual nourishment to anyone who needed it.

From Dallas the Hog Farmers went home to New Mexico, only to find the house full of strangers—some stranger than others. On waves of publicity, seekers from all over the country who had been turned on by the Hog Farm had washed up on the property and pitched their pup tents. When the dinner gong rang, long lines of people stood outside the kitchen with their plates and tin cups, waiting to be fed. Often there wasn't enough to go around.

Overcrowding almost inevitably tends to uptightness. The Daily Hogtopus, the Hog Farm paper, ran the following item about a meeting held near the Sea of Krasnakovitch (a small pond):

It was one of those occasions on which everybody got a chance to speak out. It seems that the "family" is split into two different camps, overlapping in various ways. One side, generalizing, feels that the greatest favor we can do for newcomers is to tell them, although nicely, to split. The other side, again generalizing, feels that whoever comes up the hill is here for a reason and becomes family in such a sense that whether he stays here or not, we should be able to enjoy his presence and either help him on to do his own scene, or to become a Hog Farmer. It all sounded sort of confusing, but somehow a greater feeling of benevolence prevailed.

Meanwhile, Hugh Romney—then the Hog Farm's spiritual leader and spokesman—had gone on to California to set things up for a seven-day Starve-In, which was supposed to happen on October 11. With the members' double consent, Romney committed them to be there. But the caravan buses were delayed day after day at the farm by mechanical difficulties and sluggish cosmic machinery. By the night the buses were finally ready to roll, the Starve-In had already begun. Snow in Nevada and bus breakdowns en route made certain that they reached California too late.

Romney was upset. His work had been violated. So, he chose to sever all visible connections with the Hog Farm, even to the point of changing his name to Wavy Gravy. He now wanted to get together a few people, about 20, who could be responsible for their commitments, and a fast bus that could speed to wherever it was needed.

Some members drifted back to the farm in New Mexico, some stayed on in California. Others joined Hugh Romney on his super bus and went on to other things.

Meanwhile, back at the farm, a handful of people decided to stick out the winter, put up an A-frame, and try to make the farm into a real home so that the rest of the family would have something nice to return to. Now, instead of handing out insufficient food to long lines of people waiting outside for dinner, the family could sit down together at three long polished tables, holding hands for a few moments in silence and dining by candlelight.

Conditions gradually improved during that winter—the winter of 1969–1970. Alberto organized the back room of the information house into an arts and crafts workshop, where he began turning out some very attractive jewelry. Mark Twain got into building adobe ovens. A well was dug on the property, but there still wasn't any indoor plumbing. Meals were cooked over, and houses heated by, a wood stove. The farm's animal population totaled three chickens, five rabbits, some cats and kittens, four goats, too many dogs and dear old Pigasus. And, during that winter, the members nurtured their plans for planting a vegetable garden in the spring.

There were now two adobes and a cabin, which together were capable of housing a maximum of about 26 people. The Hog Farm population was down to about 20 people ("no men, no women —all children"), and they kind of hoped to keep it that way. Subsequently, a three-day visiting limit was posted.

Lately the "children" have been out doing odd jobs around the neighborhood, pulling stumps and transplanting trees in order to earn enough money to make the farm's land payment every month. Some well-meaning idiots bought the farm a flatbed truck and half a backhoe, hoping that these would make the farm self-sufficient. The flatbed is presently out of action because it will cost $91 to register. The backhoe keeps breaking down and can't even finish paying for itself, much less anything else. But somehow, with faith in the cosmos, themselves, and each other, the members keep on trucking. They made a deal with a neighbor who fixed the backhoe the first time; in return, the "children" dug him a hole for a septic tank. Hog Farmers would really rather trade services than deal in cash. ▪

THE LOWER FARM
by Richard Fairfield

WE HAD HEARD RUMORS OF THE EXISTENCE OF SEVERAL HIPPIE-style communes in Placitas, New Mexico. So we decided to hunt them down in April 1970. Not having much luck in locating one of these communities, we stopped in at the local post office to inquire. But we were late and the post office had already closed. Noting an elderly man sitting in front of a house just a few yards away, we sauntered over to see if he'd be open to our inquiries. He was responsive and invited us in for coffee and cookies. Mr. C.W. McFall turned out to be a retired high school teacher who had taught in the South most of his life. Having lived in Placitas for two years, he was quite familiar with the people in the local communes. He offered to serve as our guide. We piled into his old Volvo and headed for the Lower Farmhome of Ulysses S. Grant who, in addition to being the self-identified reincarnation of the other and earlier Ulysses S. Grant, was a commune leader and a candidate for governor of New Mexico.

After leaving the main highway, we drove along a winding dirt road into a valley. Numerous adobe houses and several tepees dotted the hillside. The sun had nearly set when we arrived at the little village complex.

One or two people were wandering around, but the place seemed deserted. Eventually Ulysses showed up and invited us into a back room of the main house. The room had recently been vacated by a member who was asked to leave, he told us. Said member had apparently been uncooperative and the cause of trouble in the community.

"We're not a commune," Ulysses said without hesitation. "Communes don't work—we're a village. We have a mayor and courts and laws just like any other village." We learned more. The village had been legally incorporated as a non-profit organization, complete with and run by a board of directors. No one who lived there was allowed to hold an outside job. The members had almost no money. Some residents used food stamps. There was no rent to pay because the land and buildings were owned by the corporation and because maintenance expenses were minimal. The property had a long history of use by squatters. And, as Ulysses said, anyone who wished to come and build on the land was welcome to do so. People are not subject to the rules of the village unless they actually live in it, meaning in the main complex of seven adobe buildings. The property was bounded on three sides by a national forest, and on the fourth side by an uptight neighbor who continually complained that the commune's horses got into his hay.

A tall lanky fellow came into the room wrapped only in a blanket. He took a seat in the corner and laughed madly at our sporadic conversation. It was now dark, so Ulysses lit a kerosene lantern. He pulled out two books he had written. One was a 16-page watercolor presentation of his candidacy and platform for Governor; the other was a larger book, illustrated with simple watercolor sketches that explained the by-laws and purposes of the village. I turned to Ulysses and asked, "Does the village get harassed by any local rednecks? How do you handle that?"

"Oh, once in a while a townee gets drunk or bored and comes down here to make trouble. I just beat him up," Ulysses responded gruffly.

I asked how the candidacy for governor was coming along. U.S. complained that he had been kept off the ballot because he did not have the $1,300 the state required for a filing fee. A poor man cannot run for high political office in this land of the free and home of the brave, where we are taught as infants that anyone can become President if he tries hard enough. Ulysses was discouraged. He didn't feel he had much of a chance with his name not even on the ballot.

As U.S. talked about rules and beating up townees, and politics, I sensed that his attitude had developed over a long period of time that it was not a bullying or authoritarian attitude, but one recognizing that ignorance, so characteristic of a large percentage of people, required hard-headed, adamant confrontation. He was almost benign in his toughness. But then, he was not a kid but an older man past the age to be trusted.

"I've got a neighbor here," U.S. remarked, "that wants to see me in jail. He steals my horse and then, when I go to get it, he has me arrested for trespassing." (I recalled the story about the Dukhobors in Canada, about the time when their cow was shot when it was caught in a neighbor's pasture. The bereaved community men, women and children gathered around the dead cow and wailed and wailed so loud and long it stirred up the entire countryside.)

As we talked, I was looking casually through U.S. Grant's picture books. When my eyes fell on the bylaws of the organization, I said, "Hey, can I copy out these bylaws? Some of my readers might like to know how your village is organized."

"Sure," he replied, "but not now. It's time I called it a night. We go to bed when it gets dark around here.

Getting out of the village in darkness was not as simple as getting in by daylight. Before we got back to the main highway, our nerves were shattered from our being forced to explore every alternate road leading to deserted cabins and dead ends. We finally found someone who gave us directions on how to get out of that labyrinth. Next morning, when we returned to the village, we discovered that we had explored half the hillside in the direction of the national forest.

When we parked near the complex, we noticed two young longhairs busy repairing an old pickup. I asked one of them if he lived here. "Only temporarily," he replied. "I'm looking for a place way out in the wilderness. Too many people coming through here."

"It's pretty hard to get away from people these days," I said. "'Course you can always put up a sign saying 'Visitors Not Welcome.'"

"Yeah, but who wants to do that! I'd rather find a place for my family and friends that's so far out that no one will want to visit."

"All I can say is, 'Good Luck,'" I concluded, thinking about Sam Wright, an ex-professor of mine who had moved to the wilds of Alaska, accessible only by helicopter, or by several miles of hazardous trekking on snowshoes. Even so, Sam had visitors.

One Chicano guy with long hair and a Chinese-style mustache did most of the rapping, casually twirling a copy of The Watchtower in his hands as he spoke. The three others—a beautiful black cat named Tucker, the guy with the mad laugh from the previous evening, and an ex-middle-class coed with torn dungarees—interjected comments when they could.

"People go running back and forth and up and down like wild rabbits or crazy deer," the Chicano said. "What for? Just stop and open up, be receptive to the good earth, tune in to natural vibrations, no one has to work for anything. God provides all if you don't get uptight about it. That Old Man knew what he was doing when He made all of this," gesturing with a sweep of the hand and a broad grin. "A lot of us used to live in the Haight-Ashbury. You had to shoot speed just to survive in a scene like that. It was nowhere. God meant men to be close to the land, not on concrete. Cities—wow! Freeways, cars going zoom zoom here, there. Lights blinking, rush. Man, that ain't natural. That's insanity. The city is doomed. Those who get it together on the land will be the survivors. 'Course if you're really together, man, you can survive anywhere, even in the fuckin' city. There were a few cats like that in the Haight. Maybe a few still there. So high, so spiritual, you could tell just seeing a guy like that walking down the street. All the shit around him. Above it all. But if you're not that far along spiritually—and most of us ain't, man, the city is doomed anyway, and you just catch all those bad vibes by living there. So you get a place where you feel good, like this, and everything is beautiful and you don't need speed or any of that bad dope and you don't need to worry about money or anything."

We all agreed. That conversation made me high.

The Lower Farm had a delightfully relaxed feeling about it. The buildings and their interiors were all an earthy adobe color. U.S. had been hoeing in the newly planted communal garden before we arrived and one or two others were doing a little work there off and on during the morning hours. Mostly, the people were just wandering around, relaxed and chatting with one another. U.S.' wife was nursing her baby on the front porch of the main house. There was no electricity. The living environment was probably very much like that of my great-granddad, except that here there was no necessity to toil for bread or work in order to either survive or simply feel worthwhile. Consuelo and I sat on the porch and gave U.S.' books a more thorough going-over.

Ulysses S. Grant wanted to print 100,000 copies of his 16-page, full-color platform for governor. He didn't have the $5,000 to do so, but neither was he willing to print it any other way. I offered to do a four-page black-and-white summary for him but he flatly refused. No compromises: the color—the pictures as presented—was essential to the total message. Ulysses preferred that I not copy his words verbatim but he was willing for me to write them from memory. Here's part of the written portion of his message as I recall it.

1. No one would ever be forced to do anything but there would be certain things that could not be done, like industrial air and water pollution.
2. Horse trails would be developed along with roadways and people would be encouraged to use the horse for transportation.
3. The bureaucracy would be cut in half since the use of paper in government would be reduced 50% in order to conserve our most valuable natural resource, trees.
4. Police would wear white uniforms and be used to help old ladies cross the street and help motorists change flat tires; police help instead of police force.
5. A return to the one-room schoolhouse in education.
6. Legalize marijuana.

While we were sitting there on the porch, reading, Ulysses came riding up on a great white stallion. As he dismounted I could see the yellow stripe on the side of his army-blue pants.

"I don't know how he gets out. We couldn't find any holes in the fence." He plopped down in an old overstuffed chair on the porch, pushing his crumpled blue army cap back on his head.

I asked him a few innocuous questions about communal living, but the most I can recall about his answers was "Communes don't work, 'cause people don't work. There's too many people with a lot of high-minded ideas about utopia. But there ain't no utopia. Just some cats a looking to ball a lot of chicks and people looking for someone to take care of them."

"What about your candidacy for governor, Ulysses?"

"Now that's something worth talking about!" he replied. He reached into his pocket and pulled out a soiled newspaper. "There are eight candidates for Governor. Look at 'em—I'm the only one who's smiling."

He was right. The people in the seven other photos on the page looked like men who had either just swallowed a bird or had a fight with their wives. But U.S. Grant was smiling and he was the only one of the eight who never had a chance. Shoulder-length hair, beard, and smile to match—that's no way to appeal to the voters, especially if you come riding up on a great white stallion. The kids might be happy to see a beautiful white horse but they don't have a vote. "Mature" adults on the other hand can better identify with shorthaired, middle-aged men.

As part of his platform, U.S. Grant proposed to eliminate half the state's revenue "so we won't have the money to spend on things that aren't absolutely necessary." Also he called for a "reversal of the current direction society is taking. The real issues are life, stability, and taking care of the planet."

But Ulysses was very discouraged about the race. Now that his name was not to be on the ballot he felt he couldn't win. Before, though, he had seriously believed he had a chance. "There are thousands of hip, poor, and dissatisfied people in this state who would vote for me."

Later that day we visited a place that had once been a commune. It now consisted of a huge double-dome, a single dome nearby, two trailers on the hillside, and a tepee and an adobe hut across the road.

McFall knocked on the door of the double-dome, opened it, walked in, and said: "Jim, I've brought a couple of people you might like to meet."

As we stepped inside we caught a glimpse of U.S. riding up on his great white stallion. McFall introduced us and then left to visit the couple who lived in the adobe hut.

Jim, in his 30s, well-groomed hair, casually dressed, had recently bought the property. He was a salesman for Zoomworks, a company producing creative playground equipment and other geodesic dome-type apparatus. He and his wife and baby lived in this double-dome, which was as elegantly decorated inside as any hip home in suburbia. The other half of the building was a workshop. Electricity was provided by a generator. "I'm a capitalist pig," Jim noted. "I rent out the other places on the property except for the dome on the hill which Bill and Ann own."

U.S. came in and mentioned that one of Jim's dogs had killed a chicken at the Lower Farm. "I had to kick the son of a bitch to get him to leave," U.S. added.

"Oh, so that's how come he had a big gash on his thigh and was limping around here for several days," Jim retorted mildly.

"I didn't kick him that hard, Jim. I didn't draw any blood. "

"Guess he won't be so hungry for chicken anymore," Jim smiled.

"Guess not."

Another young man, Larry, entered and talked with Jim about the progress he was making in getting one of the trailers into livable condition.

U.S. explained how Larry could build a simple but adequate sewage system out of some corrugated metal and boards instead of installing an expensive septic tank. "Were either of you here when this place was a commune?" I asked U.S. and Jim.

"I was," U.S. replied, "but never really belonged. They used to have some wild times in this place. Orgies, dope, the whole trip. When I was young, I used to think how great it would be to have several wives and all of us live together in one big room. But all those ideas are just bullshit. Just ideas I had 'cause I was young and horny. All that talk about loving everybody totally and equally and sharing everything. What these people really wanted was to be free of responsibility and smoke dope and ball every guy or chick around."

"Love and sex are two entirely different things," Jim added. "One isn't related to the other."

"Not necessarily related," I interjected.

I knew what they were talking about. I had been around a lot of people who didn't understand their motives for wanting to join a commune.

Consuelo and I left the Placitas area the next day. The drive north gave us time to consider what we had seen, heard and felt.

Going back to that conversation with Jim and U.S. in the double-dome, I speculated now about why some people join, or want to join, communes. And I thought of some of the people I had known myself: the mothers who wanted someone else to take care of their children; the fathers who were tired of holding down dull jobs to support a wife and children; all those people intent upon flight from responsibility. Not fleeing meant too much pressure just to survive. No time for fun, games, relaxed and fulfilling sexuality. Communes, on the other hand, represented freedom, utopian work, all play, no one to hassle or be hassled, relaxation from stress and strain, no more senseless work at home or office.

But those who went searching for their fantasies discovered that reality all too soon slaps them in the face hard. After a brief summer of orgies and fun in the sun, the long winter sets in and darkness brings dissatisfaction and disillusionment.

Anyone not adrift in a dream world recognizes that people don't really want complete freedom from work and responsibility. A vacation, a period of compensation for their previous life's oppression, yes. But not just endless fun and games. Fulfilling work is the greatest leisure. And as someone once remarked (was it Freud? Fromm?), the two essential ingredients for mental health are represented by a balanced mixture of love and work. Even more essential, we need to stop thinking in terms of opposites: work versus play, love versus sex. Our behavior is still based on a very false but very widespread tradition of psychosocial conditioning; we insist that work must be experienced as painful but not joyful, that love is spiritual but not erotic. And once having learned irrational behavior and been conditioned to think it rational, we perpetuate it by using elaborate justifications, all of which are based on Western logic, with its faulty premises and dualistic conventions.

We need our brains and hearts washed free of all this destructive conditioning. We need to get in touch with the essential oneness of all activity, so that love-play-sex-work are neither separate nor separable. What a ball we could have if we could learn this, and truly make it part of ourselves. We wouldn't just be sitting around trying to get high by rapping about getting in touch. We'd be doing it. U.S. Grant's pessimism, I surmised, was like that of so many others. He started with the concept of what he thought people ought to be, rather than the realization and acceptance of what they were. They ought to be responsible, to cooperate in keeping the property in good condition and in planting and harvesting the garden. They ought to have the foresight to prepare for the winter as well as enjoy the summer. But "ought" came to naught (as it would almost anywhere), so Grant concluded that "communes don't work."

There is nothing wrong with having ideals. Consider the "ideal" commune, where everyone does his own thing and helps everyone as well; where rules or regulations are unnecessary, because everyone is aware enough of his surroundings and of other people, so that when something needs to be done he does it without being asked. That's beautiful, but such a commune exists only in people's minds, which constitute the true realm of possible but improbable fancy. Here on earth, though, starting a commune with nothing else but ideals will almost certainly guarantee failure. More is required of us. To get discouraged because others do not live up to one's expectations and dispiritedly proclaim that "communes don't work" is really to say: "I am unwilling or unable to find out how my behavior and thinking is imperfect, and therefore this incapacity contributes to my experience that people cannot live together in groups larger than the nuclear family."

Early in December 1970, some three weeks before Consuelo and I had planned to return to the Lower Farm for a second visit, the following headline appeared on the front page of the Albuquerque Tribune:

HIPPIE HAVEN DOUBLE SLAYING;
BELIEVE BORROWED RIFLE USED.
U.S. GRANT IS SOUGHT IN HIPPIE COMMUNES

The newspaper provided a lengthy account. According to the Tribune, this is what happened:

PLACITAS.... A rifle believed to have been the weapon used in last night's fatal shooting of two hippie commune residents near here was recovered today as officers intensified their search for commune leader Ulysses S. Grant.

Grant is wanted for questioning in connection with the deaths of Robert

Copeland, 27, and Joseph Ornas, 47, whose bullet-ridden bodies were found near his commune home last night. . . .

Bill Dolley, a Placitas farmer, told authorities that the bearded commune leader had borrowed the rifle at about 4 p.m. yesterday, adding that Grant had borrowed it on many occasions in the past.

Police also are looking for Grant's wife Helen, who disappeared after the Tuesday night shooting incident. . . .

Mrs. Grant was last seen walking through Bernalillo, carrying their one-year-old son.

Police also were trying to figure out what led to the shootings. They believe it was a dispute between Grant, Copeland and Terry D. Hardin.

Hardin and Copeland shared a house next door to Grant. Grant filed a complaint at the Sandoval County Courthouse in Bernalillo, claiming that Copeland and Hardin had stolen furniture and doors from his home.

Records show that Hardin had filed assault charges against Grant, claiming that Grant had struck his wife.

Hardin claimed Grant hit his pregnant wife with a door.

The usually calm commune was wracked by gunfire Tuesday night, Hardin told police, when he and Copeland were ambushed by Grant at the commune's waterhole about 50 yards from Grant's home.

Hardin said he and Copeland ran about 125 yards down a dirt road when Copeland was struck by a bullet.

Copeland shouted: "I'm hit," Hardin related. Hardin was not hit by gunfire and told police he didn't see Ornas shot.

Sheriff Emiliano Montoya said when he arrived at the commune to investigate the report of the shooting he found Ornas' body about 75 yards from the waterhole.

Sheriff Montoya said Copeland's body was not found until about an hour later. It was about 50 yards from Ornas' body.

Preliminary autopsy reports show that both men were shot twice; once in the back and once in the face.

On December 26 Consuelo and I arrived in Placitas to find the road into the Lower Farm completely shut off in chains and locks on the entrance gate, and No Trespassing signs. We then hurried over to see our friend and guide, C.W. McFall, in hopes that he would be able to tell us what had happened. The tape recorder took note of our conversation, as follows:

McFall: You want to ask questions?

Consuelo: I'm interested in your immediate response to the newspaper stories about Ulysses.

McFall: Well, I think it's just damn poor journalism. Because, you know,

Ulysses has been in my house, six, eight, 10 times. You know, you were there. I have accused Ulysses of being the craziest man I ever knew who didn't require incarceration. But I think his attitude was all a pose. I'm certain he knew damn well that he couldn't ever be elected governor. He knew damn well it's all right to criticize the Establishment and to buck it, but you don't knock your brains out trying to knock down a stone wall with your head. I think he was reasonably intelligent—in fact, maybe he was quite smart.

The newspaper report says this one fellow is the only person who can offer any information. And he says Ulysses killed those two people and shot at him but he got away. Then he says Ulysses returned the rifle to a gringo up here, another fellow. I don't know if the other fellow's straight or hippie. I happen to have heard—it's only hearsay, but it's something for the detectives to look up that this other fellow (who owned the rifle) and Ulysses were on the outs. When Ulysses left for a few months, part of the reason he left, so hearsay tells me, was because they had this quarrel. And he returned the rifle? After he shot those two fellows? Hogwash. That doesn't hold water. Now what happened? I'd give my option on my back seat in hell to know. I am very much afraid that Helen and the baby and Ulysses, all three, have also been killed. Because you mean our law enforcement officers are so stupid they can't find a murderer with anyone that's as easy to identify as Ulysses? And his wife and baby? And every time there's two people associated they become a square of the number, four times as easy to find. And with a baby, that becomes nine times.

Dick: They were on foot, right?

McFall: They tell me he took a station wagon and tore off, but I don't know that, not at all. People around here have actually gone up in that neighborhood where there are many—I don't know if they're caves or just mine shafts, or dry wells. . . . People around here have actually gone up there and hunted, wondering if Ulysses' body is not in there.

Dick: Who would kill Ulysses?

McFall: I don't know. Another thing that's been reported, but only hearsay— and this I don't go along with—some people say Ulysses was playing a part up here for a particular purpose. Representing somebody else. It's also been suggested that he was on the federal payroll.

Dick: What would that be for?

McFall: I don't know. But I'm satisfied there's lots more behind what happened, and I feel kind of interested in Ulysses and Helen and the baby.

Dick: When did you see Ulysses last? Do you think he had developed any unusual quirks in the last six months or anything?

McFall: I saw him a month or so before this thing blew up. He and Helen and the baby; first time Helen had ever been over here. I had bawled him out (but it's the same as I quarrel with you, you know, for fun) for coming over and not bringing Helen, 'course she couldn't, he just rode that horse. I don't know how they got over here. But I was tickled to see Helen, and she was nice enough. It couldn't have been more than a month before this a . . . well, my next-door neighbor, Mrs. B., told me, when I got up in the morning, "You know about Ulysses S. Grant?" And Joe, her husband, went over before the peace officers had removed the bodies. He saw the bodies.

Dick: So what do the local people think? Do they think he did it? Is there any other information?

McFall: I don't know, I don't know, Dick. Most of the quote hippies end quote I've talked to seem to infer that Ulysses is guilty. But I don't know what the general reaction is, among the bourgeois. I don't have much to do with 'em. I would never know what their opinions are.

Consuelo: He did have a station wagon available to him, though?

McFall: Apparently. I don't know. I never knew about it.

Dick: He disclaimed the use of automobiles....

McFall: Well, so much of his strange views were poses. He wasn't a damn fool. I know he borrowed a pickup one time. He sort of let down his hair when he came over here and drank coffee with me. He told me one time how he picked up three of those fringe hippies who were living in the commune with him, and he'd been to the store to get feed for the horses or chickens or whatever. They were going to the same place he was, to the commune—they call it the Lower Farm. The Sun Farm is up this way. And he has five or six hundred-pound sacks of feed, and these three fellows got a ride. He took them right down to the commune. When they got there, these three fellows got out and started up to the quarters. And Ulysses says, "Aren't you going to help me unload?" And the fellows each said, "No, I'm tired." The three of them. Ulysses says, "Well, you're going to be a damn sight tireder if you don't help me, because I'm going to whip hell out of you, all three of you." And he was just positive enough, mad enough, that he bullied them. Well, they should have helped him if he gave them a ride. Sure enough they gave him a hand. They weren't going to tangle with him.

This again is hearsay, but you can check it around. A few days ago, a week or so ago, maybe two weeks, a radio or TV commentator of local repute made the comment that within a few days some startling results were going to be disclosed in the Ulysses S. Grant case. That was after I had made up my mind all wasn't as it appeared to be. Now I don't know what happened any more than I know what happened with the assassination of John Kennedy. You see, I was unfortunate I had a TV at the time and I saw the assassination, whatever of it was shown on TV. Immediately then I said, "There's a whole lot more behind this than whatever reaches the newspapers." And when I heard this about Ulysses, from what I knew about the man and what I could size up of the situation, I was unsatisfied. I don't know what lies behind it, but I know it's not as reported in the newspapers. ∎

DROP CITY
by Richard Fairfield

THE NOTE WE RECEIVED READ: "AT YOUR CONVENIENCE TAKE
Interstate Highway 25 into Colorado… [turn] 'til Drop City drops on you —Jack."

Because most communes are so difficult to reach, it was a relief to have good directions and a paved road all the way to Drop City. Drop City dropped on us like a
flash. One moment we were on a pleasant drive on a semi-rural paved highway, the
next moment we had a full view of several colorful geodesic domes on a hillside.

I loved Drop City immediately: no hassle finding it; it was compact—all the
buildings in a small, neatly arranged complex, and those domes—beautiful domes
are somehow much more lovely than the loveliest of suburban mansions. The
domes, each accommodating from five to 10 members, were usually two stories
inside. One double-dome contained an office, library, workshop, living room, and
kitchen, along with some second-floor living quarters. A large dome in need of
repair was to be renovated for use as a recreation-workshop center. Another dome,
about the same size, was partially completed and was intended to be used as a
crash pad for the expected hordes of summer visitors.

We arrived at Drop City on a Monday in April 1971—a day that was promis-
ingly clear and bright. The current residents were extremely open and friendly.
None of the people at Drop City had been there more than nine months. At the
end of the previous summer, 1969, things had become so chaotic that everyone
had left. And two of the domes had been damaged as a result of accidental fires set
by careless residents.

Drop City was one of the first rural commune efforts. It was the first to construct geodesic domes as living quarters and was a recipient of the Buckminster
Fuller Award. It had water and electricity and something more—solar energy was
used to heat one of the domes used as living quarters.

When I was publishing The Modern Utopian magazine from Boston in
1966, I received mimeographed newsletters and flyers from a new community
called Drop City. They advertised themselves as a community of artists who were
innovating not only in the area of buildings and lifestyle, but also in a multimedia approach to art.

The Drop City people were the avant-garde of American society and they invited everyone to visit. They even pulled off a big art festival, which attracted young
hip types from all over the country. This open-door policy resulted in an inunda-
tion by hordes of teenage runaways, thrill seekers, sightseers, and miscellaneous
dropouts, mostly of the irresponsible variety.

At first the permanent residents accepted this invasion as part of their mission to help others get their heads together and move on to creating their own alternative lifestyles. After a while they got fed up and threatened to burn the place down. Such threats did not, of course, discourage visitors. Several of the Drop City leaders decided to move to a mountain several miles away. There they formed a new community, Libre, or Liberty.

Drop City continued to be a place for every transient commune-seeker to crash. But in the fall of 1969 conditions got so bad that even the crashers couldn't stand it (no food, no maintenance, plenty of hostility). So everyone pulled out.

That same fall, though, two couples came and stayed the winter. Then others began to trickle in. Drop City was coming to life again.

By the time of our visit the following spring there were between 15 and 20 residents. We talked casually with most of them. They were all bright, enthusiastic, and optimistic about the future. None of them were temperamentally or philosophically inclined to settle in and make Drop City their home forever and ever. What was important was that it was their home now. In contrast to the other communes of this nature, Drop City was on surprisingly good terms with its neighbors and the townspeople.

While we were visiting Drop City, a neighbor dropped by with a pickup truck loaded with goats. He wanted to know if they wished to sell their goats. "No, man, we like our goats. We need our goats."

"Like to buy some goats then?" the man inquired.

"Sure, if you'll take beads and pipes in exchange. We don't have money."

"No thanks," came the reply.

The farmer was congenial but a little freaked out by the barrage of happy and joking comments he encountered. He was used to more serious negotiating, I'm sure. "Besides, one of our goats is going to have kids pretty soon," one member told me. "We don't need any more. Grass we could use any time; goats, no."

There seemed to be an abhorrence of normal currency transactions. We tried to buy a gorgeous pipe made from a deer's antler. As a cash purchase it was a tiring effort to settle on a fair price, whereas we would have had no problem obtaining it in exchange for a lid of marijuana. In fact, this one encounter was the only negative aspect of our visit to Drop City. We were too anxious to be fair and to encourage the sale of their handmade products. The major creative effort of these people was to make beautifully unique pipes, pottery, and beads.

Still, they needed cash to pay utilities and taxes ($40 per year) on the property. Somehow, in the most unstructured way possible, this money became available when needed.

The terrain of the commune was dry and rocky. Good enough for goats, perhaps, but not for crops. The members had a small garden but it was not productive and no one thought of it as much of a resource. Food stamps were better.

When we finally got the pipe, we lost some of the positive feelings of our earlier encounters. We left too hurriedly and with regret that our business dealings had interfered with the casual friendliness of the commune.

Jack's dome looked like a small red igloo, but he was not inside on so sunny a day as this. Seated, totally nude, at one end of a large rectangular space dug in the ground, he was playing a guitar. His girlfriend, with nursing child, sat nearby. Consuelo and I sat quietly beside them. Jack began to sing a song about getting back to essentials almost as though in a trance. When the song was done he put the guitar aside, looked us in the eye, and said with a smile, "Hi."

The mood of our conversation was meditative. Jack was no speed freak—he was unhurried and deliberate in his speech. He espoused a philosophy that I did not grasp entirely. It was probably for that reason that I felt him to be far too abstract and idealistic. Yet, he, more than anyone else we had encountered on our trip to the Southwest, was deeply involved in a journey toward self-enlightenment. He spoke of energy levels and of man's relationship to the earth in its mystical sense. As he spoke, his fingertips touched the dry earth over and over, and I felt that somehow he was more at one with that earth than most of us: whatever he sensed in it, the earth simply felt like chalk to my fingertips. In this atmosphere I felt unable to ask the mundane questions I had about Drop City. How are decisions reached? How will you deal with the onslaught of visitors this summer? Do you eat communally?

I did find the answers, but Drop City had been through many changes in its four-year history. It was still changing and would continue to change, so for each answer to a question, there is another question—and another answer, and so forth. They took their meals together in the giant double-dome today. But tomorrow? Decisions in a group of this size were by consensus, but what will happen when more people arrive? Income comes mainly from food stamps, outside help, and barter of commune-made products (whatever the maker of a product receives in exchange for it he shares with the rest of the commune). But how long will these simple economics last; how will they change? The answers are not structured. Similarly, interpersonal relations are unstructured and therefore largely conventional. Couples with children live separate from singles. Males outnumber females two to one.

The essence of Drop City is change. In this respect it is a microcosm of American society, which has moved into an era of accelerated change—indeed so much so that America, perhaps more than any other country in the world, is sinking deeper and deeper into the quagmire of affluence.

In any event, Drop City is appropriately named, for it remains a place for people who need to get out of the Establishment rat race and discover an alternative route. (They may discover that the alternatives are infinite.) Stimulated from their initial experience at Drop City, they may develop the courage to venture forth in a direction of their own. ■

LIBRE

by Richard Fairfield

IN THE SPRING OF 1968 I READ THE FOLLOWING NEWS ABOUT Drop City in an underground paper:

At the entrance a large sign reads exactly like those outside the ramshackle Southwestern Indian reservations: NO PHOTOGRAPHS, VISITING HOURS WEEKENDS ONLY 8 AM to 8 PM.

"We'll let anyone come for awhile, but only those who contribute can stay," stated a resident. "It has to be that way. We've learned the hard way, by letting too many come who could only take away."

"We're thinking of burning Drop City down," he continued.

"We're going to move, start out new in Canada or Virginia or on a farm near here, but this time we'll keep it a secret."

And so they moved. Peter Rabbit and his friends moved out, not to Canada or Virginia, but to another location in Colorado. It was no secret. They wanted more isolation, perhaps even total isolation. They wanted to get away from the tourists, the crashers, the teenyboppers—all the people they had initially invited (wittingly and unwittingly) to visit them at Drop City. So the members determined that if their new community was comparatively much less accessible, they would have far fewer visitors. But it didn't work out that way. They still had to confront their own inability to turn people away.

Liberty represents an alternative route for people intent upon getting out of the rat race. But it seems an unlikely one for young energetic idealists, for it is a sort of refuge for hip artists who wish to maximize their privacy but still retain neighbors who are like-minded and cooperative. These artists have attained a measure of success and recognition. One, for example, as a novelist, and another as a painter having exhibited his works in a famous New York gallery.

Liberty, a nonprofit organization, actually began when four artists, together with their wives and children, bought 400 acres of land on a mountain far from the main highways of Colorado. Each family built its own unique geodesic dome and did so under an agreed-upon community rule that, for reasons of beauty and privacy, no dome could be within sight of any other dome.

A dirt road, several miles in length and itself on private property, leads to Liberty. Upon arrival, you follow a sign directing you to a parking lot, where only one log cabin is clearly visible. There are two huge gardens lying south and east of the parking area and woods stretching away behind the cabin.

When Consuelo and I arrived, two or three people were working in the fields while another person was trying to repair a tractor. Two campers as well as other vehicles were in the parking area. A lean, bedraggled Scandinavian-type female was hassling with two screaming kids. A bearded fellow in weatherworn overalls sat on a crate eating a sandwich. No one paid any attention to us.

We walked over to the log cabin and knocked on the door. "Come in." The voice came from the top of a staircase, which led directly from the entrance to the second floor. We were not invited up. We sat on chairs near the doorway at the foot of the stairs. To our left was a rustic kitchen with an old wood-burning stove; to the right was a partially elevated living room with fireplace, wood floor, rugs, and cushions.

The voice joined us and turned out to be that of a young girl in her mid-20s. "I don't usually answer the door, but I could see you coming from the window up here and thought you had a nice face," she said, gesturing toward Consuelo.

Most of the conversation revolved around the Liberty community's growing fear of people invading the place. The girl spoke at length: "We thought we could get away by coming up here, but people just kept following us. We've had at least half a dozen visitors this afternoon and it's only early spring and a weekday at that. What will it be like when summer arrives?

"Tell people not to come here. We're interested in maybe a few more people joining us but we're in no hurry.

"It's funny. We were here all winter and snowed in part of the time. Then, we wouldn't have minded visitors. Yes, my husband and I built this place last year. My husband had some help with the heavy work but otherwise we did it ourselves. Got moved in during the fall and kind of hibernated for the winter. I got a lot of reading done.

"We went to Denver to my parents' home once. They thought I was dirty and smelly so I took so many showers you wouldn't believe. I'd come out of the shower and my mother would say 'you still look dirty,' so I'd smile and say 'okay' and jump back in the shower. I loved it. Sure was good having hot and cold running water for a change. But I wouldn't go back to that way of life.

"Some of the places do have electricity here, but we don't. We don't have any money to spend on that kind of thing.

"The community meets about once a week to discuss issues and make decisions on things which affect us all. We don't take a vote or anything like that. We talk until we reach consensus. We'll have to have a meeting pretty soon about what to do about visitors."

She was a lot like her house: very pretty in her own way, charming—yet direct, bold, without decor, and (like the wood in her house) had an old-new or new-old quality. She seemed young in experience with this kind of lifestyle, yet old with reflection on the lifestyle from which she came. She seemed certain of what she could no longer be, uncertain about what to be now.

We decided to drop in on Peter Rabbit, the main force of Drop City in its early days and now sort of the spokesman at Liberty. Peter lived in a gigantic and elegant white dome—the most modern dome we had seen. When we arrived, he was sitting in the middle of a spacious room, with a typewriter on a tray in front of him and with lots of paper neatly stacked on the floor nearby. He seemed as tired and bedraggled as had the woman with the two whiny brats in the parking lot.

"We know you've had visitors all day so we'll only stay a few minutes," I said apologetically.

Peter also complained of the traffic at Liberty. We agreed that visiting communes and writing magazines about them wasn't really that great a thing to do. The Rabbit noted that we were using too much paper and destroying our forestlands: "It takes hundreds of acres of trees just to produce the Sunday edition of The New York Times. Who reads it? What difference does it make anyway?"

"I am writing a book about the history of Drop City," Peter continued. "I've made a commitment to do it, so I will."

"Yeah. Consuelo and I recently read a paper on how to practice sound ecology in our private lives. One of the points was that we all use much more paper than needed. It's hard to break old habits. We stopped at a drive-in restaurant yesterday and we were drinking out of paper cups before realizing what we had done. I guess it's hard only because we're too lazy and comfortable to make the effort required in order to change. It's much more convenient to forget."

Halfway through our conversation, Peter's wife entered and went directly to the kitchen to the left of us, an open and unpartitioned area. She began working on the evening meal. The level of tension in the room increased considerably.

Peter maintained a quiet friendly composure and talked of Drop City and why they had left it.

"It served a valuable function," he said, "but we got tired of doing the same thing over and over. A bunch of fucked-up kids would come through and we'd take care of them and get their heads straightened out and send them on their way. Then along would come another bunch and we'd have to go through the same procedure all over again!"

Wow—what a relevant ministry, I reflected.

Peter continued: "It gets tedious after a while so that's why we moved here. We want to help our brothers and sisters get it together and that's why we hate to tell people they can't visit. We have to have our own privacy though and we certainly aren't interested in being home for every stray person that comes by."

"Perhaps you could have people visit only on Sundays like the Lama Foundation," I suggested.

"Yes, that's one possibility. We're going to meet about this soon. We don't like to turn people away but we've got to do something."

"One thing I believe people have to learn is to say 'no,'" I continued. "Eric Berne has said that the three responses of a healthy personality are 'yes,' 'no,' and 'wow.' If we can't say 'no' as well as 'yes,' then there can't be anything to 'wow' about. Commune and hip types tend to have that problem—overly positive, idealistic. Let's face it, there are some times when we have to say 'no' not only for our own good but for everyone else's as well."

"You can say that again," Peter's wife curtly joined in.

"What would a person have to do to join Liberty?" I asked.

"Rent a house in the valley for six months or so and get to know everyone who lives here pretty well. At the end of that time we'd take a vote. If he were approved then, he'd have to build his own place out of view of any other place and would become a full participating member."

Dr. Stanley Krippner of the Maimonides Medical Center in Brooklyn, New York, has written a paper in which he describes the Liberty lifestyle as the "incorporation of the paranormal into daily rituals." He writes:

"Childbirth at Liberty is also ritualized, a local midwife and doctor come to the community. The entire group is present as the baby is delivered. Whenever possible, the delivery is accomplished outside 'under the sun and moon' with the inhabitants chanting to welcome the infant into his new environment."

Peter Rabbit, our host, does all of the commune's hunting during deer season. According to Krippner: "When he discovers a number of deer, he reportedly talks with them, asking one of the deer to sacrifice himself, vowing that the energy gained from his flesh will be used for creative and constructive pursuits by Liberty. Without fail, according to the hunter, one deer will move away from the others and will remain still until he is shot."

I didn't get these stories confirmed or denied while there. But as Peter mentioned Krippner as a good friend, the accuracy of the report probably cannot be denied. Still, the people there did not seem to behave any differently from middle-class hip types you see in the city.

Peter said, "Up here we learn from the mountain. The mountain is our guru. Time is unimportant. A day, a month, a year passes like a moment in eternity."

Words, words, words. The tension of being unwelcome visitors and the brevity of our relationship impeded my ability to see these people as types who would stand under the moon and chant to the birth of a newborn babe or convince a deer to give itself up by talking to it. They seemed far too "normal."

As we started to get up to leave Peter's home, I said, "I guess we'd better..."

"Yes," he interrupted, "why don't you go now. Perhaps someone else here who's had less company today might not mind your dropping in."

He remained friendly even as he hurried us to the door. I couldn't help feeling that it was okay for him to push a little. His wife, after all, was not happy with having visitors at that time, and he had to live with her after we were gone.

Despite Peter's passing remark, we didn't drop in at any other of the dome houses, though we walked by two which were so aesthetically pleasing, settled in a clearing surrounded by groves of tall trees, that we were tempted. Liberty was a beautiful place, like Lama, only more personal, less grandiose. ■

THE MILLBROOK TRIP

by Richard Fairfield

ALTHOUGH I WAS FAR TOO UPTIGHT, MIDDLE-CLASS AND CON-
servative to experiment much with drugs, I was fascinated by the growing psychedelic movement. When I announced to the world that I planned to begin a
magazine on experimental communities and radical social change, Tim Leary was
one of the first subscribers and well-wishers.

The first issue of The Modern Utopian contained an article on the Neo-American church. This church is a spaced-out, satirical put-on of the orthodox religion.
As an unorthodox, almost anti-Christian, theological student attending a school
that was still struggling to shake itself loose of prayer book and pomposity, I rev-
eled in the madcap iconoclasm of this church.

The philosophical position of Leary, Art Kleps (the Neo-American church's
founder) as well as other "heads" regarding man, nature and the universe was so
similar to mine that I became certain that the psychedelic drug experience was a
valuable one. They had arrived at their position through drug experience, and I
had through several years of study of religious and philosophical thought. They
were trying to live out their experience by gathering with others in a church or
commune. I was trying to express my thoughts through a magazine.

When Tord Svenson, chemist, acidhead, keeper of the divine, toad of the Neo-
American church and friend, offered to take me to visit the Millbrook estate, I
accepted with enthusiasm, though with trepidation. I wanted to know what was
going on; I didn't want to take LSD without a carefully selected guide and environment. (That was my rationalization at the time.)

The first time I saw Tim Leary was on a TV news interview. I got the impression that he was somewhat effeminate. At Millbrook my head was turned around
completely. Maybe he was totally stoned and I got a contact high but he was then
the most beautiful, soulful person I had ever met. Later I attended his lectures in
Berkeley and developed a more balanced perspective. When young militant New
Left types thank him for his contribution to the Revolution and then dismiss him
as being passé, I hastily came to his defense. The reason that a peaceful, nonviolent
man is kept in jail for months without bail and pending appeals for marijuana
convictions is because more than anyone he held the secret of true revolution:
"Turn on, tune in, drop out."

The sexual revolution was not won by pickets and protests and demonstrations
or by the assassination of prudes and postmasters. The affirmation of human sexu-

ality and the freedom from virginity and guilt among young people today has been won by each individual deciding to turn on to the joys of sex, tune in to its positive and negative aspects and drop out of the old Puritan ethic, and then DO IT.

Leary is dangerous because he is a father figure who will not conform to the traditional father-figure image. He is an exponent of joy, leisure and play. Such things do not get the work of society accomplished—we must be producers and consumers so that someone "up there" can realize a profit.

After I got back from my visit to Millbrook I published the following report (in Volume 1 of TMU) of my impressions:

The entrance to the Dietrich Estate is the gatehouse, a unique stone structure with its archway over the road. A simply lettered warning to uninvited guests is attached to the gate: PRIVATE PROPERTY NO TRESPASSING VISITORS BY APPOINTMENT ONLY WARNING GROUNDS PATROLLED TRESPASSERS WILL BE PROSECUTED.

Arthur Kleps, Chief Boo Hoo of the Neo-American Church, keeps his office and residence at the gatehouse. As a result of living there he often has the "paranoid" task of informing would-be visitors to this psychedelic mecca that the grounds are off-limits to anyone who does not present a letter of invitation from a resident on the property.

There are three organizations at Millbrook. One is Art's Neo-American Church headquarters, which, as he makes explicitly clear, has no intention of becoming a "community" and does not have the facilities for this in any event.

Timothy Leary's League for Spiritual Discovery is located at the main house, an impressive-looking mansion in good repair. The main house is about two-thirds of a mile up the road from the gatehouse. Tim's group of 20 people moved into the woods for the summer. His son, Jackie, is temporary "caretaker" of the main house and at present a rock group called the "Aluminum Dream" is living there.

Two or three miles into the woods, accessible by vehicle, in an open clearing, a communal tent has been erected. There Tim and other members of the League are free to commune with the beauties of nature in Thoreau-like contentment.

Just behind and above the main house is the Sri Ram Ashrama. The Ashrama is a religious community which has two aims: first, to seek spiritual development and growth for its 30 members through meditation, contemplation, study and the psychedelic experience; second, the application of these experiences to productive work. The Ashrama building is a large silver-painted frame structure and contains, besides living quarters, workshops for arts and crafts and printing. Members make pottery, baskets, necklaces, sculpture, etc., and run the KRNA press. The housekeeping seems well-organized and efficient. The spiritual leader and practical manager of the Ashrama is Bill Haines.

Although the Neo-American Church, the League for Spiritual Discovery, and the Sri Ram Ashrama are each unique and totally different in their approach, they are interrelated and overlap in objectives as well as practice. Bearing in mind the superficiality of categorizing, a rough division of these three into what seems like their current attitudinal emphasis might be fun and perhaps give the reader a "feeling" for the estate.

Pessimist: The Neo-American Church approaches the scene from the pessimistic edge. Art emphasizes satire, the tragicomic aspect of our strange reality. It is anti-Establishment and provides the necessary function of debunking the absurd status quo society. (Art is presently creating a psychedelic comic book which pokes fun at Millbrook as well as the Establishment.)

Optimist: The League for Spiritual Discovery, Tim's group, free from the need to be economically productive, at present concentrates its attention on tripping back to nature, living at one with their natural environment.

Realist: The Ashrama, under Bill's leadership, combines the pursuit of spiritual discovery with a productive orientation to create a meaningful and stable enterprise.

The guardian angel and benefactor of this estate is its owner—the personable but spoiled young millionaire, Bill Hitchcock.

Although the town of Millbrook's newspaper prints rumors that "Leary's Paradise is Crumbling" and some of the local clergy shout "Sin, Sin, Sin" from the pulpit, the relations between the estate and the townspeople are rather good, especially with the local merchants.

The Millbrook estate is a whole new world. It seems unhurried, unrushed, and has a quiet, tranquil quality about it in comparison with the straight world. The people there seem quite at home with one another. Most of them are not without hang-ups, a few rather severe, just as is the case amongst non-psychedelic people. But many of them are aware of their hang-ups and some are working to overcome them. This is far less the case in the straight community.

Having stayed at the estate for only a weekend does not give me a proper base for verbalizing any criticism. I wonder, however, if the people there are not too isolated and unconcerned about the "salvation" of the world. My impression is that they don't care much—which, of course, may be legitimate in the short run, as "saving oneself" is a prerequisite… I might add that going to Millbrook without having dropped acid is like going to a nudist camp without taking off one's clothes.

This was my first direct experience with a genuine hippie-psychedelic commune, ashram, movement. I was impressed, and relieved that what I had been thinking and believing about the movement was, in fact, true. Later I was to learn more subtle gradations of the truth, which were not so positive.

Leary's liberation from jail by the militant Weathermen, his subsequent flirtation with the Panthers in Algiers, his "revolutionary bust" by Eldridge

Cleaver, and his subsequent accommodation and support of a violent approach to revolution in America, has, to some, dethroned him as High Priest to the psychedelic subculture. There are no longer any heroes, and perhaps it is just as well. We, each of us, must assume the responsibility for change and not let "heroes" do it for us. ∎

STREET P

THE MODERN

EOPLE

CHAPTER 4

life in the city

UT☯PIAN $1.

PHILADEPHIA'S COMMUNES

by William J. Speers
Excerpted from The Philadelphia Inquirer, *2/21/71*

*Men and women living together experiment with a new kind of family. There are
chores and drugs and friendships and children with many fathers. . . . And, as in the
straight world, problems with sex.*

IN HIS MIND-OPENING BOOK *THE GREENING OF AMERICA*,
Charles A. Reich suggests that the spirit leading to the mass establishment of communes within the last several years is a reaction against a technologically-oriented
society that emphasizes using things instead of being with people, that creates
an anti-community life that goes unshared, where the genuine is replaced by the
manufactured and, in general, creates a culture that is hostile to life and which
substantially impairs consciousness.

Naturally, uncounted thousands of communes have sprung from the "love"
culture of the middle and late '60s. Locally one hundred, maybe even two hundred, communes are flowering in East Fall, Germantown, Mt. Airy, West and
Southwest Philadelphia, the Queen Village section of South Philadelphia, Kensington and even Upper Darby and Drexel Hill. Rural communes also are quietly
doing their thing in Montgomery and Bucks counties and South Jersey.

But the lodestone of communal living in this part of the world is that gingerbread relic of nineteenth-century elegance, Powelton Village. Vaguely bounded
by 31st, 40th, Spring Garden, and Market Streets, Powelton contained about 10
communes a year ago. Today there are 30 declared ones and, residents estimate, a
similar number of undeclared ones.

Urban communes like those of Powelton vary greatly in intent and structure,
but rural communes like the Farkle Farm, in Warrington, Bucks County, are
somewhat uniform in their goals and ways.

The Farkle Farm has a hardcore membership of six people and over a week's
time may host six or seven "crashers." Said one of the farm's members: "The city
is so fast-paced it's impossible to get your head together. There are too many illusions there. Out here you can get your head together because you're closer to
things that are real. You can find direction for the things you want to do and at the
same time see the things you don't want. Then when you get yourself put together
you can help the next guy." The junior member of the Farkle Farm is David, four,
who has spent half his life in a commune. His mother is Susan, 25. Susan believes

commune life is good for David. "It's better for the mother, too. She doesn't have to give concentrated attention to the child and with all the other adults around a child is more apt to get the attention he needs."

Eight-year-old Josh Weiss has lived in his Upper Darby commune since last summer and his father, Mike, sees it as a totally positive experience for the second-grader. "He has been exposed to a variety of people with many skills and interests. In particular, he himself has become interested in the work of an artist in our commune and he's been plastering our walls with his own drawings. He never drew before."

"He also sees his parents in less of a God-like light and that's good. He sees us challenged and he sees how we work out our problems with other people."

In general, parents and fellow commune-dwellers report that children being raised in such circumstances evidence more leadership among their peer group, are more at ease with strangers, adapt better to changes in circumstances and are better able to express themselves verbally than other children their own age.

Powelton is the largest communal colony in the Philadelphia area. In the Village there is a quietly determined anti-system, little-us-against-big-them flavor to the commune movement. (And they do refer to it as "the movement." Although a long-time communer was quick to point out that there were no leaders because "a movement without a leader can't be stopped.")

This esprit at Powelton Village has even radicalized some of the straight citizenry, like Monte Lis. Monte is over 50 and he's built like the mover and hauler that he has been most of his life. He hasn't been the same since some longhair convinced him that it was in his best interest to sit in on a tractor that was ready to turn more Village earth for the good of Drexel University. Nine months ago the divorced man moved into a commune on 33rd St., got himself a girlfriend and generally feels like maybe it's all worth it.

"Before, I lived alone and didn't care much about anything, but now I feel I'm part of the community, part of life. I go hiking now and mountain climbing and I appreciate people more. It's much better than watching TV or drinking beers at the bar. You know, your average American is going around in a state of sleep."

Last December, the 30 known communes of Powelton banded together in an Association of Communes which is dealing strictly with matters of mutual communal interest. From their deliberations have come the beginnings of a variety of new communal programs.

The most successful of these is a flourishing food cooperative which is operated by the Association members themselves. It buys food wholesale at the Food Distribution Center and resells it to communes at no profit. The savings amount to about half and the food quality is generally higher than that found in supermarkets. The food is sold each Tuesday morning in a building "liberated" by Powelton residents from Drexel.

In addition, the Powelton communes have their own babysitting service and a commune of mechanics that fixes autos for communes at cost. The Association is now exploring alternatives to dealing with banks and insurance companies and may set up a neighborhood carpool.

If you get the idea that communes are kind of down on the fruits of capitalism, you're kind of right. "Our lifestyle is a definite threat to our economic life as now structured," said one commune member. "At our place we have eight adults sharing one car, one washing machine, one refrigerator. . . I'm afraid that's not helping the old system along very much. Capitalism either expands or it dies."

People come together in communes for many reasons but most always it has to do with reasons of freedom—economic and personal—and the desire to become deeply involved in the lives of other human beings.

Monte lives in an apartment-type collective of a dozen people. He pays $40 a month rent for an apartment he says would cost him $150 a month in a non-cooperative situation.

Bob Bair, a 26-year-old resident of the Family of Peace commune on Baring St., pays only $30 a week to support himself and his girl. This means he is able to work for a peace group for $45 a week, which he would rather do instead of working in electrical engineering—a field in which he has a degree.

Barbara, a 22-year-old law school dropout, can model nude at an art school for $30 a week while making things in clay in her spare time.

Rusty Johnson, 28, a member of the Quaker-oriented Job Chiloway House and just a stone's throw from receiving a doctoral degree, placed all his studies aside to construct a potter's shop in the basement. He has already made two potter's wheels and is now working on a kiln.

"I went to school to learn what it meant to be a human being," he said. "I've learned a lot more than most but you really don't need a doctoral degree to talk with other people. Now I want to do something with my hands. I come from a long line of artists." He hopes to make a modest living by selling his pottery and devote free time to sculpture.

"We try to reinforce each other's values, to be supportive of what we're each doing," said Bob Bair. "What we try to say to a guy is, 'Look, you don't have to make money to be cool with us.'" The most viable communes seem to be those with a common thread of purpose running through all its residents like the Summer Street Gang (all mechanics) and the two Quaker-oriented communes, The Family of Peace and the Chilaway House.

The Chilaway eight are buying a century-old, 20-room house for $19,500 at $116 a month. Everybody puts up half his income for the support of the commune. While the house is structurally sound, it is badly in need of renovation and each member of the extended family donates a good deal of time to scraping wallpaper, painting, plastering and plumbing.

This commune is a lot more organized than most with a daily duty chart and dinner menus drawn up for the week.

Joyce Ennis, a trim 44-year-old editorial assistant for a Quaker publication, and her 50ish husband Bob, a state employee, are the commune's senior members. They sold their residence of 12 years in an old tree-lined white Frankford neighborhood to begin this new life six months ago.

"I like the social aspects, the interacting and just being around a lot of people I like," said Joyce. "Also, I don't have to feel odd here bringing home people who look funny to residents of a more traditional neighborhood. And I like the integrated aspect of the neighborhood and I can bike to work every day." ■

YELLOW SUBMARINE
Richard Fairfield

ON THE SIDE OF A HILL IN THE SUBURBS OF A CITY IN OREGON, there is a large yellow house, hidden from the highway by a bank of tall trees. The residents, Beatle fans, had come to call their dwelling Yellow Submarine, not because it is near a body of water (there is none nearby) but because of its obscurity from the road. I must agree that the name is an appropriate one for this commune. In terms of longevity, Yellow Submarine probably has few equals among communes existing in an urban-suburban setting. The commune got started in 1968, when several friends moved from Colorado to Oregon. Some made the move to attend college, others to be with their 348 friends while dropping out and trying a new lifestyle. When I visited Yellow Submarine in the summer of 1970, four of the original members (two brothers and their girlfriends) were still there, together with six or seven newer members (of whom only one was female). A few of the other original members who had left lived nearby and remained in close contact: "They just found they'd rather live with their families in separate dwellings," Tom told me simply. Yellow Submarine supports itself primarily through the sale of Granola and Familia, two popular and tasty grain mixtures, whose ingredients they purchase in huge quantities from other suppliers. These products are sold to the hip and college community through the local cooperative. The income from the commune's business is divided equally among the members after deduction of the amount necessary to pay for rent, food, and other household expenses. This usually leaves several dollars of spending money for each of the residents. Additional income is obtained through some outside work. When I was there, for instance, one or two of them held outside jobs and contributed an equal share of their earnings to the house fund.

Yellow Submarine is not a unique community. Rather, it is one of thousands of typical urban-suburban residential houses being used as something more than a college co-op, and something less than a revolutionary commune. Its members are satisfied with an easygoing low-income economic arrangement for the time being. It takes care of their basic needs and allows them a great deal of free time, which would not be possible if they worked at straight jobs, lived in a straight environment with separate apartments and transportation. (When I was there the commune had one truck as well as a car, although the truck was actually in a garage undergoing repairs amounting to $200, no small sum of money for a group of this nature.)

The large living-room table was partially covered with empty bottles. Several crocks of dandelion wine were being prepared under the kitchen tables and counter, while finished crocks of wine and beer were being stored in the cellar. I helped Tom and Bill pour bottle after bottle of corn syrup into one of the wine crocks.

"It takes nine pounds of sugar to make one gallon of wine," Bill's girl said.

"Fattening, huh," I repeated.

Tom got a big pitcher of homemade beer from the refrigerator and passed it around. A few friends had dropped in and we all sat in the kitchen, listening to the rock music playing continuously and loudly from a phonograph in an adjoining room. Around went the beer again; then someone passed a joint and we smoked that. It was a cheerful gathering, and I enjoyed myself.

While there at Yellow Submarine, I had the opportunity to find out more about the residents' activities. After getting up in the morning, they often would proceed to narrate and discuss their dreams of the previous night. Then they would chant and meditate. A huge chart hung on the wall of the kitchen outlining the possible activities of the forthcoming day. It told of going with friends to the park where they would dance and sing, chant and meditate, hold sensitivity groups, do psychodramas and sensory awareness exercises in the afternoon, and have an early, potluck dinner. After dark they would light a huge bonfire, take a little dope to expand their consciousness and then dance and sing and make music together. And before leaving, they would pray for good crops and the good health of all present in the coming year, and then each person would burn something from his past in the dimming bonfire. "Those are only suggested ideas," Tom noted, when he saw me reading the chart. "We may do all of them, or none of them, according to who's there and how we all feel at the time." These are after all a new and better breed of youths. They are not hung up on plans and schedules and rigid structures. They are able to adapt, change, modify, and eliminate a plan if the mood and tone of the moment does not fit the pre-described plan; they are now-oriented and yet able to project toward the future, that is, to organize and plan without disregard for the reality of the moment. Thus, they are not continually trying to impose a system on a situation simply because it had been planned.

A Common Sense of Purpose

After my visit to Yellow Submarine, I contemplated the group's way of life and its commitment to an alternative lifestyle. This commune was no band of pioneers living in lean-tos at the end of a semi-impassable mountain-goat trail. This was suburbia—or rather, a commune in suburbia where the members made no great efforts to isolate themselves from the outside world. In fact, many of the group's interpersonal and recreational activities took place outside the commune. As the male-female ratio was about 3:1, and as each female was involved in conventional monogamous pairing, most of the guys had to seek female companionship elsewhere. This kind of arrangement tends to make the membership in a commune more transitory; it also reduces depth interaction and interdependence characteristics that, if present, can create a more satisfying and permanent community.

But should every member of every commune be intent solely upon the purpose of developing depth interaction and interdependence? There are now many people, especially the young, who are content with a Yellow Submarine type of situation.

These people are not ready to make a permanent commitment to any one endeavor while there is still a whole world of alternatives out there for them to explore a universal wall chart to choose from. Only after a broad and satisfying experience of many diverse possibilities can a person really hope to find the place where he really wants to be, the place he can grow with, rather than beyond.

Few of us ever find that place. Some continue the search for quite some time, struggling bravely against exhaustion and exposure. But most of us take only a few steps before spotting what looks like a comfortable niche and snuggling safely within; thereafter, we confine our explorations to vicarious experience derived from newspapers, magazines, books, radio, television, and occasionally people.

In a world like ours, where the environmental stimuli run high, we are plagued with constantly gnawing feelings of discontent, dissatisfaction, boredom; feelings that can be traced directly to our inactivity. We cannot escape the fact that the search for self—for the true and total place (in all its physical, psychological, emotional, and social aspects)—where we know we ought to be—is as basic an urge in humans as is any automatic body function. We play all manner of games in our efforts to ignore this urge, because it offers no guarantee of fulfillment. But it hounds us throughout life and can only be outrun by death or nirvana; there is no in-between. Direct consciousness of this fact, combined with a total personal commitment to the search (not just intellectual; you must get in there with your hands and feet), constitute the only way to deal with this urge. Although some people have postulated that this urge is "the religious instinct," organized religion has no recognizable connection with it even if most clerics would like to claim it as their exclusive province (yes, including today's liberal-cum-social worker-cum-do-gooder-cum-clergyman).

I discussed no such weighty matters as these while at the Yellow Submarine. Nor did I studiously sit there thinking Important Thoughts and speculating about the ultimate meaning of it all. There was no need. My visit was relaxed and casual. It was fun. I emerged from that landlubbed Yellow Submarine much fuller than when I had entered. One useful and practical generalization was possible after my visit: homemade beer is a good fuel with which to keep a commune brewing. ∎

politics and revolution

CHAPTER 5

AY OUT/ may june / 75 CENTS
vol 2, no 5

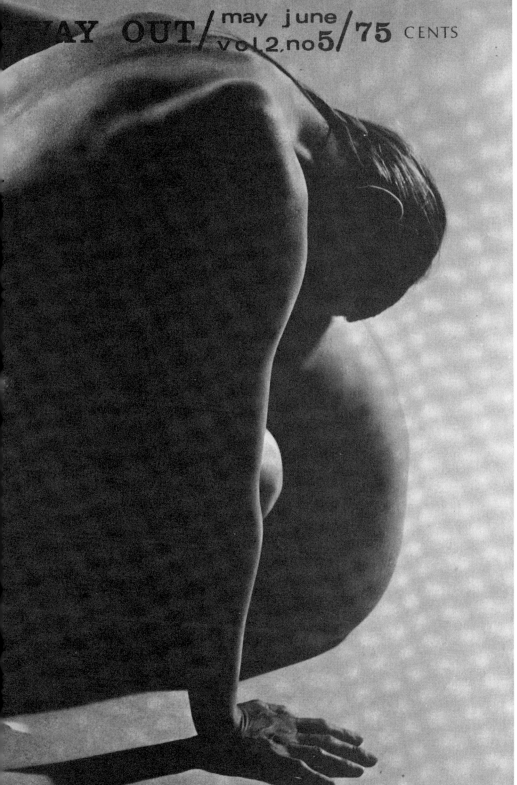

COPS COMMUNE
—Underground Press Syndicate, 1970

THE COPS COMMUNE IS A THIRD GENERATION COMMUNE. Its members live in several rented houses in Oakland and also run a ranch, The Black Bear, located in Northern California. I use the term "Third Generation" to indicate that the people who formed Cops are experienced communards, nearly all having lived on other communes. The first generation of these was probably a haphazard affair, perhaps not much more than a crash pad, and which lasted no more than two to four months. Second Generation communes are slightly better organized for the survival of their members and tend to stay together six to 16 months before breaking up. Third Generation communes are those which have lasted for at least two years.

Urban communes with rural branches characterize many of the larger and experienced communes, and it's a key feature in the expansion of communal life in California. The rural branch may be just a patch of ground off some dirt road, or a well-organized ranch. Each provides a place to raise crops, take a break from the urban chaos, tent out, etc. The communal farms have created the basis of an underground agrarian economy, which also includes mutual trade of goods and services. In April the Cops obtained an old truck which they were fixing up for use on a seaweed run. The idea was to go to distribute seaweed among the communes for use as an organic fertilizer. But the communards are not just on a fertilizer trip, they have also been organizing an inter-commune communication network. One manifestation of this is a multicolored newsletter, Kaliflower, distributed free to communes in the area. One of the people I met at Cops, an old friend from New York's Lower East Side, was in the process of teaching himself midwifery in order to provide free groovy obstetrical care. The issue of obstetrics is an important one when you consider the average San Francisco hospital charges $1000 for a delivery that occurs in an extremely alienated manner, to say the least. Natural childbirth is not sanctioned by AMA (American Medical Association) money-grubbers.

The many communes about San Francisco stay together for a variety of reasons: drugs, a leader, an issue such as ecology or revolution, which brings people together, both to live and act. Cops is a political commune. Although it is not the commune's immediate intention to organize demonstrations or storm pig headquarters, Cops people have a profound awareness of the social/political implications of their work. Last year the commune ran an elaborate print shop, until it was suddenly knocked out by a mysterious fire.

Cops have obtained another small photo-litho press and members are busily printing up leaflets and posters for the movement. But most significantly, their political third eye includes an understanding of the necessity for an organized system of intra- and inter-communal defense. Cops itself is so large that its people live in at least three different houses in Oakland alone.

A major feature of the work of the Cops commune is a free bakery, which opened in a rented store in Oakland (a flat above serves as another communal base camp and their printing shop is next door). The commune spends a huge amount of time and energy in keeping the bread baking and on its way to other communes and groups such as the Black Panthers as well as neighborhood youngsters. Cops first got the idea of opening a bakery when they heard that another commune had been given a large amount of baking equipment, which was not being used and rusting to death. Cops decided to grab the material, fix it up, and make free bread. What better way to expend one's energies, especially given the not so symbolic equation: bread=money.

How did the other commune get the baking equipment in the first place? According to the story I was told, not so long ago there lived a young baker in Oakland who slowly, but definitely, was feeling more and more fed up with his life as the years rolled on. One day, early in the morning, while making a batch of strawberry tarts, he made the definitive break with his past, to chuck the job and have some fun. He ripped off his clothes and went for a swim in a large vat of strawberry jam. An elderly lady entered the room at this time, and he ran after her. In doing so, he fell over a batch of flour and ran into the streets, naked. Our friend, the freaked baker, simply wanted to explain to the old woman that everything was okay. He never got to make his explanation since he was apprehended by the fuzz and taken to the local bughouse. There he decided that he had had enough of baking, and he donated all his equipment to the commune.

The Cops folks spent nearly six months refurbishing the oven and afterwards found a place to bake. They managed to rent a decrepit store which had once been used as a bakery, and fix it up to city standards, much to the annoyance of the building inspectors who continued to hassle the commune people almost until the day the bakery, gleaming with freshly painted walls and clean floors, was opened.

I spent an afternoon helping to bake some very turned-on bread. And a hard afternoon's work it was! The dough is tough and has to be kneaded for at least an hour to get it into baking shape. The bake room has a 12-foot-long table around which maybe 20 very beautiful cats and chicks stood kneading bread, drinking wine or beer, talking, having fun. Occasionally, some neighborhood kids would come in and have a go as kneaders too. When the dough was ready, we placed it in army surplus pans, or better yet into two-pound coffee tins. These allowed the bread to rise more evenly. Then we placed the pans and tins into a metal closet to allow the dough to set before it entered the oven. Great smells wafted from the oven as people flocked to taste the freshly baked bread.

Cops commune bakes three days a week. At other times they allow other communes or groups to use the oven and bake for themselves. This operation was just getting started at the time of my visit. The commune gets the ingredients for the bread by donations from friendly folk, and other more artful means. But the commune is dissatisfied with store-bought flour, because its vital ingredients are overprocessed and eliminated. Cops people look forward to obtaining their own milling machine to mill their own wheat.

Cops is only one of many communes organized to provide essential services for the Bay Area. Over in San Francisco The Good Times is put together by a newspaper collective, with both the newspaper and those who get it together living and working out of a large house in the center of the city. Other communes help to provide free medical care, and some even serve as freak-out centers where the damaged products of the "Great Society" can come for R&R. ■

COPS AS REPORTED BY A MEMBER OF THE BERKELEY TRIBE

COPS WAS ORIGINALLY A POLITICAL COLLECTIVE OF 20 TO 30 people which had vaguely defined politics and made minimal demands on its members. After almost a year together, about half of the members felt that we wanted more from a collective. We wanted to move toward communal living, income sharing, larger work commitments, more discipline, more personal support, training in revolutionary skills, and sexual experimentation. Most of us in this subgroup had worked closely together on the Third World Strike at the University of California, our first real experience with protracted confrontation and police terror, and we felt the need to further integrate our lives, both for support and motivation. Having drafted a document entitled Revolutionary Families, which is surprisingly close to the Weatherman's original conception of collectives, we found a vacant fraternity house and moved in on May 1, 1969. We lived there as a commune until June 1970.

Revolutionary Families was characterized by its simplistic clarity, its use of rhetorical generalities with which nobody could disagree, and its naive certainty. We discussed everything from our eating habits to imperialism. The collective discipline we prescribed for ourselves would not be abhorrent because of our revolutionary consciousness and collective spirit; we would thrive on this true merging of individual and collective interests. We were going to do everything possible to rid ourselves of bourgeois traits and mold ourselves into the best possible revolutionaries.

Needless to say, our original simplemindedness caused us all endless torment and anguish since it was impossible to live up to the personal and communal expectations we had set for ourselves.

If I sometimes sound overly critical of our experience, it is because I want to communicate a sense of the complexity and magnitude of the problems involved. The most valuable thing we gained from the experience was just this sort of understanding. The strategic problems of "smashing the state" are dwarfed next to the problems of getting ourselves together. As one of the first political communes in Berkeley, Cops was highly successful in the effect it has on its members, the services it provided the community, and its stimulation of others to form communes.

Sex is by far the most explosive and complicated problem to be dealt with. Our experiences and changing views on the subject show how we moved from simplistic to more sophisticated understandings of problems. It also shows how forces in the movement outside of the house affected the development within the commune. Our year together coincided with the year that Women's Liberation rose to its present prominence.

Prior to moving in together, our discussions of sex remained very vague, equivocal, and generally evasive. They were invariably accompanied by uncomfortable joking. When we finally moved in, there was an anxious undercurrent of excitement about all the new possibilities. This phase ended in an ill-fated exchange of partners, after which there was a general withdrawal into our customary sex lives which lasted for quite some time.

Some months later, I came home from the movies late one night and could not wait to go to sleep. When I reached the second floor, I found most of the commune members heatedly discussing monogamy. Although I knew that there was something wrong with the way people were talking about the subject, I could not yet explain what it was. This uncertainty, and my own defensiveness about being in a couple, caused everything in me to resist joining the meeting. But I knew that there was no way to avoid it.

The discussion went around and around well into the night when one of the women had a flash. She realized that the men were doing almost all of the talking, and that the heated way in which they were talking revealed their tremendous ego investments in the subject. "Smashing monogamy," at least the way we were talking about it, was a male trip. Once this was brought into the open, many of the other women admitted they had objected to what was going on but had been too intimidated to speak up. They said they were afraid of being bourgeois, unliberated women.

The two members of a couple make an implicit "deal" to never question certain fundamental aspects of their lives, for such questioning might undermine their stability and security as a couple. In collective struggle situations, when one member of a couple gets attacked, the other member protects her or him. Rather than sharing their problems with many of the other people in the house, one member of a couple tends to rely solely on the other for help with personal problems. Since a couple is a somewhat self-sufficient unity, they tend to withdraw to their own rooms and lessen collective activity. And monogamy is a bourgeois, propertied relationship where one person tries to possess another because of all sorts of inadequacies.

Throughout the argument, I had the feeling that it was not the specific principles of the debate itself that motivated people, but rather a general feeling that we were just not moving fast enough in transforming our personal lives, a fear that we were just rated, or whatever you choose to call it. It had also been the men who had always talked the most about sexual liberation and who had initiated the ill-fated sexual experimentation. It is tempting to attribute this solely to the men's desire to sleep with many women, and this undoubtedly played a part. But I think the explanation is far more insidious than the mere physical excitement and satisfaction gained from sexual variety.

To be a successful movement male, one has to prove that as well as being intelligent, militant and articulate, that he is also sexually liberated; sexual liberation is another arena for movement macho competition. It was not even the desire for the women as sexual objects, much less as human beings, that primarily motivated the men. Rather, it was the need to establish their image among the men and their position in the social hierarchy of the house.

Disturbed by the passive roles that they had allowed themselves to be forced into, the women decided to hold separate meetings regularly. These meetings continued for quite a while, but I don't think they ever attained the sense of unity and excitement that all the women had experienced at women's meetings outside the house.

Regardless of their intentions, given the situation of the commune, the women's first loyalties were not to their communal sisters but to the men of the house, whether their own individual man or the men in general. It was always agreed that they would support each other in situations with the men, but as soon as one arose, this promised solidarity failed to materialize.

Reacting through fear and guilt to the women's meetings, the men also began holding meetings. The discussion stayed within safe boundaries. It was permissible to discuss all the ways we were insensitive to women, all the ways we behaved chauvinistically. But we never discussed the ways we related to each other as individuals in any substantive way. At best, we discussed men in general. Our images of ourselves and each other, the competition between us, and our sexual feelings about one another were all verboten.

I would like to suggest two things about monogamy: We must do everything within our power to transcend it, while simultaneously guarding against the formalistic, destructive way that much of the movement has dealt with the question. There is no doubt that monogamy is an inherently insidious form. It is founded on insecurity, possessiveness and jealousy as well as economic domination. For the woman, it is nothing more than an exchange of her human potential for a chimerical security. Moreover, the relationships of domination become, through the children, the source of the slave mentality that infects all our social relations.

The error often made with disastrous consequences in dealing with monogamy is to mistake mere form for the essence. Although monogamy may manifest itself in the bed, it primarily exists in the head as a nexus of attitudes. To transcend monogamy we must wholeheartedly plunge into its attitudinal basis and not mechanistically rearrange our sleeping habits.

The key to transforming these deformed attitudes is trust and support—human solidarity. Couples must be helped to grow into a part of a larger collectivity rather than being coerced to dissipate into an atomized unit which often lends itself to hustling and being hustled. They must feel they are gaining something rather than losing something. This sort of support requires hours of patient discussion.

Every aspect of our communal life, from the quality of the meals to the productivity of our meetings, followed a surprisingly regular cycle of degeneration and regeneration. There were occasions when entering the front door was such a brutalizing experience that I seriously considered climbing the fire escape to my room to avoid encountering anyone. With tears constantly welling up in my eyes there were weeks when I experienced the house as a totally hostile "otherness." Given this potential for hostility, it is understandable that everyone wanted to protect themselves and were reluctant to take psychological risks.

To be able to function, a commune requires constant investments of psychic energy and commitment. Withdrawal of the psychic investment by any one person can cause a crisis of confidence which in turn sends all the other dominoes tumbling. The primary communal task is maintaining confidence, and this is subject to everything from an individual's unconscious to intentional politics. Most factors are far beyond our awareness, much less our control.

The physical objects surrounding us, most of them the leftover trappings of our previous lives as students, were persistent reminders of our revolutionary shortcomings. On the one hand, we were constantly paring down. On the other hand, keeping things, like hi-fi's and cars, was security for the future, although the house was glutted with them. After all, the commune wasn't going to last forever. But as security objects they also indicated the limit of our commitment to the collectivity, and how we were still keeping an eye out for ourselves. We fell into all sorts of mind games in trying to vindicate ourselves of the guilt we felt over our possessions.

A commune, regardless of how revolutionary it is, is permeated with hierarchy, competition and domination. There are real things to be won and lost. The collective interest of revolutionaries is not much more harmonious than that of any other social group. And this is the real heartbreaker: After running from the terror of functioning within bourgeois social institutions, I discovered that the dynamics of in-groups and out-groups, of pecking orders and advancing yourself at the expense of yourself and of others, is every bit as brutal as was my adolescent peer group.

To be on top was to be the most revolutionary. There were basically two paths of ascent. If one felt confident, one took the direct path, establishing oneself in traditional terms of what it means to be revolutionary—disciplined, energetic, militant, self-sacrificial, etc. The indirect path was better suited for the less confident. This path consists of redefining what it means to be revolutionary usually in more personal and cultural terms. Of course, these are the two polar positions and there were many combinations between them. Thus, on any given issue there was a continuum from the "hards" to the "softs."

I don't think we should despair over movement competitiveness. I just do not think that the Left should delude itself about humanity nor harbor any illusions about the extent to which it has rid itself of bourgeois remnants. But recently, there have been very encouraging developments, especially in the more advanced parts of the women's movement. With its critique of movement macho, its grounding of all forms of oppression in sexism and patriarchy rather than mere economics, its critique of the quality of daily life, its decentralized organization and its rejection of the elites and leaders, women's liberation holds the promise of a way out of the mire....

"Living here we learned how to communicate a lot better."   —*The Mole, 1971* ∎

BLACK COMMUNALISM WITH BOBBY SEALE

Copyright Noah's Ark, Inc. 1971, by permission of the editors

SEALE DEFINED A "COMMUNAL SOCIETY" AS ONE THAT HAS adequate wealth but is organized around its equal distribution. The people control the technology, but on a local level rather than having resources controlled and allocated by a centralized authority.

He said the most immediate task for the Black Panther Party was the implementation of the "survival programs," which he called "the people's fuel for revolution." He spoke of the Party's clothing factory and shoe factory which are being opened in the San Francisco Bay Area, and of his own plans for building communally owned, communally built, inner-city housing as soon as he gets out of jail.

Seale then began to talk again of how his inner-city housing communes would work. "I'm not designing a low-rent housing program," he said. "Low-rent housing projects turn into dilapidated ghettos. This communal housing is designed to be permanent, to last 50 years without deteriorating more than 10 or 15 percent. It's going to be communally owned and communally built.

"The houses will be structurally sound and contemporary in design. The apartments are laid out especially for black families with lots of children. Some of them have five large bedrooms. If two smaller families want to rent a place, then those big apartments are laid out so they can easily be divided. Or, if there's a group of young people who want to live communally, there's room for about 15 or 20 of them to live in one two-story unit.

"The basements will be communal and usable. We'll be able to have rooms where people can hold meetings, places that can be used as workshops, places to show films and have audio and radio equipment—all there, right within the commune. We even have figured out places where we could locate pool rooms, because in the black community a lot of young kids hang out at the pool hall. Instead of hanging out in a place filled with all that capitalist junk, they can be surrounded by some people's revolutionary posters. Of course, there are going to be washers and dryers in those basements, too, as well as storage rooms."

Seale decided that he couldn't go on talking about the communal housing unless he brought out the plans he had drawn up. I remembered then that he had been an architectural draftsman, and had done some building with his father, a carpenter. He opened the door, told the guard he was going back to his cell for a minute, and returned with a roll of drafting paper. He unfolded it on the desk.

There were about 15 sheets of professionally drawn designs, showing down to the last detail how the housing was to be constructed.

"You notice," he said pointing to one drawing, "that there is no such thing as a master bedroom in here. And look over here. See how large these windows are, facing this communal yard? That's so that parents can keep an eye on their kids down there, those kids that aren't in one of the communal daycare centers. Oh, and I forgot to mention that there will be space for free health clinics also.

"Now the thing is, this communal housing is going to be able to accommodate 40 large families, or from 50 to 60 medium-size families in a square block. That's between 350 and 400 people. The families will pay a monthly maintenance charge of no more than $150 a month. That's for the largest apartment, and it includes utilities. The smaller ones will be $90–$100 a month. At the end of 10 years, the people will own those apartments. You see, when you're dealing with the capitalists you pay rent for 20 years and all you got is rent receipts; but here, you pay for 10 years, and you know you've always got a place to live. If you want to move, you just move into a different people's commune, or a larger or smaller apartment, as you need it.

"The communal yard is the key," he said. "That's the place where black folks can get together. I can just see those yards on a Sunday afternoon, with people out there barbecuing and everything. That's what I call placing the ecology problem in the framework of the ghetto. It will be a place for people to eat and sleep if they want to, and there's enough room out there to build swimming pools. It's a place to get ourselves together and forget capitalism, greed and profit."

How was this housing going to be built?

"We'll take 20 journeymen like myself, with all kinds of different skills in things like carpentry, plastering and electricity, and then we'll take 80 unskilled brothers and sisters who want to learn those trades, and they'll work with the journeymen, helping them and at the same time learning those trades. So by the end, they'll be skilled workers. And probably a lot of them will be living in the housing they helped build. We can probably get a square block built in six to eight months that way. And I'm talking about good, solid construction, not that prefabricated stuff."

"How are you going to get the money to finance this type of housing?" I asked.

"Well, the first thing me and Ericka are gonna do when we get out of jail is to sue Arnold Markle for 10 million bucks for false imprisonment. It may take a little time to get that money, so we'll just have to raise it." ∎

TRANS-LOVE ENERGIES, 1969
by Walt Odets

ON HILL STREET, NOT FAR OFF THE UNIVERSITY OF MICHIGAN campus, stand two running blocks of the kind of Grand Victorian home long ago abandoned to the fraternity brothers due to lack of domestic help. These former nests of familial propriety now bustle with fraternal activity. At 2301, hanging from the balustrade above the front entryway, is a large linen banner reading "MASH MONROE." Across the street at 2304 it is "MUTILATE MONROE." And not half a block down, just visible from our acute angle through the neo-Grecian columns, we can barely make out "MANHANDLE MONROE." It is nine on this Saturday morning and this, of course, is Ann Arbor, Michigan.

But what is this ripple in the otherwise clear pool of a college man's dream? At 2308, just across from the Monroe Manhandlers, there isn't a sportsman's hope in sight. Has it blown down in the night? Been mutilated by Monroe? Or is this just the campus' literary fraternity?

I know, because I have it neatly down in my notebook. I have come all the way from the bannerless countryside of Connecticut to meet the occupants of 2308. 2308 is my destination and I know, or so I think, all about it. And it is my secret, I think, that lodged there, wedged there, sandwiched there between DEKE and Chi Psi, in this mustard-colored mansion, live the TRANS-LOVE ENERGIES. The what? And not only that, for the mansion is filled with freaks, 20 of them at least and all the more visible for the conspicuous lack of furnishings in a home once so grand. Pick any room, any of these high-ceiling rooms at random, and the contents can be counted on the fingers of one hand—two for the kitchen. Take the front room. There is a mattress on the floor, a wicker sitting chair, a long wooden table, a straight-backed wooden chair at the table and an ancient Remington typewriter. Clattering away. Fran is there at the table and she is busily typing. Everywhere in the house is tornado activity. On the porch, strings and strings of beads are assembled from what must be the veritable cosmic storehouse of beads in the form of a tabletop chest of drawers. Later I find that they are sold at the door of the Avalon Ballroom, Detroit's equivalent to the Fillmore West.

In the dining room, carefully etching with ink and watercolors, another girl prepares slides for use in the Trans-Love Energies' Trans-Love Light Productions, also for the Avalon. And whizzing through every room in the house, in here and out there, in there and out here, damned near the speed of light, are male freaks carrying, shoving, pushing and dragging huge pieces of black vinyl-clad electronic equipment. For tonight, the Trans-Love Energies' rock band, the MC5, are to play a gig at the arena in Sarnia, Ontario. The band numbers four and the equipment manager makes five. In addition, tea is simmering on the stove, a baby is diapered on top of the tape recorder (the only visible appliance in the house), film is developed in the basement darkroom and clothing is sewn at a small table in the back hallway. And, right off what I imagine the inhabitants of this home would call the toilet annex, but I call the foyer, in this little alcove next to the front door sits one freak, peaceful as the Buddha in this storm of activity, pants down and magazine up, on the toilet.

In the basement of the mansion sits a bear. The bear is hunched over a huge cubbyhole desk just littered with papers. The bear is busy working. The bear is wearing yellow pants with black and red five-pointed stars all over them. And a matching top. The bear is a magician. The bear is John Sinclair.

John Sinclair has, in this day of everyday longhairs, the biggest head of hair I've ever seen, like a beach ball, and he is huge and hulking. He is also friendly and talkative and, sure, he'd love to have us include the Trans-Love Energies in this book we're doing. He seems very concerned that I should know about all their activities. There is the band, the MC5 (Motor City 5); the Trans-Love Light Productions; Trans-Love Poster Productions (which is really also part of the bead and clothing productions division, which sells its products at the Avalon); Lemar (Legalize Marijuana), an autonomous but decidedly relevant organization within the organization; and The Sun, the group's newspaper and the equivalent of The San Francisco Oracle.

The Magic Bear also explains in his concerned way that all divisions of Trans-Love Energies are united in purpose and, when nudged oh ever so gently, continues by explaining that the purpose is the production of propaganda for the ferment of revolution. Or as Sinclair put it, "Rock and Roll, dope and fucking in the streets." And I, recent graduate of New England's most radical liberal arts college, begin to feel like an IBM executive.

The band, including Sinclair as road manager, is ready to leave for the Sarnia concert and I am invited to come along for photographs and experience. Although Sinclair remains friendly and we talk most of the way across the northern border of America, the members of the band view me with open suspicion and talk very little. There is a tape player in the panel truck with us and speakers as big as those in my living room. The sound is so loud. We are stopped in a rush-hour traffic jam and I, in this car of rock and roll freaks, look out the window at a 40-year-old businessman in a fawn-beige Fairlane stopped next to us on the Edsel Ford Freeway. His car looks like a sausage. He is six feet away. But he is a million miles away. This music is so loud, so intense and these people I'm with are so into it, that we are transported. Traffic noise is completely obliterated and the movie unfolds through the window in this game of rush-hour leapfrog. I do not know if we glide by them or they by us, it seems strictly relative movement and silent, for the music is my head and the outside world noiseless, the quiet creeping of this vast army of Fairlane sausages, the contents of each looking straight ahead as if just not having noticed our circus, straight in the back, eyes to the front, each in his sausage like a popsicle braced up there on the front seat. We are in, I think, the only non-Fairlane on all of Ford Freeway.

We arrive in Sarnia and I remind myself that I am doing a book and must take photographs. That's a sobering thought. The arena looks like the Cow Palace, but having just disembarked from this most extraordinary ride, I'm confident they can fill it. I mean, they have done such a fantastic job on my head. Still not fully conscious and through the front latest, we file past the orange plastic hot-dog stand, straight in the back, eyes to the front as if just not having noticed that 2500 teenagers are undeniably staring straight at us. A wave of titillation rolls through the crowd. I glance over my shoulder to see if, perhaps, Ricky Nelson is not perched atop the OrangeAide machine. He is not. And I realize that this collection of longhaired freaks with a magic bear for a leader, this American housewife's nightmare, this group of dope-smoking anti-heroes is indeed the object of such attention. And I realize that I have embarked on a book about new American outlaws, in a society of outlaws and that this magic bear walking on my left is King Outlaw of the Midwest.

We descend into the long, narrow concrete-block dressing room behind the stage with nary a posse in sight. The band must don proper attire for public commission of The Crime, but there is time, for theirs is to be the third set of the evening. On the other side of the dressing room, the first band to appear makes ready. They are a very neat-looking bunch by almost anyone's standards, a sort of Bobby Darin in quintuplet, and while one actually massages a palmful of Vitalis into his scalp, preparations on outside of the room begin. Fantastic items are miraculously produced from battered valises which I had assumed contained nothing more than clothing. Purple suede loafers, lime green bell-bottom pants and an unbelievable cream-colored brocade shirt are slathered on our lead singer. (On the other side of the room someone straightens his tie.) A complete satin outfit for our lead guitar. (They brush the lint from their double-breasted suits.) Shiny chocolate-colored leather for the bass player. (Shine the shoes.) And virtual nudity for our drummer.

Bobby Darin-Bobby Darin-Bobby Darin-Bobby Darin-Bobby Darin finish their set. The applause is moderate. The audience, still ignorant of the entrepreneur's sly programming, hopes and expects that the MC5 may be next. But no, mounting desire is to climb still higher and from the women's dressing room emerges the next group of performers, a rock and roll ensemble composed entirely of 16-year-old girls and believe me, are they gussied up. They all wear silver-glitter-flashing minidresses, coffee ice cream-colored stockings and silver high heels. And they are called, if memory does not fail me, The Banana Split Sisters. When they play, their still-pubescent breasts peek out over the tops of their Gibson guitars, except for the drummer, who has no guitar and, sitting on a stool five feet above the audience, has spent her dressing room time wisely in donning a pair of coffee-colored pantyhose. They played one of my old favorites, "When Love is Blind."

The time has come. As the MC5 walk onstage, huge throbs of teenage expectation, vast rolls of hot caramel, bellow forth from the audience. People are screaming. People are swooning. People are hysterical. The Propaganda, The Crime, the Rock and Roll Show is about to begin. Hands on thighs, Purple Suede Loafers steps to the front of the platform and, over the P.A. like a walking, talking thunderclap, he shouts: "KICK OUT THE JAMS, MOTHERFUCKERS!" which is the signal for the world's loudest, loosest and fastest rock and roll to begin. It's enough to say that if the Sarnia Arena looked like the Cow Palace and led one to expect a rodeo, we begot us just that.

Lurking in a magician's suit is the heart of a true revolutionary. Sinclair and The Trans-Love Energies are concerned with transforming precisely that which the others in this book have gone to rural communes to leave behind. And Sinclair knows so well, from the outlaw's point of view, what that is, which is why he is in this book.

But the Magic Bear has at least one Establishment ambition that I have been able to discover. He would like a steak every night for dinner. So, before leaving Ann Arbor for the more peaceful landscape of rural communal living, I went to a butcher and bought him an assorted 25 pounds of steaks and chops. He was asleep when I arrived at the house with the meat, so I went to his room and poked him. He sleeps with his wire-rimmed eyeglasses on. He grunted. I poked him again. He growled. I poked him again and he finally sat up. He unwrapped the meat and eyed it with the same incredulity that characterizes the bears at Yellowstone Park as they eye that picnic basket in the back of your car.

He adjusted his eyeglasses. "Where did you ever rip this off!?" Lurking in a magician's suit the heart of a true revolutionary. ■

SDS COMMUNAL ATTEMPTS

by Jean Tepperman
The Mole, *1971*

WHEN A FEW NORTHEASTERN SDS MEMBERS BEGAN TO LIVE together in a South End building three years ago, they had no worked-out ideas about communal living—"it was just good to live together." Some SDS people had rented one of the apartments; gradually, the four other floors filled up the building with friends.

The next day I visited another South End house where others from the first house are forming the core of a new commune. Everyone was quite willing to stop what he was doing and talk about what the house had meant over the past three years. Most of them felt it had been important, both personally and politically, due both to the mistakes they learned from as from the positive experiences.

"You can't set up an ideal commune in a desert and expect the rest of society to have no effect," one guy said. "But you have to start or you won't get it after the revolution."

"It's a collective way of solving problems of living," someone else said. "Physically and also a qualitatively different way of living, more consciously approached. One goal of the movement is to make people more conscious of how they are living—a commune is a good vehicle for doing that because you have to keep making collective decisions about how to live. It's important to break down the old ways people relate to each other and learn how to share."

While they were talking, I kept thinking about people I know who are older, who try to be part of the movement, but can't really do it, because the way they live is just like everyone else. The problem isn't how much money they have, it's the whole way their lives work—the movement is their "job" and then they come "home" which means a little closed-off apartment somewhere with their mate (and maybe children). Just because life is patterned that way, couples feel that everybody else is the "outside world," and in some way you are against everybody else and everybody else is against you. It seems practically impossible to maintain real solidarity and a sense of community. Talking to people in this commune made me realize that, by living together, you stake your physical and emotional survival on being able to work out collective ways of meeting people's needs. That means that every practical problem forces people to develop new ways of relating to each other.

The South End house soon became a social and political center for many others beyond its residents. The New England Free Press began in the basement; a mimeograph machine there produces most of the Northeastern SDS literature. The house is as a center of activity for the movement at Northeastern. But some people felt that one of the reasons the Northeastern chapter became the first Boston SDS chapter to experiment with communal living was that it was a very small and isolated one. And its isolation caused resentment among people outside the house.

Political work tied the communalists together, but was one of the main sources of conflict. Money, naturally, is a big hassle. When people first moved into the house, everyone's money was kept separate—people even paid rent apartment by apartment, rather than dividing up the total cost of rent for the house. Now in all three communes people are trying to work it out so that everyone contributes whatever money they can. This is a problem because people without jobs have felt free to live in the house without any financial responsibility, confusing the line between sharing and using other people. In the new house people suggest taking turns working for a while.

The same goes for people's personal possessions—like cars and record players. At first everyone used the available car, but the person who owned it had to pay to keep it running. This caused tension. Some felt that others used their possessions to separate themselves. Now they are talking about more extensive sharing of possessions and responsibility for keeping up cars.

Rent itself is another pressure, and people are often thrown together because of necessity: "we need two more people to pay rent" instead of choosing to live together. This is why people move in and out casually, without feeling any real commitment to the quality of the relationships in the house.

Residents in the house consider work a drag. Some people there felt oppressed by having the place become incredibly cruddy then cleaning it all up, and then the cycle begins again. They have never had a work schedule or any formal way of dividing up house jobs ("we had a list once, but someone tore it down"). Dividing up work was the main function of house meetings, but they didn't happen frequently: "I think we had three in the past year."

As in most American homes, the guys would gather around at about five o'clock and say, "When's supper going to be ready?" The women told me, "We used to just jump up and cook to avoid hassles," but last year the women in the house went on a strike and refused to serve as collective housewives. Now, everyone says, people share the cooking and cleaning more equally, and there is a greater sense of responsibility toward the work.

"You Have to Build Up Openness Consciously"

People say that they want to approach work in a different way in the new house. They see the redecorating of every room in their four-floor house as a collaborative project, an important way of learning how to live together.

The most explosive problem in the house has always been sexual relationships. Many couples have formed and broken up in the house, and people have had widely different ideas about what a relationship should be. Some married couples have lived there without changing the patterns of their marriage. Other people, especially the men, feel that monogamy itself is incompatible with real emotional openness. "People see a monogamous relationship as a kind of mutual ownership," one guy said. "They turn to only one other person for security."

The women mostly had a different view. They agreed about the importance of breaking down the idea of a couple as a closed-off unit, but felt that the men's insistence on "sexual freedom" was about fantasy. "It boiled down to a situation where one guy had several chicks, not just one." "Triangle" relationships developed that created tremendous tensions in the house. Once a meeting was called to discuss one of these problems, but everyone agreed that it didn't work at all.

These failures didn't seem to discourage people from working out emotional problems in the group. They all said that failures of emotional resolution occurred only because people weren't accustomed to talking about things together. "The main thing that has to be broken down," one girl said, "is the attitude of 'If you don't hassle me, I won't hassle you.'" If people continually make an effort to overcome keeping things inside and ignoring difficulties, a crisis would be easier to deal with. "You would know how to be with people—and you have to build up that openness consciously. Living here, we learned how to communicate a lot better." ■

PREVIOUS PAGE: HAPPY HIPPIE COUPLE, COMMUNE USA

ABOVE & RIGHT: TWIN OAKS COMMUNITY, LOUISA, VA

LEFT: TWIN OAKS COMMUNITY, LOUISA, VA
ABOVE: THE HOG FARM, LAYTONVILLE, CA

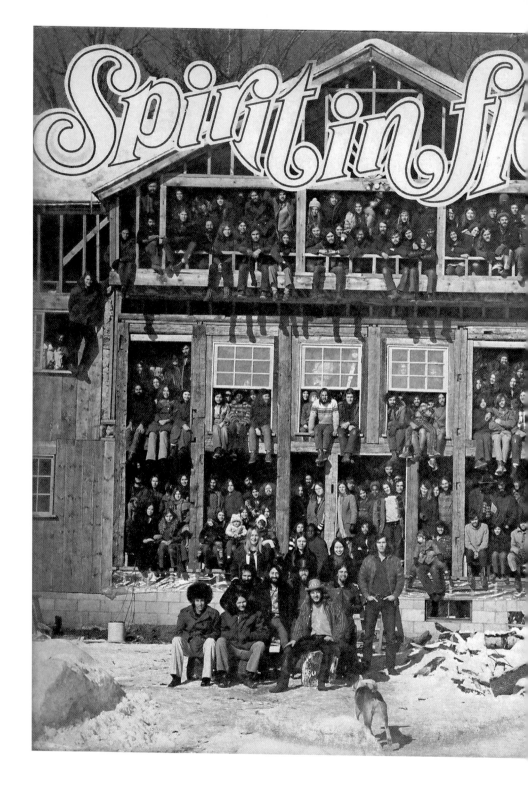

RECORD COVER FOR THE BROTHERHOOD OF THE SPIRIT
COMMUNE'S RECORDING PROJECT (WARWICK, MA)

Photo by Robert Altman

ALLEN NOONAN AND DIAN, ONE WORLD FAMILY WORLD CRUSADE, SAN FRANCISCO
Following page: The Weavers of Maine community

<small>Stephen Gaskin leading class at The Farm, Summertown, TN</small>

Top: Krishna Commune, Minneapolis, MN

Bottom: Love Israel Family

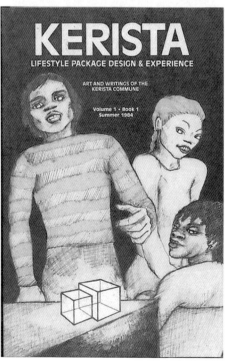

Upper left: Acolyte, Process Church of the Final Judgment, Boston Chapter

Lower left: Book cover from Kerista commune, San Francisco

Center, Mel Lyman, from *Avatar Magazine*, c. 1971

Lower right: Father Yod and YaHoWha 13, Hollywood, CA

Message to Humanity:

Hi gang, I'm back, just like the book says. By God here I am, in all my glory, I thought I'D NEVER come. But I'm here now and getting ready to do the good work. Maybe some of ya think I aint Him. You'll see. I aint about to prove it for you, much too corny, I'm Him and there just aint no question ABOUT it. Betcha never thought it would happen like THIS did ya? Sorry to disappoint you but I've got to make the most of what's here and there sure as hell aint very much. No turnin water to wine and raisin the dead this trip, just gonna tell it like it is. You've waited a long time for this glorious moment and now that it's actually HERE I expect most of you will just brush it off and keep right on waiting, that's what those damn fool Jews did LAST time I came, in fact they're still DOING it. Oh well, what's a few thousand MORE years to people who've been suffering for MILLIONS. So while most of you turn your heads and continue sticking to your silly romantic beliefs I'll let the rest of you in on a little secret. I'm Christ, I swear to God, in PERSON, and I'm about to turn this foolish world upside down. . . . .

Love, Christ

15

Lou Gottlieb, Rena Morningstar, and Vishnu, Morningstar Ranch, CA

GAY COLLECTIVES
From Come Out! Magazine, *1970*

EXPERIMENTS WITH COLLECTIVES HAVE BEEN VERY MUCH A part of the Gay Liberation Front in the past year and with good reason. Any group that calls itself radical and revolutionary must concern itself with providing an alternative way for people to live and work together than the competitive, role-oriented model which heterosexual, capitalist society offers us. The chief "virtue" in our society is individualism through which a person continually perceives what is to his or her own advantage at the expense of others and fights for the money and power to attain it. It is the institutionalized individualism in our society which leads to the oppression of every powerless group (homosexuals, women, third world people, etc.). A functional alternative to individualism is collectivism.

A collective is a group of people who organize around a common purpose and agree to function collectively in order to attain it. Collective functioning involves the idea that within the group there are no leaders and all strive to participate as equals. Every idea and feeling that arises in the group is brought forth and shared. No decisions are made until the whole group has talked the matter out long enough that there is an agreement reached among everyone as to what to do. Criticism is an essential part of a collective. It is the responsibility of the group to continually evaluate how it is functioning. Criticism of the group or individuals within that group is never allowed to go on in private but is always brought forth in the presence of everyone. The responsibility of an individual in a collective is to continually strive to see what is to the advantage of the group (which includes herself or himself). When a collective lives together it becomes a much greater challenge because it enters into every area of life.

Our collective has been functioning dynamically for the last three and a half months, and often I ask myself what internal or external bond holds us together. To me the answer is obvious that it's because of consciousness-raising, which is the process of evolving a politics by talking about our oppression as gay men in this sexist, male chauvinist society, and also through my entrance into Femmes Against Sexism. This is a consciousness-raising and an action group designed to deal with the oppression of femme males as well as the hypocrisy of the "straight" homosexual man's need to come off as straight in order to feel less pressured in this sexist society, leading to the suppression of the femme side of his personality. In my nine months in GLF I noticed that the women were more together than the men. By "together" I mean that the women did not have the need to compete and did not fight with each other as much.

153

The men of the 95th Street collective are mostly femme males. By virtue of being femme males we have the ability to love one another and have stronger emotional bonds than the "straight" homosexuals. When ideas are in conflict we collectively search for a solution that meets all of our needs. When a member of the collective is hurt, we are sensitive to the other's personal pain. There is no need to hide our pain as so many men do in order to uphold the masculine image that our society forces on males. We express pain as well as the love and anger which run rampant in all of us. As long as we let the femme in us come through, our collective will continue functioning as a whole, and not as one "man" competing against another. I feel our collective has much to offer as an example to men who are still handicapped by a masculine image that is slowly dying, and which women and femme men feel is oppressive to us.

My entrance into the GLF men's living collective was the direct result of five months of consciousness-raising. Through this group experience with my gay brothers, I learned to identify with and trust other gay men. This eased the pain I had felt as an isolated, lonely, "sick" man. Simultaneously, I developed a furious anger against this sexist society which was so oppressive to me as a gay male and as a femme. Thus I became increasingly active in gay liberation.

Collective living was the natural next step. A living collective provided the maximum politically productive use of my energies, but even more important was the opportunity it provided for an alternative lifestyle. We strive to create an environment where we are equal, where no one is oppressed. We give each the love and support we need to accept criticism and change. Each of us has grown and flowered at an amazing rate since entering the collective. I have particularly come out in this environment, expressing even more freely my feelings and ideas. I have gained immensely in strength and confidence, recognizing always that our strength is in the collective, not the individual, and that our struggle as gay revolutionaries is to smash sexism.

People who wish to form a communal collective should keep in mind that a full commitment to collective living is a must from the start. At the same time, people must be very patient with themselves and each other. We are all encumbered with all kinds of irrational habits and petty hang-ups. Some of us are shy about sex or nudity or expressing our emotions. Some of us smoke too much, or have developed little rituals about sleeping or eating or going to the bathroom.

Only when we feel a collective or personal need to get rid of these habits can we begin to observe them. And when we do so, we need to be able to trust our sisters and brothers to give us the support and love that makes them unnecessary. For this reason, a collective should never make rules governing individual behavior unless everyone can support a certain idea, and it is probably not necessary to make it into some kind of law, anyway. What a collective decides becomes a plan of action. If people carry out the plan and it succeeds, all well and good. If they do not, or if the plan fails, a group self-criticism is in order to find out why people were unable to carry out the plan, or why it maybe wasn't such a good plan in the first place.

After observing the collective living situation for two weeks I decided that no other lifestyle could offer so much or could be so challenging, rewarding and valuable. Beginning the third week as a member of this collective I have encountered many frustrations and difficulties. But I am more and more aware of a new strength and positiveness that comes from the support and understanding my collective brothers have offered. I now realize how difficult it is to make the change from an individualistic consciousness to a collective one. Yet with each obstacle I encounter, I find I have not only my own strength (which would not be enough), but the strength and aid of my four collective brothers. And when an obstacle has been surmounted, I have a genuine sense of something important gained through the experience. ∎

IOWA CITY ALL-WOMEN'S COLLECTIVE

by Everywoman, VPS 7/31/70

IN THE INTEREST OF BRINGING WOMEN TOGETHER AND IN AN attempt at experimenting with communal living, several women in Iowa City formed an all-women's collective. They're hoping that living together will do several things. First, by pooling all their incomes they can free some of the sisters from oppressive work so that they can do more worthwhile work.

Living together makes them physically close, enabling them to study together, work together, sharing the shit work, and sharing the exciting moments together. They formed the collective hoping that it would be a place where all sisters could come together and find alternative lifestyles and philosophies for the future. They have lived together in a large house for just one month. Six sisters actually live in the house and two more sisters will join in the fall. Two of the sisters help organize and run the two free day-care centers in Iowa City. Other sisters help at the day-care centers and work full-time at straight jobs. All the money earned is pooled together. Sisters contribute anything from a full month's salary to food stamps. This all goes into either the household kitty or the checking account.

Thus far the collective has made several structural decisions. We have regular closed meetings to discuss issues or problems at hand. This is a time for consciousness-raising. At first we thought that closed meetings may be elitist. But in the interest of experimenting with a small core of the same people we decided that it was necessary.

We have also decided that there will be no men in the house. This decision was made in the effort to support the goals that we have made for ourselves. If women are to truly get themselves together then they need someplace where they may go and always know that the open arms of a sister await them. We think of our house as a place where married sisters, high school sisters, and all others may come to talk if they have problems, or to have fun if they need to get away for a while. It has been difficult to not allow men in the house, because there always seem to be those exceptions. However, the rule of never any men in our house has established an atmosphere that we all agree is wonderful. It is very important that we do not become co-opted on this point. We also decided that there will be no dope in the house. Especially these two decisions came after a large discussion on how disciplined we want to become.

We try to schedule collective meetings on a night when there are no cell meetings and as often each week as we can. Initially these meetings were mainly concerned with the basic functions of the collective. For example, we discussed how housework, money, meetings, cars were to be taken care of. However, we also began to discuss theoretical issues such as sisterhood, loving women, elitism, self-discipline, group protection, pigs. All of these discussions led to consciousness-raising.

The household responsibilities have been divided so that two people cook every evening meal and two people do the pots and pans after each person does their own dishes. We all eat dinner together at seven o'clock, and usually there are many other sisters who sit down to eat with us. The weekly cleaning is done on Saturday when two sisters plan the meals for a week and buy the groceries, two do all the laundry and two plus any other sisters who come clean the house. These jobs are rotated each week, and no one is ever left to do anything by herself.

Economically, women's collectives are highly desirable. A single woman has a much harder time than a bachelor. She receives less pay for more and shittier work. Insurance companies, the government's and other institutions' policies make it harder financially to be single. However, if the woman marries, she fits right into the capitalistic system of economics. She can be written off as a "dependent" or an "exemption." A collective with other women is less expensive since costs are shared. The collective is a new institution in society, and as such, can buy food and other needs more cheaply. ∎

TWO HIP COMMUNES: A PERSONAL EXPERIENCE

by Vivian Estellachild, Hundred Flowers/UPS

IN THIS ARTICLE I WILL DISCUSS TWO RURAL COMMUNES IN which I lived for a total of 10 months. Those experiences served as a catalyst to my becoming a feminist. I did not live on these communes for the purpose of writing this paper. I joined them as an alternative to the straight world.

The major problems of the commune were male chauvinism, insensitivity, and stagnation. New ideas met with incredible resistance. In order that people notice that you were upset about something it was necessary to do a total hysterical freak-out scene. New suggestions met with laughter and ridicule. It is impossible to live in such conditions. When I saw Lottie freak out over the unwillingness of people to change, I saw her old man hit her in the face so badly that she was blinded for two weeks. She and I were called "dykes" because we were uppity. Only she was braver and so paid a higher price.

The second type of "man" was the Big Jim variety. He had the biggest penis but was not the best fuck around (just in case this should fall into his hands). He was a big macho alcoholic (as were at least six other men). He has sired six children but will never be a father. I have seen his wife thrown around and come close to a concussion. The men were basically this macho type with one exception.

The Farm

I would like to talk about The Farm, a commune of 30–50 people in Oregon. It consists of 310 acres financed by loans and parents to the tune of $75,000. The men do odd jobs like tree pruning while the women take care of the babies and wash an unending pile of dishes. They contribute their welfare checks to the communal bank account. Expenses run $2500 a month. Despite the communal handling of money there is continual squabbling and distrust as to who gets more and who is stashing money and other articles. This is particularly true of the men. The men come in a few simple varieties. The first is the Bill Ph.D., with two wives and seven kids, too good to work with his hands but not too good to fuck everything that moves. At the same time he always makes it clear that he cornered the market on brains. To him I was always the idealist whose head he never quite understood.

Fucking became the major occupation of the group. No one was capable of getting anything else done. It was a full-time occupation to prove one's manhood. Meanwhile, the house and the kiddies were women's work.

While the men played All-American on an $8000 Caterpillar and wrecked all the cars, the women were criticized for their driving and were told things like "there are three kids with dirty diapers in here and three chicks—get to it." Of course the men had just been sitting there while the women had been baking bread, making supper, and doing the endless pile of dishes left from the interminable snacks. On one occasion I was crazy enough to leave a friendly note on the wall suggesting that each person wash his own dish. The response was angry derision from the men. The note also asked that three meals be cooked daily, which would simplify cooking and cleaning. What!? Infringe on people doing their own thing? Schedule their lives?! I finally stopped helping but then the burden fell on the other women since we really did not have our shit together. There was a schoolhouse in which one woman worked tirelessly.

Education was more of an all-day living experience. So we were successfully raising kids who were free of time zones but into heavy "masculine" and "feminine" role-playing. The 10-year-old boy was getting to be an unnerving copy of his father.

I tried a few times to talk about women's liberation. I brought home a few articles. (At that time I had only begun to read the literature.) The men gradually became so uptight about it that I took the safer course and dropped the subject for almost two months. It was impossible to talk about it anyway since everything they said was really only a "joke." They would laugh and would not have to deal with me or their problems in a serious way. I wonder if the 13-year-old is a virgin (ha ha), or who has won the quest to deflower her (ha ha ha). She sure is getting to be a good cook and a help with the babies.

Gluttony and drunken brawls three to five nights a week, constant high-key frenetic living, as well as the sexual frenzy and lack of any creative activity, contributed to my misery. I wasn't about to challenge their egos over the brink. Another problem was the rapid turnover of people and transients. The atmosphere left me with no bearings at all. I left and so did a few other women (this seems to be a trend, so there is hope). The next time I saw the men they were in town looking for "some ass," and only four women were left on The Farm. If The Farm sounds repulsive I assure you that it was. The only good thing that came out of it was by beginning awareness of women's problems and focusing on them. I became more aware of why we compete and I became very interested in the women. Mostly they were warm, loving, generous people. They were and still are being used. Instead of suffering the miseries of shitwork and alcoholic husbands all alone in a house in the suburbs, they were together doing the shitwork as a group.

Although superficially there was talk of group responsibility for the children, only the women really did it. Women without children became resentful that their lives were filled with too much household drudgery. Women who were into anything interesting like music, poetry, herbs, teaching, or crafts left The Farm. Under pressure, the only monogamous couple left The Farm (the husband was uptight about his prize possession). A woman with one child left to go to a quieter commune in California. And I finally left for a commune in Minnesota. I had lost my hopes for any kind of life at The Farm and I thought I still might find another group more willing to experiment with lifestyles and macrobiotics that I was interested in. Shortly after I left, The Farm men took my car, crashed it, ran over it with the Caterpillar and pushed it into the dump heap. I am sure that it was a cathartic experience. Probably gave them a hard-on. They never could subdue me and the car was second-best.

The Outpost

Before I talk about the Outpost commune, I would like to relate one of the experiences that I had while traveling through hippiedom on my way there. I came to Minneapolis knowing only one man. The next night he took me to a friend's house where I dropped a triple dose of acid. The friend turned out to be a Leary-type guru who took us on a Tibetan Book of the Dead-type trip. Unfortunately, I had never read the book beforehand. He delighted in torturing me because I did not understand. I became more and more terrified. The acid was very strong and I was operating in the after-death plane. He started spitting in my face and accusing me of all kinds of things.

I felt bewildered. He also totally humiliated the other women in the room. I ran away. My boyfriend said it was all in my own head, certainly not the "Maharishi" and definitely not the acid. In my greatest need he totally deserted me. These were the most insane moments of my life. I ended up totally out of my mind, half-dressed, wandering the streets of a strange city. It took me two days to be relatively sure that I was on the planet Earth. Lately I have had the strongest desire to meet this "Maharishi" once more on the after-death plane. It will be his last "trip" and there will be no coming down.

It was in this state of mind that I arrived at the Outpost. The people were happy to see me and I decided to stay and try to figure things out as best I could. We lived in a rented building and farmed about six acres of land. Immediately I got into the farming. It was hard work but soothing to my battered head. Except for one man, I had really become sexually turned off by men. I began to read, study herbs, farm, and eat pure foods along with the rest of the group. In August I even helped deliver a baby at home with our whole family gathered around. New ideas were more openly received and people seemed to respect each other.

I dropped some more acid this time only with four women, and had an incredibly beautiful trip. For the first time another woman and I spoke our true feelings about the men. We were safely out in the field. It doesn't take too much to realize that we had come to the same conclusions. Pottery brought in the main income of about $200 a month. Life was much simpler but better. The core group of people had known each other for years.

More transients came through in the summer. The stability of the original group had broken down and the shitwork grew, especially since the men visitors would never do anything but sit and wait for their meals and treat the commune as a summer resort. Lack of money, disease, boredom, machinery breakdown, etc. had driven all but six of the people off the land. The members of the Outpost primarily live as monogamous couples, and each of the original group has at least one child.

The child care is basically the responsibility of the mother. In the cases where the parents are separated, the father acts as if he were single while the mother bears almost all the responsibility of the child.

Our cooking was done on an old wooden stove but was simpler because of the macrobiotic (mostly grains and vegetables) diet. When the group enlarged to more than 30 it really became a project. When I first arrived the men were into cooking and baking bread. The women worked in little groups to do the other preparation and gathering of wild vegetables. Only two formal meals were prepared each day and everyone washed their own dish.

One of the major activities was working for other farmers in the area. This was fun and relieved the monotony, but only for the men. I was the only woman free to go since I did not have a child. When I would get to the neighbor's house it was "hi fellas, let's go combine those oats," and "oh Vivian, the Mrs. will be happy to see you," and I ended up in the kitchen politely preparing lunch for the "men-folk," making sure there was first enough room at the table for them to sit, and then the women. No man ever objected to this. The other women worked in the nearby garden plots and did housework and childcare because by default it is always more "convenient" that way. By the end of the summer I was really quite tired of kitchen work, serving men visitors, illness and babies. The milking of the cow, which I really like to do, was taken over by a man because he was "faster." One morning as I was starting a fire in the stove, one man came in, said he was in a hurry, and that I had better let him do it. I screamed to be allowed to do something. To learn some skill besides the ones I had learned all my life—babies, dishes and cooking. That was a terrible thing to do. I have started a thousand fires but naturally that morning the fire went out! Later some of the women voiced their support to me in private. I finally did drive the tractor and helped with the haying. It was sort of a novelty and not a real responsibility. By September I was becoming bored. The men got jobs unloading freight cars and we were preparing lunches. The first day we did not have things together and one of the men was upset that the lunch had been late. I exploded with rage. I didn't have to take that crap since I was nobody's wife. He immediately apologized and said that he had only been "joking." At this point the other women demanded to know why he had opened his mouth in the first place. He shut his mouth and slipped away and I got my first taste of sweet sisterhood. So the role-playing had not really changed.

At least half the women were unhappy, going through crying spells, but could not pinpoint the cause. The roles women can play are so very limited, leaving two possibilities: being sexual playthings and then Madonna and child chewing at the breast. If you object, then you are accused of not being natural, not groovy with nature, not doing things as they are supposed to be. The only thing the communal woman can create is a child. After the novelty wears off, and the tiredness of the mother makes her less sexual, her old man goes off looking and she gets left with the kid. Although communal living appears to be a step in the right direction, the hip commune uses women in a group way the same as their fathers did. The communes are too fluid to create any security for a woman. Her stability lost and isolation complete, she cannot be an effective force for change. She must leave or kick the men out. Kicking the men out is hard because they own the land and are the breadwinners. There is also quite a stigma attached to being that ungroovy and unfeminine. It is hard for the hippie housewife to rebel, but it is happening. Almost every woman I know has gone home to her parents or moved to her own place (using her welfare money). More and more the communes are becoming all-male. Then the men look around and wonder where have all the "chicks" have gone. ■

KIDS IN COMMUNES

by Pedestal, *1971*

HAVING LIVED IN COMMUNES WITH MANY OTHER ADULTS, I would like to say that it is potentially the best arrangement in which to raise children: best for parents, other adults, and children alike. I have to admit, though, that in most cases I've seen, because of the attitudes of many of the adults concerned, it is also one of the worst arrangements.

Children need privacy, quiet and a sense of order to cope with the rapid physical, mental and emotional changes occurring within them. This is difficult to provide in a house with many adults, but it is essential to the child's development as an individual. All too often though, with numerous adult trips and chaos happening around them, they feel lost and confused and their confusion comes out in destructive ways—crying jags, running around, making lots of noise and destroying things.

Children need to be treated with love, understanding, and respect as growing individuals with decided personalities and temperaments of their own. They need individual attention that is not superficial, and they want to feel pride in their achievements and be acknowledged for them. Even if the communards are tuned in to the kids, you'll inevitably have problems with some of your friends treating them like inconvenient house pets, giving them superficial attention when they're feeling benevolent, or when the child does something irritating. If children are ignored and are greeted with, "That's nice, dear" when they show you something they've done that they're proud of, they do things like kicking the baby or peeing in someone's shoe because then they really get noticed.

Children need to feel identification with a group of people—the family or collective—especially for the first few years. This can only be achieved if the group is fairly constant and people are not forever splitting for Montreal or San Francisco or wherever every couple of weeks. In that case the child is surrounded by a bunch of strangers and never gets to know any of them.

Children must be allowed to assert themselves and make many decisions for themselves. This is most a problem for the communal child who is not yet talking. Unless everyone in the commune knows the child well enough to understand when he/she mumbles something, he is likely to be trampled by well-meaning adults who think they know better.

Since you are so much bigger, louder and have so much power over the child's life, you must be very careful not to lay your trips on her, or expect him to necessarily get off on your trips. A sensitive, excitable small child will not benefit from being taken to a long, loud rock concert no matter how much her/his parents dig it. He experiences things so intensely that she'll likely suffer from sensory overload and scream from fatigue and frustration. The same goes for other adult trips—blowing dope in the kid's face is extremely unfair until he/she gets old enough to ask for it; the same goes for booze, extreme food trips, loud parties with her/him in the room, and taking him/her places you want to go where he/she is not going to have a good time. For instance, we made the mistake of taking two small ones on the Unemployed March to Victoria last week. It took them (and us) two days to recuperate from being cooped up on crowded buses and ferries for hours at a time and being dragged around from place to place. Next time we'll leave them home and a good time will be guaranteed for all. At its best, the commune in the family or tribe state offers:

For the Children: more friends of all ages and exposure to many people's different trips (it's too bad old people aren't included). This prevents shyness and super-dependency on one or two people and lessens the damaging effect of bad mistakes made by the parents or others because there are more people with whom the child has secure relationships.

For the Adults: gives many their first exposure to children, a feeling of true family to those who've been floating around transient for a while and are feeling lonely and somewhat alienated by sharing the workload. Everyone is much freer and less burdened by it, and it underlines the double standard for women. In other words, if only the women look after the kids and wash the diapers, and the guys are full of shit about being communal, women can support each other in demanding their rights and equal sharing of responsibilities. Communal support helps remove financial pressures from the parents by sharing food, housing costs, and baby equipment as well as proper postnatal pampering of mothers with new babies. ■

scientific ideology and *walden two-* influenced communities

CHAPTER 6

MODERN UTOPIAN $1

WALDEN HOUSE
by Richard Fairfield

I WAS A THEOLOGICAL STUDENT MORE INTERESTED IN HUMAN-istic psychology than the behavioral form when I first read B.F. Skinner's novel Walden Two. Nevertheless, the book turned me on; it was sort of a composite of many previous utopian visions—communal dining, egalitarian economics, professional child-rearing, labor credit system, and so on.

My initial enthusiasm was so great that I immediately got out the phone book, looked up Dr. Skinner, and called him. His cordial invitation and our subsequent meeting left me as positive as ever.

A short while later I came across an interesting classified advertisement in Ralph Ginzburg's Fact magazine. It said that Gerald Baker of Cresco, Iowa was looking for people to form a Walden Two community. I contacted Baker and discovered that the rudiments of such a community had already been formed by other people in Washington, D.C.

I visited the nascent community in the spring of 1966. It was my first visit to a commune and found it located in a poor section of the nation's capital. Here, half a dozen idealists had gathered to start a new society. One of the founders, Bill, had studied at Meadville Theological School in Chicago. But instead of going into the ministry after graduating, he returned to Washington, D.C. where he and some friends began to develop his utopian schemes. In essence, Bill wanted to combine the ideas of Walden Two with the practice of group marriage. In 1965 he and a friend financed the purchase of an old, narrow four-story house wedged between similar nineteenth-century buildings. Brick walls caked with deposits of soot disclosed the building's rundown appearance. There was a tiny yard in front and a slightly larger yard in back.

The two men advertised widely and conducted meetings in hopes of finding others to join them at Walden House, as they called it. This was a difficult process. And in order to keep up payments on the house they took in boarders. George, one of their first members, was industrious and responsible. He would have been an asset to any community as he had a practical inclination and could fix things. His main interests were in various applications of the physical sciences, electronics, mechanics, etc. He was the only person in the house who had these kinds of interests or aptitudes. When I visited Walden House, George was converting the plumbing so that their newly acquired dishwasher could be installed. He had just built an electric-powered turtle that would have been a joy to any young child but there were no youngsters at Walden House.

Kathleen came along soon after George. She was a divorcée with a teenage daughter, Susan. Well aware of the pitfalls and disadvantages of the isolated monogamous family structure, Kathleen enthusiastically embraced the ideas of Walden Two.

When I was there the community had one or two other members, as well as two boarders. Members and boarders paid the same amount of money per week for rent and food and had about the same benefits. Boarders, however, did not have to do household chores. On the other hand, they could be asked to leave on short notice if new members were admitted and the room was needed. And they could neither vote nor have a voice in the purchase of equipment made from the common purse. New members had to wait through a trial period of three to six months before they could vote. It all seemed a little too complex and messy to me.

At the time of my visit, Bill was no longer a member, although he still lived in the house, in the front room on the second floor. He no longer ate with the group nor participated in its activities. He drove a taxi by day and wrote his utopian ideals by night. In the beginning, Bill had envisioned a group-marriage community where adult members would rotate sleeping partners. As Kathleen was the only adult female member at the time, she was the crucial factor in this experiment. But she did not want to sleep with anyone except George. So Bill resigned and sold the house to the group with the understanding that he could stay on for a time. Bill's original partner had sold out to him sometime previously.

Kathleen had administrative abilities, as well as a strong personality. In addition to writing and editing the newsletter the group had begun, she also handled the money, and supervised household chores; in short, she ran the house on a practical basis. She and George were an essential team to make a project like this work: she the congenial organizer and taskmaster, he the efficient handyman.

During the day each member of the commune had to work at an outside job in order to pay for the group's practical necessities of life. It is not surprising then that, exhausted from a full day's work, they had little energy left over for their own needed household repairs and interior decorations.

But it was not all hard work for all people at Walden House. Consider, for example, one short-term visiting member—a stout ex-Army colonel. He was around the house all day. He spent the time reading and relaxing. At dinnertime, I recall, he would relish the meal with audible groans of delight, mouthful after ecstatic mouthful. I kept my eyes glued to the food, not daring to look at anyone for fear that I would burst out in uncontrollable laughter.

Irrespective of their concern about improving the building, the members did not consider Walden House to be anything but a temporary home. Their goal was to find a better place, preferably in the country. Eventually they did find such a place in the adjoining state of Virginia after a useful trip to Michigan.

In the summer of that year (1966), Kathleen and George, having just been married by a justice of the peace, took a trip to Michigan to attend the first annual Walden Two convention. It was staged by a few behavioral psychologists who hoped to found a full-blown Walden Two community based on Skinnerian principles, with the aid (they fondly hoped) of a huge foundation grant and the cooperation of some pliable utopian people.

Among the other people attending the convention were Rudy and Dusty, two university students from Atlanta, Georgia. They had recently begun a newsletter called Walden Pool in cooperation with Gerald Baker. The contents of their paper included, among other subjects, theoretical ideas on how to create a Walden Two community, letters from enthusiastic readers, and a summary of important ideas from Skinner's book. They themselves were impatient with talk and theories and anxious to create the real thing.

The Walden Two convention brought Walden House and Walden Pool together. During the next few months, much discussion and exchange of visitors materialized between the two groups. A third party in this interaction was a Virginia businessman named Kurt, who had also attended the convention in Michigan. Kurt enthusiastically backed the Walden Two idea (unlike his wife, who, opposing his involvement, divorced him). He offered the collective groups money on a low-interest, long-term basis in order to buy a farm. The offer was accepted, a farm was found and purchased, and a community was begun. ■

WALDEN TWO
by Matthew Israel

BETWEEN SEPTEMBER OF 1967 AND SEPTEMBER OF 1969 I FOUND-
ed and lived in two communal houses. Both houses lasted one year and were intended as experiments in group living using behavior modification.

I also hoped that they would prove to be first steps toward a full-scale experimental community within commuting distance of the Boston area. Each of the
members of the two houses derived many valuable lessons, experiences, ideas, and
skills from his or her participation. In that sense, both houses accomplished their
objectives, and most of the participants are probably glad that they experienced
the year of communal living. However, the most important objective, in my own
eyes, was to make each house such an enjoyable experience that new members
would wish to join, and that the original members would wish to continue living
together and to gradually develop a full-scale experimental community. Judged by
this standard, both houses were failures. Although the first house had many positive aspects, when our lease was up I was the only one who wished to continue for
a second year. In the case of the second house, the issue was much more clear-cut.
We stopped talking to each other out of anger or disgust before the year was over,
and the house became something of a nightmare during its later phases.

Membership and Personal Relationships

The first house, Morningside House, was located in a large modern house in Arlington, Massachusetts during 1967–1968. The members for most of the year
consisted of one couple, two single persons, and a three-year-old child. Bob, a psychologist in his late 30s, and Betty, a nurse in her late 20s, were the couple. Sally, a
kindergarten teacher in her 20s, and I, a psychologist then 34, were the two single
persons. Evelyn, three, was Sally's daughter. Sally and I dated persons outside the
house, and had no dating relationship with each other.

The second house, Rutland Square House, was located in the South End section of Boston during 1968–1969. It consisted of two couples and myself. Jim,
an unemployed chemist in his late 20s, and Elaine, a temporary file clerk in her
early 20s, were one couple. Randy, an interior architect in his 20s, and Alice, an
interior designer in her 20s, were the second couple. (To protect the identity of the
participants, I have not given their real first names.)

The two houses were communal in that we shared the living space, ate dinner
together each evening, and divided up the household chores cooperatively. We

shared equally the costs of living in the house (rent, utilities, food, etc.). We held frequent social and business meetings for the larger organization from which our commune had developed (The Association for Social Design).

In both houses we attempted to deal with the problems that arose by using behavior modification. We met regularly to discuss and decide on behaviors and contingencies. Our biggest success was with Evelyn, the three-year-old, who started as a spoiled, tantrum-throwing, screeching, bossy, always-saying-no, and rather bitter little girl. By using behavior modification, we changed her into a sweet, lovable, well-managed girl who was a pleasure to have around. Unfortunately, her behavior reverted significantly after she stopped living in the house, for her mother never understood, liked, or used behavior modification.

Why Did the Houses Fail to Develop Into Full-Scale Communities? Here are the major reasons that come to mind today—about two and a half years after the experiences. The reasons are not presented in order of importance.

1. In many cases we found, once we were living together, that we really didn't like each other as much as we had thought we would. Before moving together, we each controlled a major reinforcer for the others—our willingness to move in with the others and thus make possible the experiment. Once we did move in with each other, we seemed to have "consummated" that particular reinforcer, and in many cases found no other to take its place. Also, once we had signed a year's lease, given up our previous apartments, and moved our furniture in, we all knew that each of us was more or less stuck with the bargain for a year. As a result, after moving in, we were no longer as careful to use reinforcement and to avoid using punishment with each other as we had been prior to living together.

2. We were not a group of good friends that had moved in with each other because we really liked each other. Instead, we were really "business" acquaintances who had come together because of a plan to form an experimental community. In some cases very warm and fond relationships developed; in others, the reverse occurred. (To avoid this problem in the future, our new proposal for an experimental community calls for a community that can exist successfully whether or not everyone enjoys everyone else's company all of the time. Each person or couple may, if they desire it, have a separate house or apartment of their own. Members will be able to interact when they wish to, and with whom they enjoy. The members will not be forced, by communal living quarters, to interact daily with persons who irritate, bore, or disgust them.)

3. Once we were living in the same house, a variety of irritations and jealousies were caused by, or enhanced by, the fact that we had to share the same living facilities. Exhibit 1 shows a partial list of some of these irritations and jealousies.

4. Once such irritations occurred, the situation was often made worse by the means we chose to deal with them. It was often easier to punish than to ignore,

or to reinforce desired behavior. As a result in some cases relationships that had once been very positive suddenly turned negative, and often so quickly that, when discovered, the damage seemed to be beyond repair.

5. Little irritating interpersonal habits in each other that we had tended to overlook before we moved in together came to be far more irritating when they had to be dealt with every day. To handle this problem in the new proposed community, we need to alert each prospective member that he or she has a duty to do each of the following the following things at the earliest possible date:

6. We failed to realize that a critical goal for any experimental community should be to accelerate the use of positive reinforcement in the member's interpersonal behaviors and to minimize the use of extinction and punishment. This means maximizing the extent to which each person shows warmth, attention, support, love, friendship, praise and assistance toward each other, and minimizing criticism, inattention, avoidance, etc. The objective should be to create a warm interpersonal environment, and to help members maintain and build favorable self-concepts. In neither house did we recognize this as an area in which behaviors should be pinpointed, and self-management and behavior modification procedures applied.

7. In some (but by no means all) cases, our living together led to overexposure or "satiation" with each other. We sometimes found ourselves running out of things to say or ask, and at such times awkward silences would invade the dinner table.

8. There were fundamental differences in lifestyles, personal philosophies, interests, and tastes. For example, Jim, who espoused a "hip" style of living and who immersed himself in the new-left politics, developed contempt for Matt, a psychologist, who tended to be apolitical and "middle-class" by Jim's standards.

9. In neither house did anyone make a real personal commitment toward personally and immediately working to develop an experimental community.

10. We neglected to determine carefully what events functioned as reinforcers and punishers for each other prior to starting the two houses. We also failed to ascertain just what were the specific activities, experiments, arrangements, services, and changes in one's life that each member was hoping to achieve. One of the most significant areas of potential life improvement for most persons is the character and condition of their day-to-day working situation. Yet neither community house was able to do anything for its members with respect to offering them more interesting or meaningful work.

11. Even if we had known what items were on the "reinforcement menu" or the "punishment menu" of each participant, we were not in a position to do much about providing the items on the former, or removing the items on the latter, due to our lack of capital and to the small size of our group. For example, Jim and Elaine very much wanted to start some kind of preschool, but we lacked the necessary manpower and money.

12. By failing to identify and provide hoped-for reinforcers, we ended up disappointing our members.

13. The development of the community houses suffered from the fact that the whole project was run on an amateur, evenings-and-weekends basis. Many of the problems I am reviewing in this paper were known to us at the time, but no one really had the time to do the thing we knew was needed. Or if something were done, it was not done with the excellence of which we were capable, had we given it more of our time. Consequently, critical things either did not get done, or got done in a second-rate manner. The projected experimental community should have its own full-time professional staff whose job would be:

(1) to measure the quality of life of the members;
(2) to administer the orientation-training course;
(3) to determine what services, experiments, facilities, projects, and changes in one's life each potential member wishes to see happen; and
(4) to administer or create these experiments, facilities, etc. Income pool might be used in part to support such a professional management staff for the community.)

14. Because most of us worked at outside jobs during the day, and because we had no "community staff" as such, the only time for performing community-building activities was evenings and weekends. Some of the members came to begrudge the use of their spare time for such meetings and activities—and this became another irritation caused by the community.

15. In both houses there were disagreements about whether the majority of the members had a right to "legislate" behavior modification. If a crisis was developing over members' irritations over crumbs on the counter, Evelyn's tantrums, or more equitable sharing of household duties, did the majority have the right, after thorough discussion and voting, to pinpoint desired behaviors, and to set up appropriate contingencies that would generate the desired behaviors? In Morningside House, Sally, who was the person whose behavior most often seemed to need changing, never really agreed to this, and consequently felt that the others were ganging up on her. At Rutland Square House, the majority seemed to be opposed to this procedure for resolving behavioral disputes, and the result was a form of anarchy that degenerated into no community at all. The reader may be asking, "How could you go into a community based on behavior modification without having a decision-making procedure for pinpointing and changing behavior?" The answer is that there were very few persons to choose from in starting these communities. The choice for me was between no attempt at all, or an attempt with less-than-ideal members.

16. Betty became irritated at the large number of times the house was used for community-building social functions such as potluck suppers. In particular, Betty

found it distasteful to discover dirty dishes in the sink the next morning, or to find that dishes had been stored in the wrong place.

Jealousies:
(1) Betty was irritated that Bob, her boyfriend, was spending too much time at community functions. Betty was irritated that Bob paid too much attention to female guests on occasions when we had open-house, cooperative potluck dinners.
(2) Betty eventually took to avoiding these dinners entirely and either stayed out of the house on those occasions or stayed in her room.
(3) Alice and I started out our year at Rutland Square House disliking each other or at least not particularly liking each other. Then Alice got interested in identifying positive and negative indicators for the quality of her life on a daily basis—something that I had introduced to the others, and in which I was very interested. As a result. Alice and I found ourselves sharing a common interest for the first time and our relationship suddenly improved. I was surprised to find myself offering to do small things for Alice, such as driving her to work and making a sandwich for her in the morning. I had no sexual interest or intention toward Alice in this. One morning Alice said, "You should see Randy [her boyfriend]. He's throwing things in the bedroom." Randy was jealous at the interest I was showing in Alice. Learning this, I stopped doing the little things I had been doing for her. Thereafter, the relationship between us eventually returned to the same dismal level it was at when the house began.

Irritating Interpersonal Behaviors

At one time or another, each of the following complaints was made: Sally's conversation struck some as boring and her ideas as too conventional to be interesting. Jim often held the floor too long when talking. Bob talked in a too-smug and assertive manner, "spraying" the listener with the facts that Bob knew and that the listener did not know. Jim tended to put down other people and other ideas too often. Matt tended to rely on punishment too often rather than using reward. Matt gave the impression of not really caring about them, of being too coldly a "mechanical behaviorist" and of not being spontaneous enough. Jim constantly attributed all problems to a conspiracy by the middle-class establishment. Matt found this irritating.

> Checklist of Desirable and Undesirable Interpersonal Behaviors
> Undesirable "put-downs"
> Too direct & aggressive
> Asserts things as The Truth
> Punishes with aggressive remarks ("brassy" as applied to woman)
> Talks professorially

Too-lengthy remarks
Not responsive to request to prove remark
Doesn't seem to think logically
Nervous laughter, nervous gesture
Not enough eye contact
Uses eyes as weapon (too much eye contact)
Praises A. & not B. when both are there
Remarks constitute a challenge to one
Frown on face
Makes aggressive gesture
Has chip on shoulder
Fails to make friendly overtures to another who is present
Ignores
Fails to respond to remark
Interrupts
Gives impression that he knows everything
You have nothing to add
Makes cryptic apparently clever "psychological-analytical" remark
Doesn't listen to one's remarks
Shows obvious impatience
Doesn't give me a chance to talk
Doesn't ask my opinion
Keeps me at arm's length
Smirks
Is trying to manipulate me
Creates awkward silence
Traps me into blurting out something to cover silence
Whines
Always complaining
Talks about self too much
"Autistic" (answers with gesture, smile. etc.)
Spouts too many facts
Seems insensitive to effects on others
Makes me feel I'm competing with him
Seems hostile to me
Intimidates me
Makes me feel inferior
Seems dogmatic
Desirable
Reinforces me

Makes qualified statements
Smile on face
Makes friendly physical contact
Builds my self-esteem through justified praise of me
Has non-punishing, non-aggressive attitude
Makes me laugh or smile
Has humility
Is cooperative
Agrees to change his position or to rethink his position
Checks appropriateness of remarks ("May I inquire about. . . ")
Asks for my opinion and seems to respect it
His remarks, eyes, cast of face say "welcome" to me
Eyes light up when he talks to me
Embraces me at start or finish of conversation
Finds a felicitous way to say things ■

TWIN OAKS TAKES ROOT

by Richard Fairfield

ORIGINALLY INSPIRED BY B.F. SKINNER'S WALDEN TWO, AND founded in 1967 in Louisa County, Virginia, Twin Oaks remains one of the longest enduring and largest intentional communities in North America. It continues to espouse non-violence, egalitarianism, feminism and ecology. According to co-founder Kathleen (Kat) Kinkade, the community avoided the problems usually associated with communes (laziness, freeloading, and excessive lack of structure) by modifying Skinner's concepts and adopting a structured, but flexible, labor system.

Twin Oaks was established at what had been a 123-acre tobacco farm near a Virginian town far from any large city. Rudy, his bride, and Dusty made the move from Atlanta. Kathleen, Susan, George, and two others arrived from Washington. They all settled in at Twin Oaks on June 16, 1967.

When I visited the community in August its population had jumped to 10. Everyone was hard at work, making rope hammocks and harvesting the crops (the previous owner had conveniently planted many vegetables and acres of corn).

Even at that time the group not only had many visitors but also a well-defined policy for handling them. Visitors were required to work a specified number of hours and to pay a fee according to the length of their stay. As I discovered, it was fun to be a visitor picking and shelling peas, husking corn, and watching the tomatoes stew in a big outdoor vat. The members had already canned enough vegetables to last the winter, but were now worried about the lack of freezer space; they had no money to buy another freezer.

Kathleen showed me around the farm. The house was small, a one-family dwelling hardly large enough for the 10 members. But it was summer, so most of the members slept outdoors. One problem they faced with equanimity was the very inadequate water supply. All baths were taken at the swimming hole across the road. The toilet was flushed only a few times a day. And nothing was washed under running water. This problem was greatly aggravated by the influx of visitors, which sometimes doubled the population, especially on weekends. Still, the situation was handled with a minimum of tension. This seemed characteristic of Twin Oaks, for an energetic and buoyant spirit permeated the place.

In addition to the tiny farmhouse and one or two storage sheds, there was also a workshop for the making of wooden sections for the hammocks. This same building accommodated the printing-press shop. The members had purchased an old multilith and were trying to produce a good newsletter. This paper was important to them: it enabled them to tell the outside world about their attempt to create an alternative society and it also brought income into the community. Dusty was in charge of running the newsletter operation, although Kathleen continued to do most of the writing.

A dairy cow and hay feed were kept in a small rundown barn. But at the time I was there the milk and butter were all being sold to the outside because the cash income was sorely needed. The members also hoped to make and sell enough hammocks to avoid the necessity of taking jobs for cash on the outside during the winter. And they were raising a few hogs so that they would have meat during the cold months ahead.

A First Interview with Kathleen: The Community at Three Months

Much of what I learned as a result of that first visit to Twin Oaks came from Kathleen, who took the time to answer my many questions. The following is part of her response:

Dick: Did you deliberately choose a farm that would be so far from any large city?

Kathleen: No. That choice was dictated by price. You can't buy a farm within reach of a large city for the money we had available.

Dick: Why did you decide to name the place Twin Oaks? I thought you would use a name with "Walden" in it.

Kathleen: The name was a compromise. We couldn't seem to come to any agreement on a name that any of us were crazy about, so we eventually settled on the neutral, descriptive name of Twin Oaks. That's the twin oak tree there, by the well. The "Walden" names were vigorously championed by some, but we couldn't get consensus. Others were opposed to using "Walden" because so many starry-eyed people would show up expecting us to be just like the book. It isn't fun to be in a position of consistently disappointing people.

Dick: Are you still accepting new members, Kathleen?

Kathleen: Certainly, provided they are people able to accept our crowded conditions and severe economics. We have a very serious housing shortage right now. We are going to build a large structure this fall which will contain several bedrooms, in addition to work space for our hammock industry on the first floor.

Dick: Tell me about those hammocks.

Kathleen: The hammocks are made of cotton rope and kept in comfortable shape by oak stretchers. They sell for $25 to $35 each, the price depending on the size. They come complete with the hardware for attaching them to trees or porches, and we are developing a hammock stand for people who don't have any trees to hang them from. We don't make a big profit on them, because the materials cost a large part of the price. But it is a means of putting our labor to use on our own premises. It is much more pleasant and better for the community than going to work in the nearby towns.

Dick: The hammock makers seem to be having a good time, not like working in a factory, for sure.

Kathleen: I don't know many factory managers who would put up with that amount of joking and singing, or with the hi-fi that alternately blasts them with the Beatles and Gregorian chants. We find that most work done in compatible groups is relatively pleasant.

Dick: Quite often people who tell about their communities tell only the good things. It always leaves us wondering what is left unsaid. How about people getting the work done? What about interpersonal conflict?

Kathleen: Dick, you must realize that we are talking about a community that is less than three months old. We are still on our honeymoon. Interpersonal difficulties are minimal. So far we find a great deal more satisfaction from each other's company than we do annoyance from each other's idiosyncrasies. Of course there is the person who always spills water on the bathroom floor, and another who can never remember to clean up after herself on cooking and baking projects. But remember we have the whole outdoors and several barns to work in, so we aren't stepping on each other's feet too much in the summer months, which minimizes petty annoyances. We realize that this kind of thing can be a problem, though, and we have thought up a means of dealing with it. Along with our other managers, we appointed one called the Generalized Bastard. His job is to be officially nasty. For example, suppose that a certain member has a habit of letting his work partner do the dirty part of the work and of skipping out on the last 10 minutes of cleanup on a shared job. If this happens once or twice, his work partner ignores it. If it keeps happening, the complaining member goes to the Generalized Bastard and explains the situation. Then it is the Bastard's job to carry his complaint to the offender, which he can do in an objective way.

Dick: Isn't that a bit roundabout? Couldn't you just encourage people to be frank with each other? It seems like a cop-out on the whole idea of community to have people unable to confront each other. What kind of depth can develop in a relationship if frustrations can't be expressed directly? I'd resent it if someone had to get another person, official Bastard notwithstanding, to complain to me.

Kathleen: Maybe you're right, ideally, but we've found the Generalized Bastard helps things to run smoothly.

Dick: You mentioned that managers had been appointed. That sounds like Walden Two. What kind of system have you set up?

Kathleen: We spent five weeks without government. Everybody did what seemed to him appropriate for him to do, and we got along all right. Occasionally we would have a meeting and try to get consensus on something important, like spending a large amount of money on some particular item. We would still be carrying on our business in that manner except for one thing: some of us couldn't stand meetings. Some objected to what they termed "wasted time." Others always got upset because of disagreements that arose at the meetings. What happened is that we had fewer and fewer meetings because they were so unpleasant. And as a result we found that decisions were going unmade, except when one member would just do something on his own initiative. Like, one weekend, one person just went and bought some wire and wired the shop. He figured that if he waited for a meeting on the subject, it would be winter before the shop got any electricity, and the printing press that was there doesn't run on treadle power. Now we have elected a board of planners with broad powers. And the board in turn appoints managers to various areas of work. I can't tell you how well this system works because at this point it is too new. We have a hammock-making manager, community-health manager, vegetable-garden manager, visitor manager.

Dick: And you're the one who manages visitors?

Kathleen: Actually, I'm three managers. All of us are at least two. There are more jobs than people. I tell visitors where to pitch their tents and remind them to pay for their meals. I'm not required to entertain them. We can't spare the labor for that.

Dick: How do you divide up your labor?

Kathleen: Our labor credit system is very much in the experimental stages. Right now we divide the work weekly by means of a kind of card game, where everyone is dealt a hand and passes his unwanted cards to the right until he accumulates the right number of credits and the jobs he prefers.

Dick: Is it working out well?

Kathleen: It seems to be fair to everyone and there has been general good will toward the system, but it takes a long time. We keep imagining what it would be like if we had 50 members instead of 10.

Dick: What would you do here if someone refused to do his share of the work?

Kathleen: Ask him to leave. That everyone works is a fundamental assumption at Twin Oaks. There is a lot to be done and we are not in a position to afford any loafers.

Dick: So you consider yourselves an experimental community in the same sense that Skinner intended in Walden Two?

Kathleen: Yes. Of course we aren't the avant-garde of the sexual revolution. So far we are sticking to patterns which give the feeling of free choice, and free choice for a woman could mean a one-to-one relationship that is fairly stable. We are different from society at large in that we merely practice marriage. Society at large virtually requires it. In our community the practice of lifetime marriage will endure just exactly as long as it is functional and no longer. Society at large regards it as a sacrament in itself greater and more important than the happiness or unhappiness it produces.

Dick: How about marijuana? Do you people smoke?

Kathleen: We are asking members and guests not to use it at all on the premises.

Dick: Doesn't that strike you as rather a conservative stand for an experimental community?

Kathleen: Yes. Most of us favor liberal legislation on the drug question. But pot is illegal. And adding indignant neighbors to the list of our difficulties is more than we can handle! We are trying to get a lot of work done.

Dick: Couldn't this sort of thing be done with discretion, so that the neighbors and the police need not be involved?

Kathleen: Conceivably. If we had a population with a strong personal desire to smoke pot or drop acid, we might have to take risks like that. But our membership at present has virtually no interest in drugs. And if we did have, we wouldn't have the money for it. A liberal stand would benefit only our potential guest population, and we don't see any reason to risk the community's local reputation just for guests.

Dick: What about free love?

Kathleen: The community doesn't take a stand on free love. We take it for granted that couples will find each other and seek the kind of relationship that they mutually consider desirable. We foresee no reason to regulate it.

Dick: You seek to regulate some behaviors and not others, according to whether you feel they need regulating. Tell me, have you found certain pressures in community living that are not found in ordinary life?

Kathleen: Some. We have to remember to clean up after ourselves, to put tools back in their places, to do our work at a reasonable time so that other work will not be held up. Community life is not entirely free of restrictions. On the other hand, we escape a great many pressures by being here. We dress as we please, our schedule is more flexible than it would be if we worked at a city job, there are no artificial standards we have to meet, such as qualifying for a degree or earning a promotion. I personally feel very free here.

The Growth of Twin Oaks [December 1970]

Since those early days in the summer of 1967, Twin Oaks has continued to grow not by leaps and bounds, but gradually and consistently. It has avoided both stagnation and abrupt change thereby giving itself a better-than-average chance for survival.

There has been a great deal of construction, as well as physical reorganization, at Twin Oaks since 1967. The new building was erected as planned and made livable before the weather became intolerable. The first floor of this building became the hammock factory, with private rooms tucked along both sides of the common workspace. In addition, part of this workspace was made into a living room and library; the printing press was moved into a new building, a photographic darkroom was set up and a communal clothes closet was built there too.

In February 1970 the members completed the main floor of another wood-frame building. They named the new structure the Oneida building in honor of that famous nineteenth-century community. With seven bedrooms on the finished main floor, the workers were now busy building a second floor that would provide another seven. Because of all this expansion, the woodworking shop was moved into the first new structure dubbed the Hammock building which would eventually be converted into shops entirely.

The tiny farmhouse, which had formerly been divided into living room, dining room, kitchen, bedrooms, etc., was redesigned to accommodate the community's kitchen, dining area, laundry, and office. And the water supply was improved, thereby remedying another of the community's initial inadequacies.

Changing the Labor Credit System

Since the community's inception, the labor credit system has been the basic method for getting the work done. Under this system, each member is required to earn the same number of labor credits per week. The labor credit manager decides how much work and what jobs need to be done. He makes and posts a weekly list. Members sign up for the work they prefer. The amount of time each person works depends on the desirability of the jobs he selects. If more than one person signs up for a job, that job is considered desirable work and its credit value diminishes; if nobody signs up, then the job is considered undesirable and the credit value goes up. This job is then assigned to someone at random. Theoretically, people who perform the least desirable job work the fewest hours per week, because they accumulate the required number of credits faster.

For three years the labor credit system worked fairly well. But then the community decided to modify the system. This change was discussed in The Leaves of Twin Oaks, the community's newsletter, in its issue of October 1970:

"We became discontented with was the overall quality of the work done. Many a hopeful member would take a managership with the intention of seeing the department thrive under his care, only to find that the other members working in his department just didn't care enough to do a good job, and good projects were continually being sabotaged by indifference... Under the old system you might clean the kitchen one morning and somebody else the next; then you were on hammock weaving, which you had only five hours of, and the next day you were mending fences. Most people had a schedule like that. Presumably, most members liked the variety, because they continued to choose it. Nevertheless, its natural results were that if you left a jar of spoiled tomatoes on the counter, somebody on another shift would have to clean it up; and if you left the saw out in the barn, somebody else would have to go look for it. The most elementary behavioral theory told us that we were not set up to get a good job done.

So with a sigh of regret we turned away from the hectic variableness of schedule and began to encourage specialization. The work shifts began to be arranged so that on every meal shift and every cleaning shift in a given week, at least one and preferably two, people were assigned throughout the week and were familiar with the work. The system quickly extended to garden work and even office work.

Specialization meant signing up in blocks of 14 to 21 hours, and this made the old competition and random assignment system untenable. For, if you lost a 21-hour block at the flip of a coin, you would have to be assigned 21 hours of something undesirable in its place. Large blocks just did not lend themselves to a sign-up system at all. Something new had to be devised.

What we are working with now is a simple preference list. Each member has a list of all the job categories and is asked to number them from 1 to 40 in the order of his preference. From there, the labor credit crew takes the preference lists and makes up all the individual schedules, giving each member as much as possible those jobs which he rated high, and assigning all unpopular jobs as much as possible to those who dislike them least.

Another change that has been made in a new way of awarding labor credits. It is now possible to give labor credits on the basis of the individual preference rather than the group preference. That is, you get 0.9 per hour for your first preference, 1.0 for the next few on your list, and so forth. Three people may be mending fences together, and each of them earning different credits, depending on how much he likes the job.

Most of the members are content with the new system. Their schedules are usually less aversive then they were under the old random-assignment rules. A few people prefer the old system because they didn't mind any kind of work very much, and could take advantage of other people's dislikes by signing up for unpopular work at high credits, thus working fewer hours than the average member. Under the new system this is no longer possible....

The improvement in the work itself is very noticeable. Managers are not so discouraged as they were. A lot of members are becoming quite interested in their work. The people on lunch are likely to recognize the leftovers, so they don't become moldy in the refrigerator; the people on cleaning remember that they didn't do any woodwork last week, so it's time to look at it this week.

This is probably not the last change the labor credit system we will ever see. It is interesting to note that we can make sweeping changes in it and still stay within the general framework of the system described in Walden Two. The principle remains the same the more aversive the work, the less you have to do it.

There have been families with children at Twin Oaks from time to time, but such an arrangement has yet to prove successful. A child-raising manager is in charge of handling discipline problems with the children in the community. The biological parents are not allowed to discipline their own children. However, few parents are able to adhere to this prescription as their life experiences have been in the structure and values of the traditional family. No such families have stayed long at Twin Oaks.

Kathleen's daughter, Susan, already mature for a girl in her budding teens, elected to study at home soon after she and her mother moved to the community. She no longer attended public school. Instead, members of the community offered to teach her specific subjects—history, English, etc. It worked so well for Susan that gradually a whole series of classes were organized for other members as well. Anyone who wanted to teach could do so; then, if there were any takers, the classes began.

New activities are constantly being devised by the members and are often reported in The Leaves of Twin Oaks. The May 1970 issue of the newsletter, for example, described the beginnings of a folk-dance group:

"About once a week these days we carry all the hammock jigs out of the workshop and set up the record player. Cramped quarters limit the kinds of dances that can be taught. We started with American square dances and have now added Serbian and Israeli circle dances to our repertoire."

Another new activity was the sleep experiment initiated by six members who decided they'd like to find out if they could "function happily taking their sleep in three-hour shifts rather than whole nights at a time." They scheduled their days and nights to sleep three hours at a stretch, and then remain awake for five, thereby giving themselves nine hours of sleep in each 24-hour period. Under the labor credit system they were free to work when they chose, so this was no barrier to arranging their time.

An experimental program of mutual criticism begun in the summer of 1969 is still in existence. Under this program (modeled on the practice initiated by John Humphrey Noyes in the Oneida Community), a different member of the community volunteers to be the subject of criticism each week. He sits quietly, listening and does not reply as each member in turn tells what is liked and disliked about him. This, from my point of view, is a great improvement over the use of the Generalized Bastard, though it still seems a bit too structured. It is important to realize though, that at least the structuring at Twin Oaks is not rigid and inflexible and that it shows no signs of becoming that way.

A Second Interview with Kathleen, Three Years Later

After writing the foregoing information about Twin Oaks, I made my second trip to the community, where I talked at great length with Kathleen (now known as Kat) and others to bring the story of Twin Oaks up to date, the date being late December 1970. What follows is the transcript of a good portion of that discussion:

Dick: How many people have been members at Twin Oaks in the last three years?

Kat: Seventy-two. There was an average of 15 members per month in 1968; lower than that in 1969. We jumped to 25 in 1970. Now we're up to 31.

Dick: With that many members are you each able to have a private room?

Kat: We've never had a private-room policy. The only time anyone's ever had a private room is when we've been real low on membership and there was space. A lot of us would really like to have private rooms, but every time you say, "we are going to have a private room," you are saying, "we are going to turn someone away who wants to join." So naturally there's pressure inside each individual. No member has a very clear point of view on this. He says to himself, "I really think we ought to have private rooms and the standard of living at this point is more important than expansion of membership." Then he turns right around and says, "But I've got this little brother, see, and he really needs to find an alternative and I'm wondering if we can take him."

Dick: How much money did it take to start this commune?

Kat: It took about $35,000 for land and one building—a little more than that counting the well, come to think of it; add another thousand for the well.

Dick: For how many people?

Kat: Fifteen people were comfortably housed, at that level. Since then we've put another five or six thousand into building. That five or six thousand has come from internal donations. A member joins who has a thousand in the bank, and he says let's build a building with this. Of course, a lot of the building fund comes directly out of our own income, Twin Oaks outside-worker income or hammock income or whatever. We put money into construction every month.

Dick: How much money does Twin Oaks need to keep going?

Kat: We live on $700 a year per member—that's food and clothing and medical and gasoline and stuff like that. But we put so much money into trying to get industry started, and one thing and another that oh, good heavens, we went through $50,000 last year. And we didn't have as large a membership then. I think we probably go through a couple of thousand per member per year altogether.

Dick: The problem is trying to find industry that will bring in that amount of money, rather than outside jobs?

Luke: Something like three or four thousand a month is what we take in at the moment.

Kat: Donations from members that are joining—

Tamara: Quite a bit comes from hammocks, believe it or not.

Kat: —and the lectures.

Tamara: Yeah, those have been contributing quite a bit too. But the highest figures on the income page are hammocks and guest meals and right after that members' salaries from outside jobs.

Dick: Who handles the money for the community as a whole? This is very crucial I would think, trying to keep the books straight and know how to budget things.

Kat: Well, it's a managership like everything else. There's a budget manager. Books are kept by fairly conventional methods, and taxes are paid just like any business would pay them. Our taxes are more complicated than business taxes, because we are not just a business, we are a living arrangement. Money is handled communally; there's no such thing as a private income. All money from outside jobs, regardless of how much it is or who makes it, comes back into the central treasury. The outside workers who might be bringing in, oh, about a hundred a week, they take their 32 cents a day for snack money and they pack a sack lunch. We try to keep expenses down as far as possible.

Dick: Do members rotate on the same jobs?

Kat: No, we seldom get anything where people can rotate on the job. It sometimes happens one member will quit a job and another will walk in and get the same job, but we each are responsible for finding whatever job we can.

Dick: All this must amount to a great deal of bookkeeping?

Kat: A great deal of bookkeeping in comparison to what? In comparison to the bookkeeping in most corporations? No, much less. In comparison to an anarchist, free-style commune? Much more. But with it we have equality; they don't.

Dick: What's that mean?

Kat: What's that mean? That means nobody rips off more than anybody else.

Dick: You mean actually dollar-wise?

Kat: Yeah.

Dick: Does that make equality?

Kat: No, it can't, but it's a start. Nor do we assume that equality equals happiness either. We may agree that inequalities produce unhappiness, though. If we can keep sort of a rough equality going by saying that everybody gets cents a week to buy candy and Coke or what ever they want. . . So you say that isn't equality? True. Some people are more attractive than others and they can get friendship more easily; some people have hot tempers; some people have placid dispositions. People are not born equal.

Dick: Has your economics been the major problem in the last three and a half years?

Kat: I would say so. It means that so many people in our community have to do outside work every day. They leave very early in the morning and they get back late at night. They have to work for at least two months.

Dick: This has been going on since the beginning?

Kat: Yeah. Well, no. The first six months we didn't have to work outside because we lived off the money we brought with us. Outside work is really very unpleasant and undesirable for us. You can't call that anything else but an economic problem.

Dick: Is economics a major factor in interpersonal relations, in terms of a group of people staying together?

Kat: Now, it's pretty hard for me to put my finger on what's supposed to be a major interpersonal problem. What's a major interpersonal problem? Sex? Problems of sexual arrangements at Twin Oaks just aren't that heavy.

Tamara: We can't supply all of everybody's needs—that's what all our problems are. We don't have private rooms and so there are problems of arrangements between two people who are sharing rooms.

Dick: Of the 41 people who have left, could you give an account of some of the reasons?

Kat: One of the major reasons is that they never intended to stay in the first place. We have a very young population. They say to themselves, "I think I'll live in a community for a while because that would be an interesting experience." So they stay six months, eight months, a year. They're young people doing adventures. And they come and they go. I don't think we can help that. Furthermore I don't even think it's bad.

Dick: Could you give me an example or two of ideological differences you have with some new members?

Kat: I think that if you're going to run a commune successfully it is necessary that competent people be in charge of industries and be in charge of the progress of the community. That's not equality, per se. Competent people have power in their hands to do something; they shouldn't have to be forever stumbling over neurotics and children and teenagers and longhairs and incompetent, inefficient types, you know, you get the general gist?

Dick: In other words, these people you're referring to aren't on the board of planners?

Kat: They certainly aren't.

Dick: So it would seem to me that what they are saying is that they want to be on the board of planners and they don't get there that quickly?

Kat: Maybe they don't get there at all.

Dick: Why do people stay? What's so reinforcing about Twin Oaks?

Kat: I stay because it's my life's work. It's reinforcing in every way. In the first place, all my basic, all my ordinary, needs are taken care of and my rather unordinary needs are taken care of too. That is, you know, the food is excellent, except sometimes it is lousy. But it's a whole lot better than I would cook for myself, or that I ever had before.

Dick: You're not so crazy about cooking three times a day?

Kat: I'm certainly not. And my laundry is done and the house is not neat, but neater than I would keep it. That sort of need is taken care of for me. I'm entirely relieved of housework. I'm supported with dignity, with honor; by that I mean—without any sense of guilt on my part—by doing things I don't mind doing, like waiting on the store and typing; and I don't have to work too many hours a day. So those are the physical basics that would really appall me to have to leave and go somewhere and work for a living again. To have to work 37 ½ hours a week in an office and travel back and forth to an apartment and clean up the apartment and do my own laundry and find a meal somewhere—oh, I would hate that! So communal living offers its physical advantages. But that's sort of minor. The quality of friendships, the quality of people that I associate with, is so much higher at Twin Oaks more so than anywhere I've ever been. One can find interesting people in college, but how do college people sustain that kind of environment when they leave college? At Twin Oaks it never stops.

Dick: You're in college all the time.

Kat: Well, in a way. I'm not sure we'd want to use that for a slogan. But it's much more than that. What one wants, what I want, is something worthwhile to do to put my energies somewhere that I feel is worthwhile, worth doing. As I see the world and as I see the social situation, working in a commune and making it a success is worth it for itself and for the people who are there now. In addition, if we can make another commune, then it's worth it for the people in it as well. In addition, if we can contribute to a movement, then it makes a real difference to the social structure as a whole, to the nation as a whole.

Dick: Are you really sharing clothes communally now?

Kat: It's just too much of a nuisance to do otherwise. There's this big closet where we keep all the clothes. You want something to wear? If it fits, wear it. You can have your own clothes if you want to, but most people can't be bothered. I think that the superfluity of clothes in this country is outrageous. Everyone's got more clothes than he can possibly use.

Dick: I remember once you told me that the interpersonal and sexual aspects of a person's life were left up to each individual.

Kat: Most of us feel that the sex-love thing is sacred. We just have a special feeling about it and we want to be left alone in it. I wouldn't say it was contrary to our philosophy or doctrine to introduce experiments in sex and love, but I will tell you this: we would not publicize it if we did.

Dick: One of the biggest problems I've seen in communes is the inability of couples to stay together.

Kat: Well, we don't call it a problem. We certainly know what you're talking about and can contribute to the statistics. There has been one marriage to survive Twin Oaks so far.

Dick: What's the reason for married couples breaking up in communes?

Kat: It's very simple. Marriage is a very weak institution. It's supported on the outside by all sorts of pressures which are removed as soon as you get into the community. We remove the pressures and make alternatives available and people do what comes naturally. They will choose to stay married only if that's reinforcing. If it isn't reinforcing, what for?

Dick: Is there some sort of dependency thing in the nature of monogamous marriage that gets taken away in a community setting?

Kat: We don't know that people are less dependent in community, but there are more people to be depended upon. Your alternatives are greater. It's not us two against the world; it's you, an individual in this community, and me, an individual in this community. If we dig each other, great. Generally one or the other will find another friend, quite often both do, and if the marriage survives multiple relations, great. Sometimes it does. There have been three couples who have gotten married because of the community, too. Three couples met in the community, left the community, and got married. But if you took a slice of married couples anywhere you would find that most of them are not happy with each other. Marriage is a bummer. Of course, I wouldn't go so far as to say that the pair has no function, because there are people at Twin Oaks who pair up and stay paired for a long time. I have not been including them in the term "married." I am using it in its ordinary sense. I don't think the reasons for marriage on the outside have a whole lot to do with interpersonal relations. They do at first, but they have to do with things like, OK, the need for sex, and a place and time to do it, reasonably and legally without parent hassles, police hassles, and so forth. Second of all there's a problem of support. Somebody has to make a living, and marriage has been traditionally a way for a woman to make a living. That tradition is also fading, but then so is marriage. Also, it's a place and a way to raise children. In a community these things are totally meaningless: everybody makes his own living, and sex is readily available and not disapproved of.

Dick: How about the emotional relationships that keep people together?

Kat: There are pairs. There are couplings that take place and stay together.

Dick: Have you ever experienced in Twin Oaks the situation where a pair got together with another pair and it's worked out satisfactorily—emotionally satisfactorily?

Kat: I don't know what you mean by "worked out satisfactorily." I have cynically suspected that group pairings take place because one of the pair is more attracted to a member of the other pair than he is to his own mate. That's the original impetus for it and of course the real goal of it. When this goal is firmly accomplished the peripheries on the side drop off. But, as I say, that's cynicism. ■

SEVENTY—FIVE

THE MODERN UTOPIA

the magazine of social cha

christian, mystical and yoga communes

RELIGIOUS COMMUNES SPREADING

By George W. Cornell, Albuquerque Journal, *5/21/71*

RELIGIOUS COMMUNES INVOLVING BOTH COUPLES AND SINGLE individuals are mushrooming across the country, says a Baptist mentor of the movement. "Hundreds of them have started up in the last three years and they are spreading so fast you can't keep track of them," said the Rev. John A McDonald of Mill Valley, California. He is chairman of a recently organized group, Evangelicals Concerned Inc., which has about 75 staff workers around the country helping guide the Christian commune development. "The houses reflect a tremendous diversity," he said in an interview here at last week's American Baptist Convention.

"The spirit is so high in them that it's infectious and they tend to produce spinoff organization of other communes." He cited estimates that there were about 600 of them in California alone and hundreds of others in Florida and areas of Atlanta, Ga.; Houston, Tex; Detroit, Mich.; Boston, Mass.; New York City; Seattle, Wash., and widely through the Midwest. "It's a movement on a wide front," he said, "There's a spontaneity about it all over the country. Many believe that the Holy Spirit is leading it." He said the houses ordinarily involve a mature Christian leader or couple, called elders, who then bring others into a close communal setting of concern, "such as dropout type young people, newly turned on to Christ."

"It gives them a basic spiritual family and a love many of them have never experienced," he said.

The Rev. McDonald, 50, was involved dubiously at first, in organizing what is considered the country's first such Christian commune, "The House of Acts" in San Francisco in 1967. He has since written a book about it by that title. "All the other communal houses are spinoffs," he said. "There was tremendous traffic going through there." He said the religious houses had a high moral code and most of them maintained daily schedules of prayer and Bible studies and share in the upkeep.

"It's cheaper for a group to live under one roof than live alone," he said. He said many of the houses are all-men or all-women houses, while others are co-ed.

Most of them carry on street projects such as the evangelism, he said, while others operate special service "Marantha House" (Aramaic for "Come, Lord") in Washington, D.C., which runs a hotline for calls from troubled youths. "Most of them are connected with the whole hippie scene and lifestyle, "he said. "As the kids turn on to Christ, they get over their drugs and promiscuous sex, but they don't leave all their mysticism and far-out ideas of life behind them. They bring that into the communal living." Concerning their evangelical fervor, he said: "Nominal Christians would consider a lot of them real fanatics." Most of them are youths who have rebelled against "cultural hang-ups imposed on them, moral codes, appearance and materialism." But through the communes "they turned back on to life. It's the most significant movement in evangelism today," he said. However, he said it also has its dangers, as shown by the description of ancient Christianity's communal living in Jerusalem.

In the Book of Acts, it is related that two residents, Ananias and Spahira, were stricken dead because they secretly held back in sharing their possessions. ■

JESUS VS. THE JESUS FREAKS

by Alan Watts, Los Angeles Free Press

A FEW DAYS AGO I GAVE A RIDE TO A RATHER PLEASANT HIPPIE couple who seemed to have no particular destination. I asked, "What trip are you on?" He said, "Like spiritual trip?" I said, "Yes." He said, "We're on the Jesus trip." "Whose Jesus?" I asked. "Billy Graham's or mine?" "Well, it's all sort of the same, isn't it?"

It is not. For Billy Graham follows a long tradition, both Catholic and Protestant, wherein the gospel (or "good news" of Jesus) has been eclipsed and perverted by kicking him upstairs so as to get him out of the way, and by following a religion about Jesus instead of the religion of Jesus.

Obviously, Jesus was not the man he was as a result of making Jesus Christ his personal savior. The religion of Jesus was that he knew he was a son of God, and the phrase "son of" means "of the nature of," so that a son of God is an individual who realizes that he is, and always has been, one with God. "I and the Father are one."

When Jesus spoke those words the crowd took up stones to stone him. He said, "I have shown you many good works from the Father, and for which of them do you stone me?" They answered, "We're not stoning you for a good work but for blasphemy, because you, being a man, make yourself God."

But the self-styled Christians, and especially the fundamentalist bibliolaters, always insist that Jesus was the only son of woman who was also the son of God, and thus call upon all the rest of us to follow the example of the one human freak who had the unique advantage of being the Boss' son. This is not gospel: it is a chronic hang-up, a self-frustrating guilt trip. It isolates the career of Jesus as an exhibit in a glass case—for worship but not for use.

It is obvious to any informed student of history and psychology of religion that Jesus was one, of many, who had an intense experience of cosmic consciousness— of the vivid realization that oneself is a manifestation of the eternal energy of the universe, the basic "I am."

But it is very hard to express this experience when the only religious imagery at your disposal conceives that I am as an all-knowing and all-powerful monarch, autocrat, and beneficent tyrant enthroned in a court of adoring subjects. In such a cultural context, you cannot say "I am God" without being accused of subversion, insubordination, megalomania, arrogance, and blasphemy. Yet that was why Jesus was crucified.

In India people would have laughed and rejoiced with him, because Hindus know that we are all God in disguise—playing hide-and-seek with himself. Their model of the universe is not based on the political states of the Egyptians, Chaldeans, and Persians, whose awesome dictatorships still hold sway through the Jewish, Christian, and Islamic religions, even in the Republic of the United States. In Hinduism the whole universe is like the Holy Trinity—one as many, and many as one. (And of course, the Hindus are the despised of the earth, having been reduced to utter poverty by Muslims and Christians.)

But Jesus had to speak through a public address system—the only one available—which distorted his words, so that they came forth as the bombastic claim to be the one and only appearance of the Christ, of the incarnation of God as man. This is not "Good News."

The good news is that if Jesus could realize his identity with God, you can also—but this God does not have to be idolized as imperious monarch with a royal court of angels and ministers. God, as "the love which moves the sun and other stars," is something much more inward, intimate, and mysterious—in the sense of being too close to be seen as an object.

So it turns out, alas, that our new breed of Jesus Freaks are following the old non-gospel of the freaky Jesus—of the bizarre man who was unnaturally born and whose corpse was weirdly reanimated for a space trip into heaven.

But to identify Jesus the man as the one-and-only historical incarnation of a Divinity considered as the royal, imperial, and militant Jehovah, is only to reinforce the pestiferous arrogance of "white" Christianity—with all the cruel self-righteousness of its missionary zeal. They may perhaps be forgiven for their ignorance, but today, when we are exposed to all the riches of Earth's varying cultures and religions, there is no further excuse for the parochial fanaticism of spiritual in-groups.

Jesus Freaks are still in a state of enthusiastic innocence as yet unaware of the frightful implications of their claims. But they must realize that Christianity would seem ever so much more valid if it would stop insisting on being an oddity.

Christianity has universality, or Catholicity, only in recognizing that Jesus is one particular instance and expression of a wisdom which was also, if differently, realized in the Buddha, in Lao-tzu, and in such modern avatars as Ramana Maharshi, Ramakrishna, and, perhaps, Aurobindo and Inayat Khan. (I could make a very long list.) The wisdom is that none of us are brief island existences, but forms and expressions of one and the same eternal "I am" waving in different ways, such that, whenever this is realized to be the case, we wave more harmoniously with the other waves. ∎

KOINONIA MEANS COMMUNITY

by Martin Kowinski, The L.A. News Advocate, *June 1971*

IN 1942 A BAPTIST MINISTER WITH HIS FAMILY AND SEVERAL friends moved to a farm in Georgia and called their new experience in community living Koinonia ("Fellowship" in Greek).

By hard work and new agriculture methods, the community prospered and grew. But not to the liking of the light-colored population of the county who saw in the interracial Koinonia Community a menace to the established order of capitalism and white supremacy.

The farm became a target for bigots who usually chose the night in which to pelt it with rifle and buckshot. Then the white establishment initiated an economic boycott against the community, refusing to buy the farm's products and to sell it the necessary supplies.

This persecution, however, caused it to be reinforced by sympathizers outside the area who joined in forming the present Koinonia Partners. Because of the enlarged community, Koinonia Partners are now able to undertake such projects as building economical houses ($6,000, $25 a month payments, interest-free) on the farm for the poorly housed of the region. The housing program called "Koinonia Village" already has nine families living in their new home and eventually will have 42 houses. Some families with better incomes even contribute to the Fund for Humanity, which will help build more houses for the poor. The sharing spirit is infectious.

"I and my wife Marie are living in the seventh house constructed and though we have paid for its construction it remains the property of Koinonia Partners and upon our death will be free to be sold to a needy family on a no-interest basis. My heart has always been with Koinonia, especially since several years ago, when I was imprisoned in Atlanta for attempting to worship at the First Baptist Church with a group of dark-colored people, Koinonia launched a mail campaign which resulted in my being released after six months of an 18-month sentence. If interested, you may read of my Atlanta imprisonment in Chapter Six of my book, After Prison What?

"On the 1400-acre farm the normal Georgian products like hay, corn, peanuts, pecans, poultry and hogs are produced. The community has a mail-order service which includes fruitcakes, pecans, tie-dyed t-shirts and hand-crafted dashikis, and records and books mostly by Clarence Jordan, our deceased founder. Profits on all sales go into the Fund for Humanity to do things like building houses for displaced rural families."

—Ashton Jones, Equality No. 28

"A Rainy Night in Georgia" is the title of a bluesy soul song which depicts a mood common in South Georgia: solitude, framed in red clay and Australian pine under heat and heavy clouds.

Cities such as Atlanta have grown in spite of this atmosphere, and have generated influences beyond their borders. Other exceptions will always be honorable and moral men and women who, alone in their consciences, prevail against hypocritical codes of conduct, often risking their livelihoods or life itself. Clarence Jordan was such a man: "... we had the deep feeling that modern man's problems stem almost entirely from his loss of any sense of meaningful participation with God in His purposes for mankind." Jordan died in 1969, after building a community of people to live after him who are hate-free, poverty-free, and growing freer.

Americus is a typical southwestern Georgia town—except for the untypical farming community of "Koinonia," begun by Jordan in 1942, dynamited by the Ku Klux Klan in 1957, and flourishing today under the care and handling of Florence Jordan, Millard Fuller, and scores of people, black and white, from Georgia and across America. But Koinonia almost died before its present success was born. During the '40s and '50s the community had considerable impact on the agricultural problems of the area, but by 1968 the giant agri-business was sweeping the sharecroppers and little farmers off the land. Koinonia had dwindled to two families and was on the verge of collapse. Jordan was plagued with a sense of uselessness.

Then one of those strange, life-changing incidents struck: a meeting between Jordan and an old friend in Atlanta. Millard Fuller, a young, self-made millionaire, also felt the emptiness; together, he and Jordan began to fill it. In mid-August, 1968, they called together a diverse group of 15 men for a four-day session of seeking, thinking and talking. They were businessmen, politicians, writers, ministers, freelancers, all with one thing in common: a deep compassion for their fellow men.

In Jordan's words: "It has become clear to us that as man has lost his identity with God he has lost it with his fellowmen. We fiercely compete with one another as if we were enemies, not brothers. We want only to kill human beings for whom Christ died. Our cities provide us anonymity, not community. Instead of partners, we are aliens and strangers. Greed consumes us, and self-interest separates us and confines us to ourselves or our own group."

"As a result, the poor are being driven from rural areas; hungry, frustrated, angry masses are huddled in the cities; suburbanites walk in fear; the chasm between blacks and whites grows wider and deeper; war hysteria invades every nook and cranny of the earth.

"We must have a new spirit, a spirit of partnership with one another." And a bold plan was begun. It is called Koinonia Partners, based on the Christian philosophy and open to all men. It has three areas of concentration:

Communication, Instruction, and Application

By Communication they preach a message of hope in a world cynical with hopelessness. All forms of mass media are used, and profits serve to strengthen the Koinonia community. By Instruction they work at not leaving this strengthening process of their community to chance, but set up a system of schools to help make all partners effective and mature human beings—to keep spirit with one another through the teaching of sound ideas and encouragement. But the first two areas actually serve the third. Application is just that, but in a dynamic, concrete, measurable system of material support to people. "What the poor need is not charity but capital, not caseworkers but co-workers. And what the rich need is a wise, honorable and just way of divesting themselves of their overabundance. The Fund for Humanity will meet both of these needs."

Money comes from gifts, non-interest-bearing loans, and from voluntarily shared profits of the partnership industries and farms.

FARMING. Working units on the 1400-acre farm consist of one to four partners, grouped closely to share machinery and labor. There are also social, recreational, and spiritual benefits which are really the backbone of the operation, keeping it expansive and self-generating. Among the crops raised are peanuts, corn, and some vegetables.

INDUSTRIES. At present there is a flourishing pecan-shelling plant, fruitcake bakery, candy kitchen, sewing enterprise, pottery, and mail-order business. More industries are planned. Technical assistance is provided, and partners work together in the same principle as in the Farming operation. No capital outlay is required of them, and no rent or interest must be paid. As the business becomes successful the original capital is freed to foster other undertakings, and the Fund of Humanity is enlarged.

HOUSING. Perhaps the most exciting is Partnership Housing. It is concerned with the fact that the urban ghetto is to a great extent the product of rural displacement. People don't move to the city unless life in the country has become intolerable or impossible. So a degrading life in a big-city slum is forced upon these people, unless decent housing and work are available to them in the country. Now there is Koinonia Village. At present at least eight new families are living in their own new homes; seven additional houses are nearly completed, and the goal is to have 30 houses occupied by the end of 1971.

These new houses are purchased by rural poor families who desperately need adequate housing. They are purchased on a 20-year, no-interest mortgage. There is no heavy burden of conventional financing and the monthly payments are between $25 and $32 per month.

Forty-two half-acre home sites are presently being made available, with four acres in the center being reserved as a community park. The houses are two-, three- and four-bedroom dwellings with baths, kitchens, and living room, and cost between $6,000 and $8,000.

For a poor person such a house under these easy terms make the difference between owning a home and not owning one. The real asset of Koinonia Farm, its industries and village, is people. Visitors come from all over the U.S. and Canada to see it. Some stay.

Community living is growing in popularity among dissatisfied Americans. Communes vary in size and purpose, and attract like-minded people. The central purpose of Koinonia, it seems, is human dignity under God.

Koinonia is an experiment and a model. It is growing in the South, and may be the seeds of a New South. At Koinonia, "a rainy night in Georgia" is a lush, poetic experience which promises good crops. The best crop of all is itself and its people: may they flourish.

As Clarence Jordan quoted from the Bible: "Come, let us build ourselves a city, and a tower with its top in the heavens, and let us make a name for ourselves, lest we be scattered abroad upon the face of the earth." ∎

THE OREGON FAMILY
by Richard Fairfield

IF YOU VISIT COMMUNES LONG ENOUGH YOU WILL EVENTUALLY trek up a long, narrow, dusty road that winds through the woods and opens onto a clearing filled with beautiful naked maidens. At least that was my in-person introduction to The Oregon Family.

Friends had told me about this group, which was now in its third year of existence. Its founders were devout fundamentalist Christians, mostly in their mid-20s, very industrious and committed.

I had listed The Family's post office address in the Commune Directory (published annually by Alternatives Foundation). So when I began to revise the list of communes, I wrote to The Family in order to find out if they cared to continue the listing. The secretary, EI Twig, replied:

Dear Brothers and Sisters

The Lord bless you and fill you with His Light. We wish our name and address to be immediately deleted from your magazine.

This is our home, not a tourist vacation spa. We are trying to gain, spread, promulgate the love of Jesus the Christ and find it necessary to control the number of brothers and sisters who share here with us. We also seek more subtle methods of soul-mating than computerizing. We appreciate your inclusion of our address, and now would appreciate your exclusion of same. Kindly R.S.V.P. that this has been done.

Love and Peace
EI Twig, secretary

When I arrived on a Thursday morning to R.S.V.P., I found a sign at the entrance that read, "No vehicles beyond this point. Visitors on Saturday only." Hoping to respect their wishes, I decided not to go in but to drive farther north instead, visit other communes, and stop back there on my return. I returned on Friday afternoon, still too early, although several other vehicles were already parked there.

There in the forest, somewhere in Oregon, The Family had erected an immense circle structure, architecturally a rural gem for communal living. Constructed of logs and timber, the building had an interior that consisted of a single room, space uninterrupted. The kitchen, occupying the end of this room next to the entrance, was amply equipped with stoves, cupboards and counter space. A long, wide table extended from the kitchen area into the middle of the room. Toward the other end of the room were two semi-circular tiers of connecting bunks. Adequate space between tiers enabled a person on a lower bunk to sit up comfortably without hitting his head or straining his neck.

When I entered the main building, I noticed a few people resting on the top bunk tier. And someone sitting near a corner was lightly strumming a guitar. Most of the women were in the kitchen baking bread and preparing other foods. A few sat outside nursing their babies. It was a warm day and all of the women were either totally naked or naked from the waist up. All, that is, except for several visitors and one resident couple who were talking to some of their guests.

The few men present were visitors. I talked with several persons in the area of the main structure. They were all visitors. Finally one of the younger naked ladies mentioned that many of the residents had gone away for the week. The men who remained were working in the huge garden at the foot of the hill or constructing new housing in different areas on the hillside.

Some families had decided to build their own separate dwellings among the trees along the winding road beyond the main communal area. The landscape was beautiful, the buildings rustic and sturdy. Among them stood a large food-storage house near the main clearing, a spacious and green garden well irrigated and promising a good harvest.

I had heard that The Family had experimented with group marriage for a time, probably with everyone housed in the main communal structure. But the marriage "hadn't worked out"—that was all the information I could obtain. Now, those who wished to could live in the main building and others could take separate shelter. Since warm weather had arrived, the hillside was speckled with campsites, tents and tepees belonging to the many visitors as well as the residents.

At a large, wooden picnic-type table near the main building, I found the resident couple talking with three women and a man. This couple, as well as the rest of the men and women members of the commune, could only be described as hippies. Their dress (what there was of it), their manner, their hair all reflected this new lifestyle; yet they seemed as fanatically committed to Jesus as were any of their more conservative, straight-type brethren, four of whom were sitting around the table discussing numerology and the Bible and Sin and Salvation and the Glories of the Lord.

"Bless you." "Be born again in Jesus." "Love God." These seemed to be the prevalent slogans as I brashly took a seat at one corner and listened in. I had nothing to say.

All four visitors were almost middle-aged and seemed to me to have just come from some Baptist prayer meeting. One of the outsiders, a seedy-looking man with short black hair and huge grim smile, seemed to be the numerology freak, as the others listened to him with indulgent Christian kindness. One woman dressed in her finest suit, probably straight out of a Montgomery Ward catalog, was talking with relish about how she believed in sin. And she elaborated lavishly when her hippie friends humbly disagreed with her assertion that "without evil how would you know good." And somehow, without actually agreeing, they all came around to the conclusion that Jesus was the answer. It was a mind-blowing scene. Four uptight, tight-lipped, straitlaced, well-groomed, conventionally dressed, knit-browed Oregon Okies talking with two dusty-clothed, freaky-hatted, longhaired, land-loving, out-of-sight Christian hippies.

The visitors—unconverted by any of this, as were their hosts—left with nervous smiles. They had spoken with "objectivity" and had assumed an unbiased demeanor. But never had they dared to discuss their feelings and beliefs about their personal lifestyles. I felt certain that the old gal who believed in sin would soon be telling the others how sinful were those who wore no clothes.

I was tired of being a reporter and of harassing people with questions about their home, which is, after all, what a commune is. It is not a tourist spa. Anyway, I didn't feel too comfortable with Bible-thumping Christians, however hip, though no one had collared me with a "have you been saved, brother" routine. The sun was going down so I decided to split.

Getting It Together in the Woods

The following account of The Oregon Family comes from a long interview with Bob Carey, one of the founders of the commune. The interview was conducted by Edmund Helminski who has omitted his questions here in order to give continuity to the interviewee's responses. Here are Bob Carey's words:

One of the things that is noticeable here is that when we first came out here, we had the idea that by coming here, by dropping out, by making this move, we'd all drop all our hang-ups; but everyone brought all their little things with them, their little things. So the first thing was to bust the bubble of how we imagined it would all be and then go back to working things out for real. There is nothing here to blame your hang-ups on. You can't say it's society, because it's your society here. I used to sculpt. That was my thing before I dropped out. The whole transformation from doing individual things for myself, from making little pieces of sculpture, that whole thing was transformed into making myself into a piece of art and finding art in the daily things around me. Like the cabin we built, it's not the best piece of sculpture I've ever seen, aesthetically speaking, but it's a beautiful, funky piece of sculpture.

This county here has a large accumulation of surplus food and they give it out to anyone who wants it. So we go in and get it. Oregon happens to be one of the down-and-out states as far as the economy goes. The only thing it has is logging and tourists. There's hardly any other employment, so the government ships in surplus food to this area since it's one of the poorest in the nation. Right now anyone who does farming is self-employed and anyone whose net annual income is less than one thousand dollars for a family is entitled to surplus food. A lot of these farmers don't make any more than that because most of their business is carried on in trade. They don't have to handle much money. Everything like machinery and most of their supplies is knocked off and so they hardly ever have more than a thousand dollars cash. Now I don't want to have anything to do with the system, because the more we stay away, the better off we are; but I went down there with this guy just to see where it was at and they were really nice, they were open, they welcomed us, and they gave us the food. We get cheese and butter and it really saves us a lot of money.

It's really unbelievable what those chicks have learned to do over a fire that's nothing more than a hole in the ground. I think we're really lucky and I've been in a lot of communes before this, three of them before we got together. If the chicks aren't making it, if the chicks don't have any energy and don't want to do anything, like be chicks, you know, wash dishes, cook, then you're in for trouble because there's nothing worse than not getting your food, having all the dishes stacked up. We used to go through so many changes in the other communes. A lot of the young people don't want to center their energy, they're afraid to, they're afraid they're going to get hung up, so they stay so scattered that they're useless, they're like parasites. You've eventually got to say, 'Dig, man, you want to eat, you got to work like the rest of us, because that's what's happening here.' And then they say, 'That's just a cop-out, man, we'll just lay around here and God will feed us.' So I say, 'OK, you go find some other God, because this God ain't going to feed you unless you work.' There's got to be a certain inner strength, not the-world-owes-me-a-living theory of man. Some of these people have had such rough times with their families that they think that anything that has anything to do with the system is really ugly and anything like work is a bummer. The Zen monk that was up here was really good about that. He really laid a trip on everybody. He was about 43 and his trip was that work was where it was at, He got a lot of them off of their asses. I work about four hard hours a day and I feel healthy too, I feel clean. Five days a week, four hours, and it has to be done anyway because we need cabins. We need shelter, we need the water developed, we need our garden. It gives you an inner strength to be your own feeder.

Down in Santa Cruz we had lots and lots of people always coming in and out, but things got so out of hand, you know, stuff all over the place, and nobody was doing anything. Everybody was just smoking and watching television and then we got up here and it was a whole different trip, man. People don't smoke and they're meditating, and occasionally we have a good session. It happens maybe once a month, when everybody will really get high at meditation. In the morning and right after lunch we have an hour for meditation, and Sunday's the day when we usually go off and fast.

There's one thing about drugs, and we all realize that it wasn't an end in itself, but it sure brought us a long way and fast. I don't know where we're going, but we've left drugs, and I believe what we're doing is right, or not even 'right,' it's just good. A lot of love is being generated, a lot of energy is in our place. Very magnetic, because even isolated up here we get visitors every week. We have people come in here from Maine, and we don't even know how they found us.

The right diet and a little physical exercise really puts people into shape after they come up from the city. All the girls are healthy. They're beautiful. Some of the girls are a lot stronger than some of the male members of the family. I don't know what it is, but sometimes there are a lot of ego games involved, sometimes with the males.

I've got a pretty strong will, but I don't try to impose it on anybody. I just try to flow with the group consciousness. But a lot of times, especially when I bought the property and said, you know, 'Let's all move to Oregon,' there was an immediate ego clash with some of the males, who would say 'Well, Bob's taking us on his trip,' you know, 'I don't want to go on his trip.' They'd start separating themselves. But it's not my trip, man, it's everybody's trip. This is just a piece of property that we can use. But that changed too after everybody saw what was happening.

Jim, the Zen monk, has a degree. He's got a doctorate in psychology. Ron has a BA, Twig has a Master's, and Sonny has a BA, and they're figuring on getting their certificates, you know, to teach the kids. During the year we'll have eight children altogether. The people with graduate degrees won't have any trouble at all and those with bachelors can get temporary certificates. I'm sort of into the maintenance part of it all, and the economics. Everybody's got their role, where everybody's got something they've done previously that's going to play an important part in the community. I want to set up a complete workshop for ceramics. All my education was in art-casting, metal work, welding, forging, and pottery. The workshop would be something for everybody to be able to trip on. If you don't get on an ego trip with art, going into shows and all that, it's really a good catharsis, therapy. Right now everybody's making vests and leather pants. Rat Face makes drums. We use a lot of that Indian print material for dresses and shirts and things. Another thing is that everybody's interested in occult things, so some people are into the tarot and some are heavy on astrology, some read the I Ching all the time.

Everybody's sort of waiting. The people from the communes in this area sort of get together south of here occasionally, and everybody's going through very heavy changes about what's happening. Everybody's questioning it, so to speak, like it's awfully heavy, but we don't know what's happening. But every time we get together, it comes up. Kesey, too, says his group is experiencing something. It makes you feel good. You know you're not alone.

Most of the people have been into a life something like this for at least a couple of years. I think Ron is the most recent. He was a computer programmer in L.A. only a year ago, until he turned on, until he saw cops beating people, old ladies, straight people even, just for demonstrating against the war.

Whenever somebody comes here from the city, the energy, the vibration is changed. They bring in a lot of the scattered energy. A lot of strange games come in too, but it's really fun. I'll have to go down to San Francisco this week to pick up the tepees. It'll be my first time out in a few months. It should be interesting. At least I'll have something to compare it to. If you're in the city all the time, you have nothing to compare it to. Your whole center is right there, while our whole center is right here. What goes on in the city means nothing to us, but when you go in you have some kind of measuring rod. Now, of the people in the city, there are those at the temples and ashrams who manage to turn out some very positive vibrations, but I don't want to get into positive and negative because that's not what's happening either.

Last Sunday we had ourselves a family gathering. Everybody came up from the city. There were about 40 people here. It was really powerful, because the people who were up here were so much more serene and flowing than the others, who have so much nervous energy.

There's a fear toward the unknown. To make the change, to go through it sometimes seems like hell when you're doing it. It's very intense and maybe you experience a fear trip, but then when you pop out on the other side, it was nothing. You wonder why you were fearing the change when it was nothing at all. Because once you're out here, you don't want to go back. I don't know what's going to happen here, but I know there's no going back.

Most of the local people have been very open and beautiful. They're really very hip in their own way. One of the reasons is that we don't try to freak anybody. A lot of hip, turned-on people try to freak people. We just try to go on their trip and love them for what they are, and then it's just beautiful, because they really give themselves to you. There's no reason to freak anybody. People will blow their own minds when they're supposed to, that's the Buddhist way.

This piece of property here has everything we need on it. We've got lumber to market, if we should ever want to. We have 180 acres that have never been logged. We can just cut poles down if we want to. They sell them for seven bucks apiece. Then we have a friend who is psychic and pretty dependable. He's already told us where the gold is on this land, maybe $8,000 worth. But we don't want to get into that yet. There's a slow changeover going on because some of us are still making money privately and we intend to be a nonprofit religious organization. But people can give us things and deduct it from their taxes, and there are a lot of people who want to do that. We have a deal with the rice company, where they give us various grains, like a donation. Right now, in Florida, my parents have really turned on to our trip and they're going around collecting blankets and ponchos and things like that for us. They're getting companies to donate materials so that we can build more. It's coming about slowly, but it will work itself to the point where we will be able, without having to go out and get jobs, to live and work on our land. This year, though, we plan to do some work for local farmers and bring in just a little bit of money that way. We also have a good friend who owns a leather shop in San Francisco, and he'll sell some of the things we make here. But I don't want to get into that kind of thing yet. I want to see if we can do without it. I want people to make their own clothes, and for people to make clothes for others in the community. I want that exchange to happen before we ever get into a commercial thing.

When I first joined up with Kesey, someone asked me why I thought I should be with them and why I thought I should be able to travel on the bus with them. I said that I didn't know, but that it seemed like what I was supposed to do, and immediately that was a good enough answer. If I had laid some bullshit on them, they probably would have told me to get out. I can't say no to anyone who wants to live with us or to learn or to share or whatever. Your whole trip is to be open and to love and when people come up, it's hard to turn them away. Once there was a guy along the road who stopped us and said that he wanted to follow along. We were all going down to the river. When we got to the river he was almost crying, man, he got out and said, 'You people are really beautiful,' and then he said, 'I don't know what's happening, but I want to learn, can I come with you?' And I said, 'Sure man, if you want to, we're all brothers.' So he followed us and everybody was walking barefoot. We were used to that kind of thing. He wasn't. He took off his boots, and I imagine he hadn't walked barefoot in his life. I told him that he should wear his boots, but he wouldn't listen to me. He started following us and we walked for about three miles, but he only got halfway, his feet were hurting him so much. He had this ego thing about him. He wasn't ready yet. Water seeks its own level. If he had listened to us, he could have come. We never saw him again. See, everybody was carrying things and he wanted to carry things, and that only made it worse on his feet. He really went on an ego trip. It was a bummer. He just wasn't ready for our trip. None of the hang-ups are out here, you bring them, they're all yours. ■

THE LAMA FOUNDATION

by Richard Fairfield

IT WAS PRACTICALLY IMPOSSIBLE FOR US TO FIND THE LAMA Foundation. We drove up and down, back and forth, along a wet, snowy mountain road in northern New Mexico. The road was rutted and downright goddamned dangerous. In exasperation we decided to give up and return to the main highway. Rounding a curve, I almost hit a truck coming toward us. Its occupants were friendly. We explained that we had been looking for Lama. "Well, follow us," the driver replied, "we're on our way there."

It was unbelievable. We had been on the same road before, but we couldn't see how anyone could live that far out in the woods. We drove and drove, fearing all the time we'd lose another muffler. Finally, we came to a parking area and the driver of the pickup pulled us over and said, "You better park here and ride the rest of the way with us. It gets even worse from here on in." I gladly parked; Consuelo bruised her leg as we jumped into the back of the truck.

"This is as far as we can go." The truck couldn't get through the ruts of mud, so the driver pulled off the road. "We can walk the rest of the way. It isn't far." He was a young, clean-cut, collegiate-looking guy with an equally all-American hip girl companion. They made their way up the road on foot. We followed. They stopped at an old school bus, now their home, and we continued on toward the central area.

I had seen pictures of Lama, but I now saw that they had not done justice to the beauty of the place. It was situated on top of a mountain, commanding a view that extended for miles. Even though we arrived at dusk, the view was almost incredibly fantastic. It was like standing on top of the world.

Midway between the main building and one of the smaller domes, one of the leaders greeted us. Consuelo and I stood there in the cool night air, explaining who we were and why we were there. We were given information about the Lama Foundation, most of which was contained in a descriptive brochure.

One fellow hurried by, stopping briefly to chat. He was another of the basic support group and sort of the overall administrator. He was busy trying to get an old Peace Corps kerosene slide projector to work for the evening's entertainment.

Our reception was rather formal and businesslike, in contrast to the more casual response at other communes we visited. Lama had the vibes of a rather hip Esalen-style retreat; its inhabitants seemed hip because of fashion rather than lifestyle. When we looked inside the main building, people were gathered around a warm fireplace and appeared comfortable and snugly middle-class.

Each family or individual who takes up residence at Lama has to provide her or his own separate housing on the land. But no one is allowed to build winter housing until he has been there one whole working season.

This residency requirement seemed to explain the apparent middle-class quality of the place. Not only would a person need the wherewithal to construct his own living quarters but also he must have previously accumulated enough money to meet his living expenses. This would come to $660 for a six-month period ($360 for room and board, $300 for tuition, limited scholarships available).

The full working season at Lama extends from early April through October. The busiest period of operation is during the summer months—June, July, and August—when guest teachers are added to the study program. Many students from all over the country attend this program, called "The School for Basic Studies." The daily schedule, we were told, includes "meditation, chanting and body movement exercises such as Tai Chi Chuan, Yoga, etc., depending on the availability of suitable instruction."

From its modest beginnings as a nonprofit foundation in the spring of 1967, Lama has grown impressively. Physically it is an imposing community, with constructed roads, greenhouse, garden, summer cabins, year-round living quarters, and the gigantic domed main building. The architecture of this central structure is a massive combination of old adobe and new wooden dome work. Without doubt, Lama is well on its way to even more growth.

Steve Durky and the Development of Lama

Learning about Lama came not so much from admiring the fine dome work as from talking with the people responsible for and living in this isolated community. The following discourse about Lama is taken from this interview with Steve Durky, one of the founders, when the community was only about 15 months old:

"How did it all begin? Five years ago someone sent me a letter, and in the letter it was said that the only place that one should live is where the heart is and where there is love, a radiance of love. Prior to that I had only heard that from people in India. So it was obvious that one should find out who that person was, and we came to this area on a camping trip and met this man. He said that nothing was possible at the present due to the fact that the psychic vehicle was oscillating and spinning from the effect of drugs at too rapid a rate; in other words, that the only possibility for spiritual growth comes when your flame is burning steady. So he said, you know, 'Go on about your business.' At the same time someone said that it was possible, if we found some land, to get it.

"Whereupon we spent many summers driving back and forth across America looking for land. And we sort of narrowed it down to here. At the same time you see, this is a very strange place, because this is actually is a place for graduates, graduates of high school. When you really want to be high because none of us really know how to do that yet. That's what this is all about. We have to find a mountain. So then, after many times of seeing Him, the flame was beginning to burn steadier. You know, we drove trans-continentally back and forth and this is where we would always stop. And He'd like always tell you where your flame was at. So the last time, which was about two and a half years ago, as I came through, He said, 'If you want to come back, go to New York and finish what you have to do.' So we went to New York, and all of us at that time did something together in New York. It started on Mother's Day and ended on Father's Day. My father died the night we left. We left and that was the end. There was a decision that was reached that year by a number of us. Before that, we had always tried to fit ourselves into shells; in other words, it was the end of the shell period. And it was the beginning of trying to create something out of nothing, of furnishing our rooms.

"That was the beginning. We came out here—there were three of us at first—and we'd drive around every day looking for land. We were living on an Indian reservation south of here, and we made a map and kept looking. Finally that man said, 'Why don't you look at a place called—' Well, New Year's Day was the first day we came up here, New Year's Day 1967. We had $4,000 in our pockets and we came to look at this land; but it wasn't this land, it was over on the other side of the mountains, same acreage but twice as much money. The person who had so kindly offered to help us was only into it for a certain amount, about half of what this other land was going to cost. In other words, that land was 44; this was 21, the number of the tarot and also very meaningful. But we had come with $4,000 in our pocket and were going to buy it, but this man said, 'Don't do it.' Now, that night an angel came to see this man, and the angel told him to see another guy, and when this man went to see this other guy, this other guy had only two weeks earlier decided to sell the land we've got now for exactly the sum that this very kind person had offered to begin this world. So, boom! We clicked in and this was the place.

"It became apparent to us that we had reached a crossroad, and we had come by many different ways, by car, by foot, by boat, by train; we were all at the same point. The point was that we could see our way up, but it was obvious that if we were to go up by this path, we had to leave a lot of things behind us, like drugs and that whole world. In other words, to grow you have to sacrifice. I don't know if everybody here agrees with that, but that's how I see spiritual growth. It's not really a sacrifice but you have to let go of something, because the body, the being on whatever plane, can only hold so much. So we let go, but a lot of us who were originally involved didn't want to let go. They wanted to maintain it. So those of us who wanted to did let go, plus new people; that's why I say it's like graduation, I mean that this is a new thing, a new grouping, a conglomeration of people who came out of a lot of different scenes, out of the very straight world, out of Indian scenes, out of bhakti, raja, hatha, etc. In some way, all of these disparate things have to be woven into one seamless garment, and that's what this is an attempt to do. And each person, like this person over here, his head, his being, is rooted in the Tao and Chinese philosophy, and this person here comes out of the ethos of the eternal living God as manifest in human form, and another person comes out of the world of the university, which is no longer alive. The university, you know, began when a number of teachers came together and people flocked to them because they were alive, which, to a great extent, the university world isn't anymore. And what I've just said is about the mental side of how this all happened. But the thing to realize is that it's always this weaving of different threads.

"The other thing that's important to say is that we're not so much against the government as for changing it. My forefathers signed the Declaration of Independence and the Constitution, and if you read those things, and really understand what they say, you'll realize that something's gotten lost, and when something's lost, it either has to be found, or you can just forget it.

"So what we did in relation to the government is that we became a nonprofit, tax-exempt foundation, founded for educational and scientific purposes, because, as we see ourselves, we are a center for basic studies. And by basic studies I mean how to make an adobe brick, or learning how to plumb and how to carpenter, learning what's basic, learning what it is that people really need and what are their desires, and what is the relationship between needs and desires. And also, what is basic, is the relationship to the earth, to the sky, and to each other.

"We're learning how to provide for ourselves as much as we need and no more, living with the grace of God. Very much of it has to do with our limitation and understanding that limitation. The fact that certain societies are cut up in a way, a certain way, where the spiritual is divorced from the practical, this is what we wanted to change for ourselves. The world that makes sense is a world where each man and each woman lives out time and the cycles of the seasons, where no man is a priest and every man is a priest, and where the duty to maintain the cosmos is dependent on everybody instead of just a select few. In other words, we're anti-priesthood. There are no priests here because everybody is a priest. There are none other than the select.

"The real basis of the whole thing is that growth can only come about through the direct experience of that ultimate that is all around us, and that when you have a direct experience of that ultimate, you know who you are. You begin by understanding that you're only beginning. That's the first understanding. Then you also have to understand that growth comes out of a sincere desire to know the truth about yourself, and as much as I am able to help you, I will help you, and as much as you are able to help me, you will help me, and that all our growth has to occur on three planes simultaneously: the physical plane, the mental plane, and the spiritual plane.

"We applied for a federal tax exemption and got it, and then we got a small foundation grant which handled about 50 percent of the construction costs last year. We hope to put together a brochure next year to raise more money. We have a five-year plan, and by the end of five years we hope to be financially independent. It's based on three different approaches: a school, the establishing of workshops, since a lot of us are artisans or artists; and publishing, because we're obliged to publish under our federal tax exemption. This year we'll be publishing two books: The Dome Cookbook, which is about zonal polyhedral construction, and The Eight Sacred Directions. Each year we hope to have a technical book, which is a help to people starting communities, and a spiritual book, one oriented toward growth. We believe that the essence of spirituality is practicality. It's not up there, it's right here, right here, right here, and every time you go up there you're forgetting what it's about. As Jesus says: the Kingdom of God is within you. Or as the Buddha says: when you get high, bring it back with you. The other thing about publishing is that as explorers we should bring back, you know, a map. And another thing is that the community is only one aspect of all this, the residential aspect.

"Another thing is that we consider very slow growth an important thing. I've been into communal scenes for seven years now, and some communities are in are rapid expansion mode and believing that you're further along than you are. For instance, you're my brother, right? And she's my sister. On the other hand, I still need my individuality and my privacy, let's say, and you need yours. Many groups say, well, if you're my brother and so forth and we're all one, let's live in a heap. But you look at these people around here, and at people all over the world, you see that they've evolved something, not by going against nature, but by going with it. If something is to be, it will be. It's not to be had by simply saying that I'm ready for that, because we know from experience, from having tried it, how far we are from it. It's like understanding all the time where you are and not trying to say that we're enlightened.

"Our ideal is no more than 30 people. Let me make one thing clear. We have two levels going here. One is to establish a firm focal point on the physical plane, and to do that we're going to grow by about one family a year until we have eight families that live here all year. Those will be the building blocks. We want to do it slowly so that we can integrate things well. Then there's the summer thing. It's kind of like life: in the summer everything expands and in the winter things shrink back. One of the screens we have against too rapid expansion is the rule that you cannot build any winter housing until you've spent one whole working season here—April to October, when all your energies are spent on the communal thing. It's just very natural.

"Now, all of us here have a very strong belief that this is the time of the coming together. Now you can call this East and West. The way of the West is exploitation, rape, and also a brilliant mind thing, you know, solving the material thing first;

and the East is much more the way of flowing with it, you know, if you don't have crops one year you don't let it get you down, you meditate in hunger. In the West if you don't have food you do something about it. Now is a time when all this is coming together, and you see this in many ways, like the war in Vietnam, where the only way that East and West can get together is through killing, which is an act of love in itself. It's the same as when you kill a deer and start taking its guts out—you establish a very close relationship with that thing. It's easy to see unless you're hung up on death. If you think that this is it, then it gets pretty scary, but if you see that it's all part of a whole, if you can see beyond the end, then you can get someplace.

"We make certain requirements of people. The reason for this can be simply explained. We have all found that there have been things in our life that we've wanted to do but found ourselves incapable of doing. We've lacked the necessary discipline to do them. We all admit that we're undisciplined in relation to the spiritual life, and we believe that through the centuries there have been very clear precepts for spiritual growth. Now 99 percent of us, especially those who have dropped out of the drug or hip world, are still very undisciplined people, out of tune with ourselves and one another. By applying from the outside a form of discipline, so that everybody gets used to it… Why do we get up every morning at six-thirty? Why do we chant? It's not just to get up early. It's not just to chant. It's to begin accustoming ourselves to a new rhythm. A good word is tuning. The instrument is still being tuned, both in terms of the individual and the larger organism. You're talking about a community, you're talking about an organism which, to some extent, is greater than its components. It is not merely that there are 20 people here who have accidentally come together, but that there is something that's evolving. I keep reiterating this, but it's just a beginning. Our feeling is that you cannot just jump all the way from the bottom all the way to the top.

"Something that's above and beyond all of this is just the wonder of it all. It just feels good."

THE ANANDA COOPERATIVE COMMUNITY

by Richard Fairfield

ON MY WAY TO THE ANANDA COOPERATIVE COMMUNITY IN Nevada City, California, I reread an article by Jim Mitchell that I had reprinted in The Modern Utopian magazine: He wrote of the "… new and young people who have come here to settle the Sierra foothills and give them a loving consciousness. Bare or sandaled feet, long hair, beards and blue jeans, Pakistani or Indian prints, a Hari Krishna chant rises above drums and cymbals, a marriage of expectation and inward peace."

The community described hardly lacked facilities: a 70-acre Meditation Retreat with geodesic domes consisting of "a common house (for meals and meetings), office, and large temple arranged near a wooden water tank and small garden." And a mere three miles from the retreat lay the commune's 270-acre Farm Community, with A-frame cabins occupied year-round. The article concluded, "At Ananda, each person is free to build a new and beautiful reality, for such a reality need only be the sum of the spirit and body of each member—you become a new society and the strength and beauty of that society depends directly on your own spirit."

I arrived first at the Farm and was told to hurry to the Retreat for the regular Saturday afternoon outdoor concert. I wanted to look over the Farm first, but I was informed that this was where most members lived and worked and that the Retreat was for visitors. Besides, the members were all at the Retreat now and I'd better hurry if I wanted to get to the concert on time. As I drove away from the old farmhouse where Ananda members made candles and incense and published books on Yoga, I also noted a few other farm buildings: sheds, chicken house, and barn as well as several tepees, small houses, and shelters scattered over the landscape.

Numerous signs pointed the way to the Retreat; there was no chance of getting lost or misdirected. The visitors' parking lot was clearly marked. Another sign read "Visitors Please Register At Office," and a helpful arrow pointed toward a small, bright red geodesic dome with sliding aluminum doors and windows.

I was given the official guided tour of Ananda. First a look at the huge communal kitchen, which was being built with the help of students from Pacific High, a free school in the Palo Alto area of California. (Pacific High students had built many unique and beautiful domes at their school and many outsiders were now hiring them to help construct domes elsewhere.) The new kitchen-dome was soon to be connected to the present kitchen and dining facility "common house," another dome-like structure also used as a meeting and social facility. The temple was

215

a large geodesic dome surrounded entirely by an exercise deck. We took off our shoes and walked inside. It was lovely and peaceful. The temple floor was covered with multicolored mats and the walls were decorated with rugs and colorful murals depicting Yogananda, Ananda's spiritual guru.

Back at the office, my guide presented me with a brochure that explained the history, purpose, and program of Ananda. Since Ananda is only a three-hour drive from San Francisco, many people make the journey for a weekend of meditation and spiritual regeneration. The location, some 3,000 feet above sea level, in an area of pleasantly rolling terrain that is heavily wooded with large oak and pine trees and manzanita bushes, provides a breathtaking view. Facilities for visitors at that time included a central bathhouse with hot and cold running water, several small residences, and (according to the brochure) "roomy cabin-type tents with large windows set apart from one another in secluded nooks among the trees. Campsites are also available for people with tents of their own." There are daily meditation and exercise periods at the Retreat, though no one is explicitly required to attend them. Most of the members live at the Farm, where a separate but similar schedule is maintained. On weekends, however, a full schedule of activities at the Retreat is planned:

FRIDAY

5 p.m.	Recharging exercises and Yoga postures
6 p.m.	Meditation
7 p.m.	Dinner
8 p.m.	Evening Service

SATURDAY

6:15 a.m.	Strolling Kirtan (chanting)
6:30 a.m.	Yoga postures and recharging exercises
7:30 a.m.	Meditation
8:30 a.m.	Breakfast
10:00 a.m.	Classes in "Creative Arts Through Yoga"
12:30 p.m.	Lunch
2:00 p.m.	Concert
5:00 p.m.	Recharging exercises and Yoga Posture
6:00 p.m.	Meditation
6:30 p.m.	Dinner
8:00 p.m.	Evening Service

SUNDAY

Morning	Same as Saturday, with a service at 11 a.m. instead of classes
Afternoon	Tour of the Farm

These planned weekends run from mid-spring to late autumn (as long as the weather permits). Only a few people remain at the Retreat year-round ("facilities for the life of a hermit" as they call it). The Farm, however, accommodates a larger number of married couples and families throughout the year. Visitors to the commune are charged nominal rates according to facilities used and the length of stay.

Ananda permits no hallucinogenic drugs of any kind on the property. Smoking is permissible, but only in the privacy of one's own tent. No dogs are allowed, a restriction because barking distracts people during meditation. Although not specifically excluded, young children are not particularly welcome to remain at the Retreat. Babysitting arrangements are provided at the Farm.

While I was sitting in the office, three young people with backpacks arrived. The director and guide had left the office in the care of John, a young artist and resident member. The most aggressive of the three began to inquire about the Retreat. "We want to stay a few days or longer, if we like it here. Can we set up camp anywhere we can find a convenient space?"

"Well, I'm not the one in charge here," John said. "The man who is will be back in a few minutes. I think only designated campsites can be used, though, and there is a daily or weekly fee for their use."

"Well," said the backpacker, "we don't intend to get in the way. How about if we just camp outside the campsite area in the woods somewhere?"

"This is an organized meditation retreat," John replied with a slight grin. "If you want to stay here you have to be part of the Retreat, not live on the edges. There are plenty of woods elsewhere, if all you want to do is camp out." Then he added, "Visitors are expected to participate in our programs and eat at least one meal daily with us."

1 felt compelled to add, "If everyone who wanted came here and just camped out around the edges of the Retreat, before you know it the whole hillside would be loaded down with people. I wonder whose toilet and bathing facilities they'd want to use? And where they'd leave all their trash?"

"Yes, I know," John replied, "we had that kind of open policy here at one time. It was a disaster. Now we've become organized. It's necessary. Unfortunately, most people aren't aware and sensitive enough to treat other people and their environment with the same care and attention they themselves would like."

"Well, you see, I'm writing a book on communes," the aggressive one replied, as if to explain why he should be an exception.

"God!" I exclaimed. "Everyone is writing a book on communes these days." (I get two letters a week from people writing books, articles, and masters' theses on the subject.)

"I'm not writing any ordinary book about communes," he retorted. "I'm writing a book on how to start a commune."

"Oh, show him your book," I said to John.

John moved meditatively toward the literature table and picked up the book Cooperative Communities—How to Start Them and Why, by Kriyananda. He turned abruptly and smiled broadly. "Have you seen this book?" he asked. The budding young author didn't seem to be very interested.

John was one of the most beautiful guys I had ever seen. His physical appearance was strikingly healthy; his manner was graceful and pleasant, yet direct and authentic. He was the one who had done the beautiful murals in the temple, and he was now setting up a display of some printed drawings of the past Yoga masters in history. These included Jesus seated in a cross-legged position, several Indian masters, and Yogananda.

John was a year-round resident at the Retreat. He told me of spending his days without seeing or talking to another person. His solitude, together with a painstaking devotion to drawing portraits of great religious leaders, had obviously contributed to his own development as a spiritual being. Perhaps someone would come along to draw him and thereby gain a little of his beauty as well. I asked, "How come there is no picture of Kriyananda here?" (Kriyananda, a disciple of Yogananda, was the founder of Ananda.)

"He is a great teacher; he is not a guru, an enlightened one," John replied. "But he is well on the road," John hastened to add, "much more advanced than most of us." ∎

SRI RAM ASHRAMA: AN AMERICAN YOGA COMMUNITY

By Richard Fairfield

"I WAS ANGRY, AND IF IT HADN'T BEEN FOR THE TEACHINGS I would have quarreled with her. But instead I went back to my house and meditated until I understood what was going on." More than the Yoga books lining the walls of the library, this comment by one of the residents seems to sum up the religious spirit of the Ashram.

The Ashram has many faces. The first one the visitor sees is the exquisite natural beauty of the Ranch—a thousand acres of starkly lovely Arizona countryside, ringed by chains of mountains. To reach the Ashram, one must bounce along over seven miles of unpaved dirt road, through arid, sandy terrain past mesquite and yucca, past the grazing cattle of neighboring ranchers, past an abandoned movie set (which everyone first takes to be the Ashram). Around a final bend in the road, one comes to a green oasis of rose gardens and cypress trees. Startled by the noise of the car, a flock of pigeons rises against the vast blue sky, circles the house, settles back on the rooftop.

Inside, the main house is cool, serene, fragrant with incense. One is surrounded by the art works of the East: statues of Shiva, a glass case with replicas of the avatars; an altar with a statue of the Buddha, burning candles, an offering of water; Indian music in the background. One treads softly, not to disturb the gentle peace—and one treads warily, waiting for the expected onslaught of heavy religiosity. Will we all have to gather for chants at the altar, sit for hours in impossible postures, listen to sermons on obscure Hindu myths? One is relieved, but surprised, when none of these rituals is imposed.

Instead one is invited to tour the Ashram. There are numerous buildings, in a variety of architectural styles. The main house, part of the old cattle ranch that formerly occupied the site, is Mexican-style white stucco. A large, airy dining hall has been built of fieldstone. There is a pottery shop which looks like a direct steal from a stage set for "Hansel and Gretel." A meditation hall is going up on the site of an old swimming pool. Most residents (members of the Ashram "family") have constructed their own dwellings: a log cabin made of railroad ties; a multi-sided house, built on the foundations of an old tipi, with a skylight made from a tractor disk and a weathervane shaped like an Om.

Everyone seems constantly busy, occupied with housework, meals, laundry, building a house, firing a pottery kiln, or planting a garden. There are young people around—students at the Desert Sanctuary—learning to cook or to use a

219

saw by working alongside the older residents. Yet for all the busy-ness, for all the activity, there is no feeling of frantic haste. People stop to talk with you, to explain what they are doing, to share your wonder at the beauty of a desert sunset.

So the day passes. But at its end, you find yourself perplexed. The rituals and religiosity you feared never materialized, but why, then, the sign at the entrance: "Sri Ram Ashrama—Yoga Community"? If this is a religious community, where is the religion?

The answer lies in the comment made by the girl who told how she overcame her anger toward another member of the family. It lies in the warm courtesy with which a guest is greeted. It lies in the concern for young people which led to the founding of the Desert Sanctuary. It lies in the friendly dinnertime teasing among family members, which can only occur between people who love and trust one another. It lies in the joy and cooperation with which the work of the Ashram proceeds.

God at the Ashram is not a word or a ritual. It is a living force of compassion, concern and love.

The Sri Ram Ashrama is an American ashram; I say this not to stress nationalism, but to emphasize the fact that we were not born in India or in Japan. The fundamentals of Yoga should be taught and then assimilated into our own background and culture. Do not develop rituals; tradition is useless. All courses taught at the Ashrama will be for practical application and direct experience. We do not depend on the practice of rites to found a pseudo-religious atmosphere. True spirituality lies beyond forms and symbols, and can only be realized in the absence of premeditation, in spontaneity and immediacy of the mind.

Our Yoga is union with Life.

Talks With AHIMSA

Because of the hundreds of visitors to the Ashram, Swamiji has instituted a Saturday night or Sunday afternoon meditation with questions and answers. The following are some of the questions:

Visitor: Please tell me what is the Ashram.

Swamiji: That is a question to which I have given many years of my life and much meditation. The Ashram is land set aside as a center for Yoga, but not only to study Yoga and philosophy but to live it. I believe in Ahimsa, "nonviolence." This center is set aside for that. In the struggle for self-sufficiency the Ashram has been pushed aside and Yoga Foundations and Desert Sanctuaries formed, and now the Psychiatric Treatment Center. But my purpose is still the Ashram, even though we seem to be both lost in the shuffle. I even thought of running a want ad: "Swami Available." I have asked the Yoga Foundation for land—50 acres to be exact—for the building of the Ashram. We have too few Yogis here. Where are those who are searching an Ashram? Where are those who are searching a Guru? The Ashram is here and the Guru is here. I am not interested in saccharine spirituality or teachings. I am searching for those who have the spirituality and who have become the teachings. Let me strike at the heart of the matter: Are you now ready? There must be some Yogis who are interested in building and living in such a center. You who have asked the question—are you ready?

Visitor: No, Swami, not yet.

Visitor: What does Swamiji mean when he says spiritual nonsense?

Swamiji: There is nothing more energy-consuming than spiritual dilettantes—those who run after the guru of the month, those who dabble in the teachings, those who know all the theories but do not live them and do not become it. All is in the Being. All else is spiritual nonsense.

Visitor: Does Swamiji consider himself a master of Yoga?

Swamiji: Swamiji is the teachings.

Visitor: Why do people leave the Ashram?

Swamiji: Like in a garden, one must weed.

Visitor: What does Swamiji think of the World Congress of Enlightenment, or congresses of Yoga?

Swamiji: All are public relations for the teachers who are promoting the congress. Most congresses on Yoga limit yoga in trying to institutionalize it, like the Christian Church. Too many of these convocations are administered by those with great limitations. One should always question the reason for holding such convocations—meditate on the motive.

Visitor: What do you mean, "Life is a game"?

Swamiji: There are two extant books on the subject: The Games People Play and The Master Game. Of course life is a game—the problem, perhaps, is that too many are involved in low-level games or our greatest enemy: selfishness.

Visitor: What must I do to become a Yogi?

Swamiji: Find out who you are, meditate upon it and live it. Glorify your limitations. All the answers are in our weaknesses.

Visitor: How can I find peace?

Swamiji: Question "Who am I?" Limit your wants. Peace is found through renunciation.

Visitor: Should I think about the future?

Swamiji: What future? Why give up living in the here and now? Thinking of the future is an escape from the here and now.

Visitor: Can I be a Yogi and also be a Christian or a Jew?

Swamiji: What foolishness! Man has put limitations on belief in God. How can God have limitations? Bhakti is with limitations until one becomes one with the object worshipped. God is without subject and object.

Visitor: Would Swamiji name some enlightened men and women?

Swamiji: Why do you spend so much time with such nonsense? I have heard people argue whether Krishnamurti, Buddha, Christ, Ramakrishna, etc., were enlightened. To enter such discussions is to keep putting off what you should be doing. It is what the young people call "copping out." Buddha said, "Work out your own salvation." Why are we always looking for someone else to do the work, the holy man, guru, etc.? All teachings are within you—you are enlightened. Everyone is enlightened. What keeps you from it?

Visitor: Would Swamiji name them?

Swamiji: Find out who you are. That truth will name them. Do you not have truth, intuitively, spontaneously? Who are you? There is truth, there is enlightenment.

Visitor: Why does the Ashram need money?

Swamiji: Because my motive is pure. I ask for monies not for myself, but to help others. There are a great many in need. If you have money I expect you to give it. If you have none, so be it. I do not charge for Yoga, I do not sell Mantras, I do not assume your Karma, I do not charge for Initiations. Examine the motive. To continue the work of the Ashram costs money.

Visitor: What does Swamiji think of the many gurus in America?

Swamiji: Some are true masters. Others are like little boys and girls away from home for the first time, doing things they would not do at home and if they did some of the things at home they would be thrown out.

Visitor: Is there a death?

Swamiji: A death of this manifestation, yes. But life continues. Life is eternal. Live your incarnation and, I pray, with nonviolence. But be careful—you might be dead already. ■

CHAPTER 8

gurus— east and west

THE PROCESS

by Brenda Lyons, **Fusion** *magazine, 1971*

IN 1967, ANOTHER RELIGIOUS BAND CAME TO AMERICA: THEY call themselves the Process Church of the Final Judgment. The Processeans are members of a relatively young religious organization, founded and run by serious young members who predict an end to the world, a prediction based upon their increased sensitivity toward realizing and understanding the growing tensions and chaos within contemporary society—the threat of nuclear annihilation, pollution of the biosphere, genetic decay, overpopulation, racism, man's inherent sense of inhumanity.

They are young men and women who believe that escaping to the country will accomplish nothing, but who have accepted as their life's work the spreading of their prophecy, an inevitable doom, and of salvation only possible through the overcoming of fear, the fear to love. They feel that they have conceived a comprehensive, practical lifestyle by which man can develop the control (rather than the abuse) of his humanity, and thus achieve a pure, moral society. The only alternative they can see is death.

The Processeans are in reality a group of intelligent and sensitive human beings who have been repulsed by the forces of bad Karma, and who are desperately trying to maintain hope or faith in an utterly self-destructive world. They cling together for the need of understanding and fraternal love which they cannot find beyond their own circle. They have totally rejected the materialistic world, and have adapted a set of beliefs which leaves their minds in peace. It is somewhat ironic that these harmless beings are often shied away from on the streets, mistaken for devil worshippers, panhandlers, hippies or druggies.

Process was founded eight years ago in London by Robert de Grimston, apparently an extremely charismatic leader referred to by his disciples as "The Teacher." He is technically not their god, but is certainly worshipped and revered, and considered by them as having achieved an ultimate level of consciousness. He is English, married, approximately 34 years old, a Libra, and was formerly an architect. One Process member spoke of visiting with de Grimston in a dream and found him to be a divine supernatural character. His inspiration has found believers throughout most of the free world—the British Isles, Central Europe, Greece, Israel, Mexico.

Since Process came to America it has spread to New Orleans, Chicago, San Francisco, and to Boston. It seems that people, disillusioned by the same things Process denounces, and manifestly believing in a divine control, are ripe for the acceptance of new answers, new spirits, new cults such as Process.

Boston's chapter comprises approximately 60 full-time members in addition to a number of "O.P.s" (Outside Processeans), members of the church who live outside the life commitment but who attend functions and devote a certain amount of time each week to augmenting expansion and assisting the church in any way possible. There are two houses rented in Cambridge, one primarily for housing "I.Ps" (Internal Processeans), the other for the church central. Their church is located at 46 Concord Avenue in Cambridge; here are their offices and devotional rooms; here, too, is The Cavern, a pleasant basement coffee shop and free kitchen and shop, a quiet center for conversation, listening to music, enjoying a very tasty menu of organic foods and drinks, and getting to know the innermost thoughts behind Process. The atmosphere is one of calm friendship and tranquility, even that of a naive alternate reality. It is open every day except Sunday, between six and eleven p.m. Also, the following activities are open to the public: the telepathy-developing circle, midnight meditation, the Sabbath Assembly, and the Processscene, a highly dramatic presentation of knowledge of the Gods and how one relates to them.

The essence of the Process philosophy is that only through the reconciliation of opposites in self, only through the unity of Christ and Satan (symbols of good and evil in mankind), can truth, which lies in the balance, achieve peace and harmony as a reality.

The root of Process lies in basic fundamentalistic belief and interpretation of the Bible. The prophecy of inevitable self-destruction is taken directly from the Book of Revelations, last chapter of the New Testament. Continuing wars, increasing drug addiction and alcoholism, the increase in crime, the poisoning of our environment, the vivisection of animals for industrial purposes, all stand as living testimonials of man's self-destruction. According to Process, only those individuals who realize this universal truth and cleanse themselves from the madness of a linear world can survive. What is their answer? How, according to the Process, will man be able to overcome his innate state of fear and trembling? Their answer lies partly in passive acceptance of the past as reflected by their motto, "As it is, so be it." Their immediate effort seems to concentrate on the preparation for a new beginning after man's inevitable fall. This is all that can be done. Only those who are strong, extremely strong, able to endure beyond good and evil, capable even of bypassing the resigned Sisyphus and attaining "superman" qualities, will possibly survive. And so they are themselves in the "process" of learning and practicing self-control, self-discipline, of overcoming fears, of increasing sensory awareness, and, like the woe-begotten Christian missionaries in China from an earlier century, spreading the word.

The attitudes of the Processeans on such topics as drug addiction and alcoholism appear surprisingly tolerant, almost radical. Their philosophy of acceptance prevents them from condemning outright any man's poison. They do not judge others, only their collective self. They personally abstain from both alcohol and drugs. Their sense of morality extends to the tenet of celibacy before marriage, and full-time members of the church can only marry within the church. They live a basically monastic life, surviving on private donations and the private means of their membership. Cautious frugality is practiced by all. They do, however, allow themselves certain indulgences—jewelry is permitted but is usually restricted to handmade silver rings, quite simplistic yet beautiful; cigarette smoking is permitted but kept to a minimum, occasionally an ice cream soda, a movie, an appreciation of the innocent attributes from the good life. Moderation seems to be the key.

Despite their seemingly innocent, childlike approach to life, the Processeans project the frightening aura of the macabre while spreading their message on the streets. Moving in twos and threes, stopping to talk with any who'll listen, theirs is a marvelous sense of theatre. Entirely robed in black, save only for the silver of their low-hanging crosses and the hellish-red Goat of Mendes decal on their collars, they silently canvass Boston and Cambridge projecting their prophecy, their entire being expressing the destruction which they predict.

Black is their color, that of mourning for a dead world; the cross is worn to express the active presence of' Christ in the world; the Goat of Mendes is the balance of evil, the active presence of Satan in the world. Their presence is intended to and does shock many people into an awareness of evil, if only on a subconscious or semi-conscious level. In addition to the bizarre utility of their dress is the significance of their rings. Some signify particular levels in the "hierarchy," the organizational structure, others merely personal indulgences; most are hand-wrought in silver, often by the members themselves, some with inset stones. The very dress code of Process is an expression of their philosophy—the blackness is Satan, the jewelry is Lucifer, the cross of the Lord is Jehovah—a carefully combined expression of unity and harmony, possible through the balance of three perceived realities.

Against the backdrop of their religious philosophy, one can see how very dedicated a lifestyle is that of the Process. Daily life as viewed on an individual basis is governed primarily by one's level within the "hierarchy." This functional structure is an organized pattern of development, and is set forth in detail in their "Document."

The beginning of the "progress" marked by one's induction into the church, is that of "acolyte." Anyone may join; this stage is quite simple and mostly comprises a beginning of awareness and increased contact with others. One remains an "acolyte" only briefly, usually passing relatively rapidly to the next level of "initiate." For an unprescribed, though again limited, number of weeks, the "initiate" continues his "progress" with the emphasis on a constantly increasing awareness. In addition, he performs various physical duties about the community—carpentry, cooking, cleaning, general maintenance, one's abilities and desires generally governing one's responsibilities.

Marking the end of this new beginning, at such time as is decreed by the upper level of the "hierarchy," is "baptism" and the discarding of one's former name for one assigned, a name of biblical origin intended to embody the innate character. It is at this point that one chooses for himself either the path of partial commitment (as a "D.P."), or that of total commitment, of the internal Processean (the "I.P."). The role of D.P. is self-limiting: when one chooses this path he becomes a "disciple," the ultimate level of a D.P. At any time, however, one can move horizontally to the I.P. position of "messenger" from which level he can then continue to advance.

From "messenger" to "prophet," from "prophet" to "priest," and finally to "master," the highest possible level attainable. Only "The Teacher" remains above, to be accepted, respected, and followed unswervingly, considered by his believers to be the instrument of a divine inspiration.

Every level of the "hierarchy" has its own responsibilities and its own rewards: "prophets" organize and conduct activities, "priests" are responsible for the day-to-day chapter life as well as for the "trainings" of others. "Masters" most often handle inter-chapter relations and activities. Each respective role becomes increasingly difficult to attain: each, on the other hand, bestows the reward of increased respect, power, and confidence through achievement. The various levels are identifiable by certain established insignia: the silver cross, for instance, identifies a member as having attained at least the level of "initiate."

One must be a "prophet" to wear the sacred silver ring bearing the symbol of Process. Life is itself a "process," according to laws of the "hierarchy." Within the rigid structure of this system the daily individual lives go on—the seemingly dull, intensely determined lives of the "brothers" and the "sisters" and on upper levels of the "fathers" and the "mothers." In Boston they have been, for the most part, welcomed—easily accepted by students and young working people, at least tolerated by an older general public, even finding sympathy in Cambridge's Mayor Velucchi, who has recognized and approved their role in the community as well as their contribution to the physical and mental health of his city.

The members themselves come generally from middle- and upper-middle-class white families. Well-educated and quite positive about their places in Process, they seem relieved to be free of a meaningless and hypocritical society. Many of the members were formerly students, most often of psychology and the sciences. Others had been architects, computer programmers, salesmen as well as artists and writers. Some had served prison terms, others had simply been unable to cope with the straight, conventional life. Now their pasts are behind them, to be learned from and forgotten; the present and the future is their ultimate concern.

Each member is important in his function, yet never irreplaceable. Many have joined; only a very few have returned to the outside world. Each member is unique, each highly personal in appeal. There's young, English-born Father Christian, presently the only master in Boston, extremely calm and controlled, his passion his devotion to the church, married and quite settled for his youth. There's Brother Dan, energetic, intense, searching, formerly a psychology major in college and now a messenger of Process; Brother Jethra, formerly a science major at Boston University, now a messenger of Process who contributes by giving Tarot readings at the Cavern; Mother Greer, formerly an architect in England, now provisional master of the Boston chapter; Sister Hagar, who abandoned the life of a wealthy London socialite for that of a humble hard-working Processean.

These people are not without their pets, and Beelzebub, Seth, and Jeremiah (three Alsatian shepherds) and Geronimo, the grey cat, are much-loved members of the community. Animals are obtainable only as presents to certain chosen individuals from "The Teacher," and are considered examples of purity to be loved, cared for, and learned from. One of their 12 publications, The Ultimate Sin, exposes animal vivisection as "the blackest of all sins." This book reveals with words, photographs, and quotations the worthless horror of vivisection.

For the most part, other Process books contain serious rhetorical statements by Robert de Grimston explaining various aspects of the religion and commitment to this lifestyle. Such titles include As It Is, a tract written for those "who want to break away from the futile human pattern of seeing reality," If A Man Asks, answers to basic questions concerning the philosophy of Process, and The Gods and Their People, a discussion of the three facets of God. One of their most relevant and informative titles is Drug Addiction: A Process Statement by an English junkie writing under the name Lord Shayne. This booklet not only explains the physical and psychological effects of numerous hallucinogenic and addictive drugs, but provides spiritual inspiration for heroin addicts seeking help. Their magazine, Process, offers heavily designed excerpts from all their books as well as candid photographs of the membership at large. Resembling an old evangelist broadside, but psychedelic and somewhat satirical, the magazine provides light reading for anyone even vaguely interested in this cause. Considering the rigid morality and the firmly structured existence within Process, their various attitudes are somewhat surprising. For the record, here are some randomly voiced comments and opinions:

On astrology: "... accepted as a real and valid science." On President Nixon: "... appears to be quite Satanic." On war: "... opposition, not only to war, but even to the most minute of conflicts," On Hare Krishna: "... much admiration, very good vibes." On the Beatles: "... artists who have disseminated much truth but who were caught up in the human game of success and failure." Generally speaking, the professed attitude of Process is one of acceptance and toleration; observation of their lives better expressed their extremely rigid sense of morality. They can perhaps even be considered a new breed of Puritan. In a sense, here in the progressively academic, quasi-liberal atmosphere of Boston and Cambridge, we observe a rapidly expanding cluster of conservatives, a group of very straitlaced, serious young men and women, self-pledged to a prophecy of death. What has affected these young people to cause such a pessimistic prediction tempered by such intense dedication? Is it possible that they have been freaked out by a society too complex to sustain itself and too competitive to remain human? Are they reacting to what Whitman called "the "mania of owning things," or are they simply expressing through their own sense of theatre a revival in fundamentalism so appealing and so indigenous to the British and American character?

At any rate, they are only one of the many groups that seek to sustain religion in this decade. The impulse is probably timeless, the circumstances perhaps unparalleled. But when a large enough number of people embrace with what must be described as fervor, a life organized rather firmly on moral principles, the impulse toward religion makes a kind of sense, while the circumstances often cease to overwhelm. ■

THE KRISHNA PEOPLE: SERVING GOD 24 HOURS A DAY

by Richard Fairfield

FROM THE OUTSIDE IT LOOKS LIKE EVERY OTHER HOUSE ON the block, but there are no television sets, dogs, cats, kids or harried housewives inside. Instead, there are three immaculately clean rooms devoid of furniture except for a stove, sink and table in the kitchen. Photographs and drawings of East Indian men and women dressed in dhotis and saris line the walls. Carnations, roses and strings of beads adorn what appears to be an altar set in an alcove off the living room. A steady chorus of '"Hare Krishna" emanates from the phonograph in the kitchen.

The three young men and three young women who live here dress in flowing East Indian garments. Two of the men have shaved heads. All have daubed white clay on their foreheads and each carries a cloth bag containing a long string of beads.

Despite their non-Western attire, Goverdhan Das, 25, his wife, Sitarani Dasi, 24, and four other young persons who live in a three-room subdivision of a large house in Minneapolis, Minn., are not from the East. They are Western—born and raised in the United States and Canada. They call their house a temple, and the altar is for their Supreme Lord, Krishna.

As members of the growing International Society for Krishna Consciousness (ISKCON), the six young persons worship Krishna, a Hindu god who is said to have appeared in India 5,000 years ago. Their faith is based on principles set down in the Bhagavad-Gita, the traditional Hindu scripture.

Swami Prabhupada, who introduced the Krishna movement to the United States five years ago, urges his followers to reach Krishna consciousness—constant awareness of God—by repeating Krishna's name and leading an ascetic life.

Since 1966 the Krishna movement has grown until it now enlists several thousand followers worldwide. There are over 70 international temples, half of which are in the United States. And the devotees who live in the recently founded Minneapolis temple are spreading their transcendental message throughout that Midwestern city.

The Minneapolis temple has grown slightly since Goverdhan and Sitarani arrived in the Twin Cities in August, 1971. The couple was sent by the president of the ISKCON temple in Detroit.

Lance Nally, an 18-year-old devotee from Aberdeen, South Dakota, joined them in September, while Dan Holliday, 21, and his wife, Elaine, 21, came from

Detroit early in October. The sixth arrival, Judy, 21, a pigtailed blonde from California who declined to give her last name, came in late October. Since all four are uninitiated devotees, they use their outside names.

Since my visit with the Minneapolis devotees in November, they have moved to a larger apartment and have added three more followers to their numbers. Lynne Walden, 22, from Minneapolis, her husband Allan, 26, from San Diego, and Walter Grundon, 25, from Minneapolis, joined the movement in December. Lynne and Walter are former University of Minnesota students who dropped out of school when they became interested in Krishna consciousness.

As president of the temple, Goverdhan assesses the devotees' willingness to accept Krishna's dictates and decides who will stay in the temple. "I see that everyone makes (spiritual) advancement and works cooperatively," Goverdhan says.

His authority is delegated to him by the president of the Detroit temple and the Swami Prabhupada. "My superior in Detroit is in charge of all the temples in the Midwest," Goverdhan says. "The whole globe is divided and subdivided to facilitate spreading this movement to every town and village."

Since Goverdhan is also a priest in the movement, he performs marriage ceremonies and formally admits to the movement devotees who have lived in the temple for at least six months.

All the devotees are friendly and very earnest as they describe their way of life. No sacrifice is too difficult for someone who truly wants to devote his life to God, they say.

Followers of Krishna are prohibited from eating meat, fish, eggs, or from consuming intoxicants including drugs, liquor, coffee, tea or cigarettes. No gambling is allowed—not even mental speculation (expressing a personal opinion instead of citing authorized scripture), Goverdhan says. Furthermore, no sex outside of marriage is allowed and sex within marriage is only for procreation. (Namely once a month during the most likely day for conception, after chanting the Hare Krishna mantra for five hours.)

Men shave their heads as a means of sacrificing their identities for Krishna. Women wear little jewelry and as Goverdhan says, "there's no chance for women to raise their skirts here."

As he speaks Sitarani and Elaine make supper. Lynne Walden, who later moved into the new temple, sits quietly in the corner, seemingly enthralled with what is going on around her. In the next room Dan walks and chants "Hare Krishna."

There are 108 beads on a string, and every time a devotee chants "Hare Krishna," he slips a bead through his fingers. Devotees go through a string of beads 16 or more times a day. "Chanting purifies your mind—it frees you from thinking about material things and brings you to a spiritual level," Goverdhan says.

Each day everyone at the temple wakes at 4 a.m. for about three hours of chanting and reading scriptures. After a breakfast of fruit, milk, and hot cereal made from whole grains, the men clean the temple while the women wash clothes in the kitchen sink or sew.

Four days a week the devotees take a bus to the University of Minnesota where they sing and chant for students as they hurry to classes. Sitarani usually plays small finger cymbals while Goverdhan keeps time on a large drum called a mrdanga. Other devotees distribute copies of Back to Godhead, a magazine on the Krishna movement. Devotees also explain the concepts of their faith to students who pass by.

Two days a week they take their message to downtown Minneapolis. Most people are friendly and many stop and talk with them, Goverdhan says.

But a few persons have insulted the devotees. Goverdhan tells of a department store employee who slammed a door in his face when he attempted to market incense made at a West Virginia temple through the store. "So far only a shop near the University of Minnesota has bought our incense," Goverdhan says. "But it's been a great success there."

Most ISKCON centers are financed by a wholesale incense business. But because only one shop in Minneapolis handles ISKCON incense, the Minneapolis temple is funded primarily with donations, magazine sales, and a few lectures devotees have given at area high schools and the University of Minnesota.

Although Minneapolis devotees are full-time evangelists, ISKCON followers may retain their outside jobs as long as they "do their work for God," Goverdhan adds. The temple's monthly income is approximately $600, Goverdhan says. About $180 is sent to the magazine publisher, leaving $420 for temple support. Devotees spend $85 a month for rent, $10 for transportation and $240 for food.

"We spend a lot for food because we have a feast (for anyone who wants to come) every Sunday," Goverdhan says.

Followers spend a negligible amount of money on clothing. "Most of us ask our parents to send clothes from home or we buy old clothes in a cooperative store," Goverdhan says.

"Our neighbors have given us many sweaters and coats for winter," Sitarani adds. "They're very nice to us."

Each day about 4 a.m. the devotees return to the temple where they take their second shower of the day, because, as Goverdhan says with a wry smile, "Krishna people believe cleanliness is next to Godliness."

Daily the devotees eat a supper of organic food that never varies: unleavened bread, spiced vegetable soup and a vegetable, such as cabbage, fried in farina. They use no silverware and lay food on a cloth spread upon the floor. There is a plate for each person and one in the center of the cloth—an offering to Krishna. Before eating they give thanks for their food, touching their foreheads to the floor in deference to Krishna. Then everyone eats a little of Krishna's sacred food before consuming his own share.

Supper is usually followed by more chanting and everyone is in bed by 10 or 11. You must get used to the regimented life, but it's no harder than adjusting to anything else when you sincerely want to attain your goal, Sitarani says. "Material life is really much harder than spiritual life because material life is full of anxiety—you never know where your next problem is coming from.

But now I have real security."

Sitarani didn't always think Krishna consciousness was right for her.

Originally from New Jersey, Sitarani attended college for two years, then dropped out four years ago. She lived in San Francisco communes for a while as she searched for alternative lifestyles. Last year Sitarani moved in with some friends who were living on a farm near Detroit. "I started chanting with them... and I became peaceful and happy and more detached from material things."

Each Sunday she went with her friends to the ISKCON temple in Detroit. "It seemed too austere at first," Sitarani says. "Then after three months of visiting there I decided to stay for three days. Once I got there I never left."

Goverdhan first met some Krishna people two years ago in Boulder, Colorado, where he worked as an artist. He is a graduate of an art school in New York, his home state.

"I found that the movement offered a solution to fears and anxiety and lack of purpose," he says. Goverdhan became a devotee in 1969 and has lived in temples in New York City, Chicago, and Baltimore.

"I was in Baltimore when I decided I wanted to get married," Goverdhan says. "After a year in the movement everyone decides whether they'd like to be married or single. Marriages are always arranged by presidents of two temples."

Like others who marry after joining the movement, Goverdhan and Sitarani had never met before their wedding in July, 1971. They were married beside a huge fire and afterwards their robes were tied together for a week. "It was very beautiful," Sitarani says. "Everyone wore a flower garland and there were vases of flowers all around."

Goverdhan and Sitarani didn't seem to mind that they had not met before their marriage. "We believe in falling in love with God and that can bring people together," Goverdhan says.

Sitarani explains that once a female devotee marries, her husband becomes her spiritual and secular master. At first it's difficult to accept what women's liberation-ists would call a condition of servitude, she says. "But later you see it's true that women need guidance in spiritual matters and every day matters. And husbands are better equipped to give it."

Most of the devotees say their parents don't understand the movement but do respect their way of life.

"My mother is very pleased, although she doesn't really comprehend the movement," Goverdhan says. "Our parents equate success with responsibility and marriage means responsibility, so my mother has more respect for the movement since my wedding."

"My parents visited me when I got married," Sitarani says. "As long as I'm happy, they're happy... and they liked Goverdhan—they thought he was a nice boy."

Dan says his parents thought he was completely out of his mind when he joined. "But the more they saw I was developing nice qualities, the more they liked the movement."

Goverdhan and Sitarani think the response to the movement in Minneapolis has been good. About 30 persons share the devotees' Sunday feasts and 12 attend their weekly cooking classes. Several persons come regularly and are thinking of joining the movement, Goverdhan says.

The day I visited the devotees' new temple, three high school students from Minneapolis-St. Paul suburbs were seated in a circle around Walter who explained the principles of Krishna consciousness to them. All three seemed to hang on every word he said.

They stayed for two hours but declined to share supper with the devotees. As she slipped on her coat, one high school girl said she had to be at church soon.

"But this is church, too," Dan said. They promised to come back the following week.

Sitarani says she and Goverdhan will remain in Minneapolis as long as it takes to establish a significant following there. "We don't know how long we'll stay here—we don't know what Krishna wants." ∎

THE ONE WORLD FAMILY: THE MESSIAH'S WORLD CRUSADE

by Richard Fairfield

I FIRST BECAME AWARE OF THE ONE WORLD FAMILY OF THE Messiah's World Crusade some three years ago (1968) through the Berkeley Barb. The news report in the Barb told how Allen Noonan, founder and leader of the Crusade, had been busted for possession of marijuana and dragged off to jail. The report continued, "Noonan, who is 52 … is hoping that flying saucers will intervene in his behalf by blocking traffic on both sides of the San Francisco bridges. Help may be offered at 1387 Haight Street. Flying saucers should be directed to either bridge."

Oh well, I thought, another kooky commune leader. Haight-Ashbury communes had a very short and chaotic lifespan at the time, so I dismissed this group as typical of the genre.

Time passed and I still heard whispers of the continued existence of a group called The Here and Now Commune or Messiah's World Crusade. In the summer of 1969 I read an article in another underground paper that described the group in more detail. It stated that the commune consisted of a core group of about 20 people, together with temporary visitors who came, experienced living there a while, and then left. This experience involved working to create Allen's vision of a world environment containing "creative schools of experience, providing food, clothing, shelter, care, recreation, and transportation for all of the people on the planet as one family." The people of the commune held all things in common, with each person giving according to ability and receiving according to need. They operated a pure-food macrobiotic restaurant in San Francisco and published a newspaper called The Universal Communicator.

I was sympathetic toward the humanistic ideals of The One World Family, but as a "liberal" I just couldn't stomach all that strange talk about flying saucers and an inspired Messiah.

In 1970, the Messiah's World Crusade took over the famous Forum restaurant on Telegraph Avenue in Berkeley and turned it into a natural foods restaurant named the Mustard Seed. Thursday through Sunday, from 7 to 11 p.m., The One World Family Band and Chorus performed at the restaurant.

One day I received a letter from Dian, the group's secretary, inviting me to do an article on their commune. With the literature she enclosed a letter talking of Allen as a psychic, "adept at channeling high potent energies from the Higher Extraterrestrial Beings who are guiding our planet into the New Age … He is a

Messiah, a Messenger—not a Savior, for there is nothing to save. Each man must save himself from becoming a slave to matter, by raising his consciousness through service to humanity."

I could not help being reminded of Robert A. Heinlein's great novel Stranger in a Strange Land, and I wondered why at this point in history so many minds were turning to a communal vision as a solution to societal stress and alienation. Sociological answers seemed inadequate.

As my own attitude toward Messiahs had broadened, I had come to feel that perhaps only a divinely inspired leader could possibly bring so utopian a vision into being. The literature from Dian continued:

"Right now decide to no longer go along with the worn-out status-quo system. Begin to form together with your friends into communes, holding all things in common, helping, loving, and lifting one another into the New Age ideas. Use our U.S. Constitution and Bill of Rights in their true essence. Only by building a complete alternative healthy environment now will we ever avoid a violent revolution.

"Right on!" I exclaimed, and rushed to the phone to call Dian to make an appointment to visit the commune and talk with Allen.

"Allen has been taken to Vacaville for three months' observation," Dian said. "They want to figure out what makes him tick." She invited us to interview her instead. Consuelo and I arrived at an impressive, two-story house that was situated on a hillside and surrounded by trees and luxuriant greenery. We tried the front door but there was no answer. Hearing voices around the back, we made our way there and came upon Dian, sitting in the sun, totally naked and unafraid, her belly large with child. She was sure to have that baby (or several, I imagined) any day.

Dian went inside to dress. We sat talking to her amid constant interruptions from the telephone and the people of the commune. She was a friendly and conscientious hostess. Despite all the interruptions, she kept coming back to us to continue explaining about the commune and responding to our questions.

Dian was in charge of things at this house in Larkspur; she was also the community's secretary and bookkeeper: she who controls the purse-strings controls the commune.

Allen, as we already knew, was at the California State Correctional Institute at Vacaville, where he was being examined by a team of psychiatrists. The history of how he got there begins with his early days in Southern California. There, beginning in 1947, he preached his gospel and set up communal living groups. Whatever his success or lack of it, he eventually headed north and wound up in San Francisco in 1966 to begin his glorious mission in the Haight. He was greeted with enthusiasm and became the focus of a commune, which materialized around him in a big mansion on Oak Street.

Allen became well known in the area, and the word leaked back to southern California where a Bircher-oriented businessman (who had attended one of Allen's meetings) informed the San Francisco authorities that Allen was dangerous and a source of corruption regarding the morals of youth. An undercover agent was sent to entrap Allen. He succeeded. Allen was charged with the sale and possession of marijuana, with bail set at $10,000. (Marijuana is known to be used by most hip citizens in the San Francisco Bay Area. But the police rarely invade the privacy of people's homes to find it. If they did they would have to build hundreds of jails to house the offenders. The people who are charged with selling or possessing marijuana are usually those who the authorities decide are misbehaving on moral or political grounds, not legal ones.)

Allen's followers responded by sponsoring benefits at The Straight Theater in order to raise money for bail. Although these benefits did not raise the required funds, they did bring the commune together and, as Dian observed, "we had a lot of fun." Bail bond was finally obtained for Allen, but the police then charged another commune member with possession of marijuana. Apparently connected to this was the judge's decision to increase Allen's bail to $25,000. So Allen had to return to jail, where he remained for five and a half months more. A hip lawyer came into the case on Allen's behalf, but it was still impossible to raise bail. As money paid for bail bonds is forfeited, the commune was not enthusiastic about spending $25,000. Finally, someone put up a building as collateral and Allen was released.

In November 1969, Allen was put back in jail for the third time; the property put up as collateral for bail had been foreclosed upon. At his trial almost two years after being charged, Allen was found guilty despite a great deal of testimony on his behalf. The judge acknowledged the special nature of the case and offered Allen two options: first, to go to jail for two years; second, to go to Vacaville for a 60–90 day period and then be returned for further consideration. Allen chose the latter.

Allen's incarceration provided him with the time to continue the writing he had been engaged on for the past 22 years. Because he is such a high person, Dian explained, people wanted to be around him all the time, especially when he was at the commune. Under those circumstances, he had little time to write. Now, in prison, he was writing much more, preparing the text of his gospel to spread the word of the New Age across the planet Earth.

"Allen [at that time a commercial artist] was painting a sign in 1947," Dian explained, "when a bolt of white light hit him and his astral self traveled to another planet where Higher Extraterrestrial Beings, known as Angels in the Bible, asked him if he would like to be the Messiah of mankind. He thought a while about how Socrates was forced to poison himself and how Jesus was crucified. After ridding himself of these negative fantasies, he said 'sure.' Through automatic writing, letting the Higher Beings guide him, he began to write The Plan that would create Absolute Freedom, Security, and Abundance to all People as One Family."

I was anxious to discover how they actually ran the commune, so I abruptly changed the subject.

"What about the current practical operations of the commune?" I asked. "You advertise openly. Don't you get a lot of people here who just want to be taken care of, who don't really want to do any work?"

"Yes, we do once in a while," Dian replied. "But we find that most people want to serve and if they aren't doing anything it's because they don't know what to do. That's what we're here for—to show them. Sometimes all people need is a little push. Everyone who lives in our communes has to work eight-hour shifts at one of our restaurants. We've had a few people who thought they were being sent off like slave laborers. Well, they just weren't ready to join with us, so they left.

"Some people haven't learned the joy of service yet. We're working toward a time when everyone serves everyone else. From each according to his ability to each according to his need.

"Most people come into the commune with far too many material possessions. Many do not need more clothing, for instance. But when they do, they simply go to the bookkeeper and get the money to purchase what they need. Yes, everyone tends to think he needs something over and above what we really know he needs. We talk it over and come to an understanding.

"Ideally we share all things in common, including sex. But, of course, people are in different places and we feel it's okay for there to be couples who rely more heavily on one another, or who want to share the same room together. We make sure that each person in this transition stage has a physical place he can call his own. A place where he can go to be alone. We know ideally that privacy can be had without the necessity for private space, but at this stage we know also that people have to work through the conditioning of the old order. We allow for that. We deal with the jealousies and hang-ups of the Old Order as best we can by continually keeping aware of our vision of the New World Order, where all will share equally all the resources of the world as One Family.

"This house is becoming the children's house. We have 17 adults and eight children here. Two adults per week take turns with the children. Just being around helping them when they need help. We believe children are happier when they spend most of their time with other children.

"Our other house in Berkeley operates as The Basic Schools of Experience. Our band and chorus practice over there and we're putting together a light show and multimedia environment. We encourage outlets for people's creative and artistic talents."

Dian stopped, and then asked, "Would you like to see this house?"

She showed us around. When we first entered the meditation room, a young man with a crew cut and athletic shorts was sitting on the floor bending and flexing his legs. He looked like a college basketball player just off the court. There were lots of colorful rugs spread out on the floor, with chairs and a couch against the walls—no table or plants. On one wall hung a painting, on another some flyers with photos of Allen. It was called the meditation room for still another good reason: the children obeyed the rule of no shouting or loud noise in this room.

The house had two children's rooms to accommodate both older and younger children. Several smaller rooms all tastefully and simply decorated provided living quarters for single adults and couples. One room was occupied by a painter who was doing signs for the restaurants. None of the rooms were occupied on a permanent basis as each person rotated from place to place according to individual and communal needs. We found the somewhat cramped kitchen crowded with members, for it was approaching the dinner hour. And in a room adjoining the kitchen, bread and pastries were being prepared for one or both of the restaurants.

Outside near the sun porch, one of the members had recently built a sauna bath from wood and other scavenged materials. It cost less than $100, he claimed. It was a fine-looking structure resembling a huge square puff of cotton candy at a fair. The pink fiberglass insulation was still to be covered by plastic. Near the sauna was a small homemade pool, and in a large open space off to one side, four old doors had been covered with aluminum foil and braced on their sides at right angles to one another to create a solar bath. Jim, the architect of all these healthful creations, asked us to stand inside it. "Hot, huh! Stay in there for a few minutes and you can get scorched." Consuelo and I exclaimed our delight, and he offered to furnish plans for The Modern Utopian so that every commune could have its own inexpensive health spa. We said "Great!" He seemed to want more approval so we repeated our exclamation. He followed us around the yard. We finally slunk away, returned to Dian, and agreed to visit the Berkeley house on Sunday.

Rejoicing in the Words of the Messiah

Sunday, every Sunday morning, the Messiah's World Crusade meets as a whole family—One Family—at the communal house in Berkeley. The restaurants are closed and the Larkspur and Berkeley members come together for song and for rejoicing in the Word of the Cosmic Messiah, Allen.

The house was a new structure, a few years old at most. The furniture and decor included wall-to-wall carpeting, ceiling-to-floor windows, and sliding doors in the front. Consuelo and I entered the living room and sat on the floor next to a couch, which I leaned upon. There were perhaps a dozen other people there. One fellow was stretched out on the floor drawing a mandala of sorts on a huge pad of paper. Mostly, the people just sat quietly and waited. After about 30 minutes a lightly built, well-tanned man entered and sat on the floor. He wore a small cap on his head, casual clothes, and a slightly ascetic look. He was older than the others in the room, probably in his late 30s. He completed his image with two bright solid-colored socks, one yellow and the other Chinese red. The woman who accompanied him was also well tanned, possibly his age or slightly older. She had long gray hair and a brilliant smile that showed a large set of sparkling white teeth.

There were now 30 or 40 people in the room. They made up the most varied crew of people that could be imagined under one roof—longhairs, shorthairs, guys who looked like they just got out of prison, guys who appeared to be inmates of business corporations, girls who appeared bright and active, girls with a spaced-out look, and a few children for whom many of the girls enjoyed playing mother.

Someone shouted for musical instruments. While these were being obtained, a young girl distributed the Crusader's songbook. We began to sing a combination of gospel and rock tunes, mostly written by the commune members themselves. "Victorious Gospel" was one.

> *We're going to love you right into Heaven—*
> *It's here on earth*
> *We're going to give it birth*
> *Come on and kiss the earth.*
> *Victorious Gospel*
> *We're going to take it to the world.*
> *If you want to take part in the start of a miracle*
> *You can be of and in the Messiah's World Crusade.*
>
> *Shouts erupted from various members of the audience.*
> *"Right On!"*
> *"Far Out!"*
> *"Let's Get It On, Brother!"*

Then Michael—he of the yellow sock and Chinese-red sock—got down to the first order of business, which was to introduce Sid. Sid was the man responsible for helping the commune obtain and set up its current natural food restaurants. Although not a member of the commune, he was a sympathetic businessman with 22 years of experience in restaurant sales and service. However, many of the members felt that Allen's latest message, a five-page typewritten article, should be read first, before Sid addressed them. Allen's message was of such import to them that they did not want to wait. Dian had given me a copy of it when she arrived. I followed along as one of the commune members read aloud:

Out With The Old, In With The New

To proclaim anything less than absolute freedom, security and abundance for every person on this planet as one family is sheer nonsense. Absolute freedom, security and abundance now for everyone must be the VISION OF THE PEOPLE'S REVOLUTION ... There are no shortages of anything except the will and understanding to make things right. Righteousness begins with self-sacrifice and self-discipline. What will you give up so that the Kingdom of

God or the true communism combined with the true democracy can come in at this time?

When we try to give up things, we see that only the things that were not good for us in the first place are falling away and a new government is emerging in our midst. This is not a government made by men, but a government made by the Universe which is now being written in our hearts.

It is unnatural to buy and sell merchandise for profit. No one is condemned because they have done this, but at last the time has come when it is no longer necessary. The One World Family is demonstrating in our communes the way all foods and services can be freely at everyone's fingertips, so there are no hang-ups to creating a world of absolute freedom, security and abundance for all who share and care. Those people who care enough about their eternal evolving to put first things first are now coming together to build a completely New Age.

After the article was read, Sid told the group that the Berkeley restaurant was not financially viable at present and he urged them to set up a system of more efficient operation. He suggested that the restaurant was not only a possible source of income but also a possible means for recruiting new members into The One World Family. He told them that another restaurant could be opened by them in Berkeley in a prime location if they could handle it.

The commune saxophonist gave a long and enthusiastic discourse about how they had already improved services at the Berkeley restaurant and were now ready to expand facilities in order to communicate the Word of The One World Family. He interspersed and concluded his talk with a few "right on"s and "let's get it on"s in which he was joined by several other people. It was now noon and time for the shifts to begin work at the two restaurants. Michael noted, "Well, if we're a little late getting started today it means this has been an important meeting." Plans were then made for the discussion of various projects. People who were interested in more information about the Crusade or who wished to join were to meet in an adjoining room following the meeting session. Some members planned to meet in the music room later that afternoon to record tapes for playing at the restaurants and elsewhere. People interested in working on construction of a multimedia environment also planned to meet. Still other plans had to do with a recently purchased bus which was to convey band and chorus to schools and churches or any other organizations that might invite them. Michael then asked all people who were supposed to be working on a shift to leave.

A guitarist and a slender girl with bright eyes and a round face led the session for potential new members. While waiting for everyone to get settled, a baby-faced young girl sang a few songs of her own composition in a soft mournful voice. Everyone was called upon to introduce himself and state his interest in The One World Family.

One very straight-looking guy smiled pleasantly and said he only wanted more information. He told us he worked in Planned Parenthood. The guitarist leader appeared not to have ever heard of that organization. When he finally understood, he explained that the birth-control method used in the commune was the natural way; members followed "vibration levels." Now it was me who did not understand; I guess I was not alone, though, for the Planned Parenthood employee left. The baby-faced folk songstress said she lived in a similar commune in Minneapolis and had been called by God to come to this one to live a while and find out if the two groups could collaborate.

A long blond-haired guy with a pinched look about him said he was ready to join and do the work of the Crusade. I had thought he was already a member; his enthusiasm was such that he had joined in on every exclamation of "right on" and "let's get it together" during the morning session.

A guy in old khaki pants, shirt, and jacket he looked like an Army reject stated quietly that he wished to join.

A young Jewish girl curled up on a chair in the corner said she didn't like the religious nature of the commune although she believed in the ideals. When pressed to explain, she got angry and said she never could find a place to join as there was always something about it she could not go along with. When the five Crusade members tried to convince her of the true nature of their religion, adding doses of liberal comments like "You can accept all or any part of this that you wish," she came back even more angrily with "I don't want to join a commune now; I'm too fucked up to join anything right now."

Then Michael came in and began to talk about a number of topics: first, about how important the shift schedule was to the Crusade and everyone had to take his turn at the restaurants; then about Allen as the Cosmic Messiah, bringing the true message to the world. Next, Michael asked those present who wished to serve in the Crusade to see him in order to get on the shift.

A girl with frightened eyes said she was joining and planned to live at Larkspur near her boyfriend, Brian, who was already a member. Michael continued discussing how the shift schedule worked. He noted that it always worked out fine when certain people wanted to be near other people on the shift schedule. There were two shifts for each restaurant and one for each house, it was all worked out. "But isn't that extremely difficult?" I inquired. "Aren't there many who prefer to be with one person or another, at one time or another?"

"Yes," Michael smiled, "but they learn that it isn't necessary. I get it all worked out," he pointed to a schedule book he had on the floor.

"I want to be with Brian," the scared-eyed one emphasized.

"Okay, my dear," Michael replied indulgently. "Let me make a note of that." The schedule book fell open and miscellaneous scraps of paper flew out. Michael hastily gathered them back into the notebook and began to talk of the importance of the Crusade in creating a New Age where absolute freedom, security and abundance would be available to all the peoples of the world as One Family.

Consuelo and I introduced ourselves next. I remarked that there seemed to be no mechanism for personal growth operating within the commune. Also, I did not see them dealing with conflict and personal frustration adequately. For instance, I observed, during the morning meeting one fellow had made a negative comment and either it was ignored or subjected to such pressures as "Wow, man, you're bringing us down; we only have one meeting together as a family per week and now you're trying to bring us down."

One member explained that personal growth was achieved through service to others, by the work and activities of the Crusade. Another noted that the despondent member had been dealt with adequately in the meeting. Now Michael took up the Bible and began to read and interpret the book of Daniel as the prophecy of the Coming of Allen, the Cosmic Messiah, and the Messiah's World Crusade: "And at that time shall Michael stand up, the great prince which standeth for the children of thy people: and there shall be a time of trouble, such as never was since there was a nation … and at that time thy people shall be delivered, everyone that shall be found written in the book…"

Michael read and interpreted for about an hour, and the Jewish girl got up and left. I went to piss. When I came back Michael was explaining a passage and its relationship to the present. At some point, our ex-group leader, the guitarist, said, "Okay, but I think we'd better get on with—" he gestured toward the other two potential new members, neither of whom had yet had a chance to introduce themselves.

"Right!" said Michael, and resumed reading aloud, picking up where he had just left off in the passage from Daniel.

I laughed heartily as an obvious cover-up of the hostility I was beginning to feel toward Michael. He reminded me of a New England preacher I had to work with one time while in theological school. That man, too, had been caught up in the flame of his own ego, reading the true word, impervious to others around him.

The pinched-look one continued to intersperse his enthusiasm—"Wow! Far out! Read that again! You know, I really believe it!" Michael responded to the compliment by fanning his ego.

Soon, however, even the intersperser was saying, "Yes, Michael, I believe it but I'm hungry now. Let's go eat." It was mid-afternoon. I urged Consuelo to go, but she insisted on staying until the other two strangers had been introduced.

But Michael talked and read on. I began to look vacantly into space.

"Astrology is an important science to study in this day and age, isn't that right, Dick?"

"I don't know. I haven't studied it very much," I replied. Michael and others then talked about the relationship of astrology to the Messiah's World Crusade. "Wow, Michael, I really love your socks," I said abruptly yet sincerely.

Michael stopped talking and beamed for a full five minutes. The most beautiful smile I've ever seen shined on his face and washed away all my hostility.

We decided to make a day of it by eating at the Berkeley restaurant. When we arrived, the place was crowded and there appeared to be only one waiter on the floor. We sat there, waiting, and passed the time by watching several commune members going to the kitchen and bringing out elaborately prepared dishes of food and then leisurely eating them. After about half an hour, the waiter, balding with long hair in the back, took down our order. I noted that there were now two waiters, but that several tables had been occupied and vacated without service. We too almost got up to leave after waiting still another half hour, but finally our food arrived. We shared a delicious meal of rice, vegetables, and so-called "macroburgers."

The crowd thinned out. Then Michael, his sidekick, and several other commune members arrived to eat and serve. Several members took up jobs, waiting on tables. Michael came up to us and began his spiel about the Crusade. We told him that they hadn't had enough help on the tables earlier.

"We operate on a plane of higher consciousness," Michael replied. "We came in because we felt the vibrations that we were needed."

A Letter from The Messiah's Secretary

At my request, Dian kindly provided me with more information about the current activities of the Messiah's World Crusade. She wrote me the following letter in late February 1971:

The Mustard Seed Natural Foods restaurant was closed in June 1970 when the gentleman who was collecting our rent went bankrupt and the IRS requested we stop paying him and pay them. As soon as we did that, he closed up... the restaurant confiscated our musical instruments and forced us to move out. Since that time we've been maintaining our family at about 40 members, caring for our 11 children, baking organic whole wheat bread and distributing it to local health food stores and the Co-Op supermarket, catering natural foods to churches and happenings, presenting feasts at our Berkeley commune at the beginning of each zodiac sign. We've also been working hard on the Messiah's World Crusade newspaper which explains our mission and how the MAS-TER PLAN, channeled from the Higher beings and written down in trance by Allen, is the plan to synthesize the struggling yin and yang forces on this planet.

Now we are presently operating our two communal homes and offering room and board in the New Age style of living for a nominal fee to help pay the rent... This also is a good way for interested people to come slowly into the communal activity.

At the beginning of March we will again open up at the corner of Haste and Telegraph. This time we have the entire building at half the rent we paid previously, plus our band equipment Good Karma. This is the People's New Age Center....

We will be featuring benefits starting March 15 with all kinds of musical and live entertainment.... Our band and chorus are ready to do a recording of their original songs, inspired by the channelings of the Galactic Command through Allen.

Allen (out of jail on appeal bond) is compiling his channelings compositely called THE EVERLASTING GOSPEL and they soon will be published in several different books. Revelations Revealed, Nature's Potions, The People's Emergency World Government.

If you wish to help, let me hear from you,
Dian ■

FIVE WEEKS IN A NEW MEXICO YOGA COMMUNE

by Jan of Neverland Community

IN ORDER TO LEARN MORE ABOUT KUNDALINI YOGA AND BE-
come a teacher in this type of yoga I traveled to Santa Fe. About 12 people have
a small piece (15 acres) of desert land. The climate is tough, that is, when I was
there—freezing cold before sunrise, very hot in the daytime. We woke up at 3:30
or 4:00 in the morning, then it was cold. We chanted and meditated 'til sunrise
at 6:15 and then gradually everybody put away his three blankets, shirts, two pair
of socks, and gloves until only swimsuits lasted. There were about 12 visitors who
came to the Ashram for this summer program.

Dawson and Kara Hayworth had put together with other people of the Ashram a good program in which they taught organic gardening and composting,
herbs for healing, natural childbirth and much more. A prosperous health food
restaurant was part of the setup.

The garden was about one acre and had irrigation canals. The water came from
a well with a pump and a big water tank. Twice a week the garden was irrigated.
The idea was if you water too much and shallow you get roots near the surface. If
you water not much but a lot each time, then you get a deep, healthy root system.
There were all kinds of vegetables in the garden and there were also fruit trees.
They got fish extract stuff. The compost system delivered excellent compost in
three weeks. A one-foot-deep hole was dug, eight feet by six feet, and a wooden
frame of old orange crates was placed around it. Now layers of kitchen waste,
leaves etc., horse manure, and bloodmeal were put in the pile. About two or three
of these combined layers made up the pile. The pile has to be moist, so we sprayed
now and then. The first four days it heats up. Each week we turned the pile. Black
plastic was put on top.

The health food restaurant is, in terms of straight business, a disaster, but if you
don't pay wages, which was the case here, then this can change the picture. The
restaurant was called "Nanak's Conscious Cookery." Nanak was one of the most
important gurus of the Sikhs; he lived in the sixteenth century. Kundalini Yoga's
mantra and spiritual teaching is given for a large part by Guru Nanak. About four
people work in the kitchen and two or three people wait on customers. The place
specializes in East Indian food. The people make a yoga of the restaurant work
and the results are clear. People come back to the restaurant because of the good
vibrations put in every drink and dish. The yoga commune has a very good name

in the Santa Fe community largely through the excellent public relations by way of the restaurant. This is an important side effect! Also, you can buy cheap food for the commune itself.

The life in the commune was all directed toward god-realization. This meant people chanting during work in the garden, kitchen or wherever. Meditating together. Going to sleep with sunset, reading from the Adi Granth, the holy book of the Sikhs, with every meal, so the whole life was permeated with it. This can be a very heavy trip, too heavy sometimes when God is used for an escape in working out trouble on a personal level and problems pile up. "Relate to the God in the other" is fine, but emotions have to be expressed even if you relate to the personality for a little while. This is my personal opinion, of course. The yoga (postures, meditation, chanting, working, etc.) gave the people a great amount of energy and feeling of togetherness. Without it the commune trip in Santa Fe, with the poor soil, rough climate, short growing season, would be very hard to do as well as it is done here. The people of the ashram eat organic food and use brewer's yeast, lecithin, whey, herb teas, homemade yogurt and much more. In this way, all the people are in a very good condition and medical bills were unknown for a long time. Back to Eden by Jethro Kloss was the bible for all kinds of minor problems. One of the main health philosophies was one connected with digestion. If you are constipated regularly a lot of poison gets reabsorbed in the intestines and all kinds of illnesses are the result, not only illnesses of the digestive system but you can get the reaction everywhere. You are constipated if you cannot empty your bowels three to four times a day, the first time immediately when you wake up! Watching the food combinations you eat will get you there.

There is no visitors problem. Only 3HO (Happy, Healthy, & Holy) Kundalini Yoga people stayed and this was no problem. There is a kind of exchange in people between the ashrams of the organization (led by Yogi Bhajan). The five weeks were a very interesting experiment. I felt too constricted by the structure of the life, though. An easier-flowing lifestyle with more room for experimentation, also in the spiritual field (the incorporating of more trips) attracts me more. ∎

MEL LYMAN, AMERICAN AVATAR

by Fusion, *Underground Press Syndicate, (4/16/71)*

BACKSTAGE AT THE BOSTON TEA PARTY, THERE IN THE SAME room with The Incredible String Band. I want to speak to them, simply because of the effect that their performance has had on me. I have nothing to say, though so I wait, sort of dazed, looking on.

Robin Williamson talks with someone else someone from Boston. Suddenly I am listening sharply, that name has floated by again. Here is my excuse.

"Excuse me," I manage to say when their talk begins to dwindle and wander off, "but did you just mention Fort Hill?"

Robin Williamson turns to speak with me. "Yes, I did. I was saying that I had my dinner there last night." Friendliness, with distance and curiosity.

There was no other question to ask. "Do you know Mel?"

"Well, I've met him... I don't think you could say anyone knows Mel."

I smile and nod, but don't jump in with anything else to say. He begins looking away from me, glancing around the room. But I haven't had my conversation.

"I've heard a lot about him, but I've never known anyone who actually met him. What's he like?"

"He's like you and me, you know. He's a human being. He's got two eyes and a nose, and a mouth. He eats, sleeps and craps just like you and me..."

"Oh, yes, I understand that. But what sort of a person is he—what did you think of him?"

A careful moment. Then, "Mel Lyman is a man of strong intentions. Very strong intentions."

"Strong intentions... yes, I see..." still smiling. I look hopefully at him.

Then suddenly his face turns very cold. "You're asking quite a few questions, you know. Come on, out with it... you're fishing for something, aren't you?" Flash to the face of Robin Williamson on stage—joy and warmth, while in command of The Incredible String Band, now it seems a little, just a little, unreal. "Come on, what is it you're fishing for?" Hostility, and the eyes are hard to meet, so piercing with sudden anger.

I look back frightened and try to say evenly "I'm not fishing for anything... I'm just interested in Mel Lyman." But I can only hold his stare for a very few seconds.

Melvin Lyman comes from the state of Oregon. He was born in April, 1938, grew up and attended junior college there. In 1955, at the age of 17, Mel left home for California where he married and took a job as a computer technician.

Six years later, 1961, now 23, Mel Lyman dropped out of his job and life in California and headed across the country looking for a new life. In Asheville, North Carolina, he found Oberey Ramfay and learned from him to play the banjo. He became a superb banjoist; music was his new life. He played with The Jim Kweskin Jug Band. He was successful.

But he was more than a musician. He had an amazing personality. He had an enormous knowledge of people, and not only made friends but helped them to solve their problems. People would come to him with their difficulties and after a while he was teaching them how to live their lives. He taught them to live with the utter loneliness and pain of human life, not to try and escape into the scrabble for material goods or the dream of a drug existence. Above all, he taught them that they had to work.

Soon these friends of his, among them Jim Kweskin, gathered around Mel Lyman in a family commune. They could be open with each other. And they had something meaningful to work for—not for a new car or weeks of tripped-out cosmic consciousness—they worked for Mel. He was the beginning and end of the only life that they had ever come close to finding happiness in. Mel was God.

Mel Lyman and his family made a home for themselves. During the Revolutionary War, a tower had been built atop the highest point of land in Boston, overlooking the city and hundreds of miles beyond. The tower still stands on the top of Fort Hill in the middle of Roxbury, Boston's black ghetto. There is a small park there, for the tourists, and a number of old Victorian mansions. It was here on Fort Hill Terrace where Mel moved his family. The first purchase was made in August of 1966, when the Lyman family came to move in, remodel and clean up their first home. Today the Lyman family owns most of the houses around the park, and claims the Tower as well, although it still officially belongs to the city. It is an impressive sight to drive through the squalor of Boston's worst slums, up Fort Hill nearly above the smog, to find the neat, well-kept houses of the Lyman Family community.

When they moved in in the middle of the 1960s, Boston, perhaps more than the rest of the country because of its great student population, was bursting with a revolution of values and ideas. It demanded communication and expression. The new counterculture in Boston needed some outlet for the energy exploding from revelations that were happening every day, but there was none. In every medium that reached the Boston community, the establishment world had strict control.

So Avatar was born. Organized by writers and intellectuals from around Cambridge and Boston and members of the Lyman Family, it would be the medium for the Boston underground, allowing expression beyond the limits of local papers and magazines. It would bring the people together, give them the power to communicate and ally, a power they urgently needed as the city of Boston grew resentful of the growing legions of longhairs. The new underground paper would be named Avatar after Meher Baba, the god-man avatar who was just then gathering a name and recognition all over the world as the possessor of ultimate knowledge and experience. For equipment, Broadside Magazine offered the use of its offices. And Avatar became a reality.

The original editorial board was made up partly of Lyman Family members and partly of people who weren't disciples of Mel, but the actual power structure was confused and nebulous. No one wanted to be responsible for the slightest editing or censorship, yet not everything could be printed, and no one was at all organized—no one, except the Lyman Family.

Mel never came down from the Hill to involve himself in Avatar. He wasn't officially on the editorial board at all. But the determined force of disciples who represented him gently pushed through any measures he felt necessary. When one of the pieces he had written was corrected grammatically by Sandi Mandeville, managing editor of Broadside, before printing, the Lyman Family insisted that the same article be reprinted in its original form in the very next issue. Mel was a perfect writer, they said, his exact words were the absolute truth, and they were not to be tampered with. The next issue of Avatar carried Mel's article the way he had written it, along with an explicit note of reprimand to Sandi Mandeville.

As each new Avatar was created, the Lyman Family always grew stronger. They were the only ones who were unified, and with ferocious determination. For nearly a year, Avatar was the only underground voice in Boston. Their circulation was excellent, and each issue carried more of Mel's message, and more devoted praise of him by followers.

Avatar was suffering, though. The people in the Lyman Family simply didn't have the experience to produce as good a paper as they wanted. Gradually, new writers and editors, and not disciples of Mel, were allowed power on the Avatar staff. These people were interested in reporting news, and not simply communicating Mel's message to the world. Avatar assumed a new format: it came in two parts, an outer section, basically a newspaper devoted to underground news, and an inner supplement section devoted to Mel.

The inside Avatar was written by and about the Fort Hill community. The cover often consisted of a portrait of Mel by artist Eben Given of the Lyman Family. Mel himself wrote a number of columns: "To All Who Would Know," "Message from Mel," and "Telling It Like It Is," usually accompanied by one or more photographs of Mel or a sky shattered with thunderbolts. There were two write-in sections, "Letters to Avatar" and the lengthier "Letters to Mel." In his columns and replies to interested readers, Mel developed and spelled out the teachings of his personal philosophy. He was the Avatar, and the paper was his voice.

In December 1966, Avatar was brought on trial in Cambridge District Court on charges of obscenity. Between the time the charge was made and the arraignment in court, Avatar devoted its entire centerfold to the words FUCK SHIT

PISS CUNT. Avatar was now the cause of free speech. Attorney for the defense was a well-known Boston lawyer, Joseph Oteri. The trial developed into a parade of qualified experts and scholars from universities in and around the Boston community testifying to the redeeming social value of Avatar. They won the case, garnering immense fame and glory for Avatar, and for Mel Lyman.

In its edition for early April of 1968, Avatar carried the charter of the United Illuminating Corporation. In it, Eben Given pledged himself and the rest of the Lyman Family:

Dear Friends,

I have written a charter that includes and defines everything I know. I have lived a thousand years in a day and a night, talked with you all, been still, slept, gotten up again and written—knowing through the sharpest pains of my own inadequacy and Limitation—the greatest that I have ever known in all my life—that what must finally be written and signed by all of us today, can only be written as my first picture of Mel could only have been drawn—when the last resources of my own separate talent had been exhausted—when I had seen so deeply, and suffered so deeply that there was finally nothing left of me to draw WITH. And the picture came.

It is not my own private pain. I suffer it as each of you has suffered it and will continue and must continue to suffer it. It is the pain of being consumed, of having every last vestige of separateness between that which we have felt and come to know more deeply than all else, which is incarnated forever, for all of us in Mel which is our heart, burned away that we may be free that HE may finally be freed. It is the pain of being born.

Today we simply incorporate ourselves as Mel Lyman. The definition rests with all that we can attest together as the larger embodiment—through us to all men of the purpose and the practice of one pure man. Today is our birthday—March 21st, 1968.

Mel rapidly became one of the most controversial figures in Boston. His advice to readers seemed sincere and compassionate, yet he claimed to be God and answered his detractors with ruthless hostility. Much of the writing in Avatar was terrifically creative and sensitive, but whole pages were often spent in what seemed to be pointless praise of Mel—his looks, his words, his every characteristic described as most beautiful and sacred. When the Lyman Family, with Jim Kweskin, performed at the Club 47 and stopped playing to relate Mel's wisdom to the audience, the evening ended in fighting.

One day in the late spring of 1968, one of the non-disciples on the Avatar staff, a powerfully built black man who wrote under the name of Pebbles, made his way to the top of Fort Hill and demanded to see Mel. Naturally he was told that he couldn't just see Mel, that he would have to wait until Mel wanted to see him. No one could stop him, though, and he went right to Mel's house and knocked on the door.

It was opened by Mel's wife, Jessie Benton Lyman, who refused to let Pebbles in. They argued for a while, then finally Pebbles loudly announced that he was in fact God, and that he was a greater God than Melvin Lyman. Then he left.

The incident was a shattering experience for the people on Fort Hill. It was, above all, a fearsome breach of Mel's security. It was that day that Mel said, "Build me a wall."

Immediately the entire Lyman Family fell to work constructing a thick stone wall around Mel Lyman's house on Fort Hill. All other activity ceased. Work on Avatar by the Lyman Family stopped.

The people outside of Fort Hill were thrown into turmoil. They had obligations to advertisers, they had articles and news to publish, but the Fort Hill editors had abandoned Avatar.

After some squabbling for control of Avatar, a new editorial board was formed and voted in, headed by Charles Guiliano and David Wilson. The paper was completely redesigned. The cover of this edition, issue 25, nowhere included the title Avatar. It was a triumph for the unbelievers: the paper carried nothing but news, underground writing and photography, and Melvin Lyman wasn't mentioned.

In the early hours of the morning, just after the production work had been completed and the papers lay stacked around the Avatar office, a truck pulled up and Mel's disciples piled out. Without a struggle, every copy of the paper was surrendered to them. After it had all been loaded into the truck, the Lyman Family returned to the Hill and deposited the papers in the Tower, later to sell them as paper scrap.

The battling was not quite over. The Lyman Family now no longer had enough voting power on the board of corporate Avatar to produce a paper their way and still be able, legally, to call it Avatar. Soon, two papers appeared, Avatar and American Avatar. The two forces continued to struggle against each other but the fighting grew weaker and weaker. The revolution which they had borne had swept past them on to San Francisco and L.A., to Chicago and Woodstock. By the end of the summer, 1968, Boston Avatar had ceased publication. American Avatar appeared sporadically for another year, then it too disappeared. Mel's influence outside of his family and following rapidly dissipated.

Since that time, Mel and his family have been quietly working to ready themselves to bring Mel's word to the world. They have founded Lyman Family communes in New York City and Los Angeles. A magazine produced by the Lyman Family called Pluto appeared in New York, but it lasted only one issue.

Members of the Lyman Family work to keep up the houses on Fort Hill. Many of them hold outside jobs where they work during the day and turn their pay over to Mel. At night they return to help in repair work and to continue the construction of an intermedia studio. This studio will have facilities for four-track tape recording and a film center as well as a theatre for live performance. Meanwhile,

Mel has already made several films which he is waiting and negotiating to present entirely under his control in cinemas or on television. The Lyman Family has also released an album on Reprise with Lisa Kindred, and it was called American Avatar. Mel himself wrote the liner notes:

I've been waiting to get this record released for three years and it is finally only possible now because I played the tapes for Mo Ostin a few months ago and he loved them. Everyone I have ever played these tapes for has been deeply moved, it is great music. The force that drew us together to record this music is the same force that is always evidenced in great works of art, and like all great works of art this music was created to elevate men, we were merely the instruments. We played this music but we didn't make it, it passed through us like light through the darkness. And like all great works of art this music had to await its time, it even took a while for us to appreciate it. I have marveled at these tapes for years and have never ceased to find more and more in them, more grace, more perfection, more magic, more God. And now I have passed them on to Mo and he is passing them on to you in the form of a record album. This is no album, it is a miracle.

Mel Lyman

Today, Mel and the rest of his family are preparing and waiting: waiting for the day when the world is ready to receive Mel Lyman's message, when Mel Lyman's smiling face will appear on your television set to announce to you that he is God.

The message that Mel relayed to the world through his writing is, on close examination, a little confusing. He takes on, at different times, the postures of a number of history's well-known gurus and messiahs, while at the same time asserts only his own particular truth. Thus in Avatar number 14, in his column "Telling It Like It Is," Mel says of Eastern philosophers,

The sickest people I have ever met were long-term believers who could spout all this crap about "we are all one" and Karma and "reincarnation" till kingdom come, they explained the whole fucking universe away to their sick little satisfaction and then they curled up and died. Talk about insanity, that's IT!

Yet in the issue of American Avatar whose cover pictures Mel on a television set (it carries no information concerning date, volume or edition number), Mel seems to have something else to say. On page four, beneath a photograph of Wayne Hansen, one of the members of the Lyman Family closest to Mel, he writes,

The Buddha is with me. Never before in the history of this planet have we appeared simultaneously, this may give you some idea of that which we are going to accomplish. I am going to operate as the heart, CENTER, and Buddha is going to serve as the World

Mind. He will put into effect, as World Government, all that I am. In the past he has assimilated and become all the wisdom of the East. In this present incarnation he has undergone all Western experience and is now the master of World Thought. This is not the proper time to reveal His Name as he walks among you as ONE of you but believe me he is HERE. Rejoice, we are going to unite the WORLD!

This is also the issue in which Mel reveals that he is Jesus Christ. "I'm Christ, I swear to God, in PERSON," he writes, on page one, "and I'm about to turn this foolish world upside down... Love, Christ." On page 15, Mel is pictured sitting atop a television set. His legs are crossed in Yoga fashion, while the upper part of his body, with his hands clasped and his face turned upwards in a rapture of saints and apostles as portrayed in religious paintings of the Middle Ages. In the "fourth cycle," first issue of American Avatar, this letter appeared:

Dear Mel,
Now that Meher Baba has left his body, are you Meher Baba?
Love, Stephanie
New Mexico

Mel replies, "I am all that Baba was. But what's more, I am all that he wasn't." Mel leaves room for all of his readers to assume that he is into their trip, too, or that he has been, and now passed beyond it. Furthermore, by making these assertions in such an absurd fashion, Mel always leaves himself the out by saying to his detractors, "Can't you see that I'm joking? You must be a fool if you take me so seriously."

On top of this spiritual fence-straddling, Mel deliberately makes certain points confusing and unclear, after first saying that they represent his most important ideas, stated in the simplest terms possible. Avatar number 15 carried this exchange in the "Letters to Mel" section:

Dear Mel,
Saw my letter printed in Avatar No. 14. You do admit, then, that pride can be expressed as love. But by saying you are at war with everybody's pride, you put yourself in the position of one who would destroy rather than transform. Perhaps your choice of words did not really do you justice.

Sincerely, David Ames

"YOU certainly don't do justice to my choice of words, my ultimate meaning seems to escape you. Let me sum it all up for you so there will be no further misunderstandings in translation: I'm out to transform; the kind of pride that destroys transformation and destroy the kind of pride that transforms destruction; Got it!"

In one of Mel's earliest works, a paperback book entitled Autobiography of A World Savior, he simplifies 40 preceding pages of his philosophy like this:

Now I want to review all that I have said concerning the process of creation. We start with space. Space is nothing, it is neither life nor death. It is nothing. Nothing cannot exist and so nothing comes into existence as SOMETHING, as BEING. Space becomes BEING and being creates LIFE and life includes its opposite, non-life or DEATH. Life is CONSTRUCTION and death is DESTRUCTION. Construction is establishing ORDER and destruction is returning to CHAOS and the two are inherent polarities in all that is in existence....

... and so on for another five pages or so. Using the same sales technique as the one that sold the emperor on his new clothes, Mel closes his book on this note:

And now I have said my piece. And you may THINK you have understood. You may THINK you KNOW. I caution you not to take these words lightly. If you really know everything I have WRITTEN here then I hold you responsible to APPLY what you know. If you UNDERSTAND, if you KNOW, then YOU are a world saviour Too and if you DON'T you AREN'T...

Mel's exposition of his personal history and philosophy of life, particularly in this autobiography, contains a number of statements in addition to his identification of himself as God whose incredibility may confound even more than those who try to understand and criticize him. Autobiography opens with this startling pronouncement:

Long long ago in another time in another dimension on another planet I volunteered for an assignment the nature of which I knew little and in fact little would be known as I didn't possess the particular equipment necessary to translate such knowledge into contemporary understanding... I was to be an embodied purpose and that purpose was THE purpose.

Elsewhere in the book Mel articulates some more facts concerning the history of the world. Mel describes the emergence of the mind in men on earth as passing through three stages. The first of these developmental stages was the "concrete mind." The concrete mind was capable of organizing man's environment to suit him: that is, to deal with the material world around him. It appeared in an early race of men.

The second stage in the development of the mind was the "abstract mind." A second race of men were so put off by the use of the mind on a purely material plane that they avoided dealing with it at all and left the concrete side of their mental composition to lie dormant. Mel points out in some detail that this was just as bad as being concerned only with the material world since neither the concrete mind nor the abstract mind can realize complete spiritual fulfillment without uniting with each other.

Finally, a third stage was reached by the human mind. A third race of men developed both the concrete and the abstract mind at the same time, very nearly bridging the gap between themselves and spiritual fulfillment.

... This third race was the race of Aryans and they made it possible for the finer tuning and further development of the spiritual instruments to continue by their efforts to perfect the lower instruments whereas the orientals negated the use of the lower instruments and became insensitive to the material world which soon led them to believe it to be invalid and the Jews became insensitive to the SPIRITUAL world and soon believed IT to be invalid. Aryans never learned to SCHEME like the Jews or DREAM like the orientals but held both worlds to be equally valid and sought to UNITE them through the process of intellect and the descendants of these Aryans are the intelligent reasonable men of the world today, the THINKERS of this planet, and though they still have a long way to go it's at least a good start toward creating a heaven out of earth and an earth out of heaven.

All of these statement, like the statement that Mel Lyman is God, are so very outrageous that it is even a little difficult to believe that anyone would dare to say them if they weren't actually true, particularly when they are couched in such impressively intellectual and seemingly reasonable terms. They are even easier to believe when they are mixed in with ideas that are reasonable.

And much of what Mel has to say is indeed reasonable; not only is it reasonable but it is deeply moving, and evidences a great sensitivity to the human condition. It may not be entirely original—great proportions of it are very similar to the philosophies of Zen, Buddha, Nietzsche, Heidegger and other existentialists but this is hardly relevant, for Mel's words convey a sense of profound belief; they have the strength of deep sincerity.

The basis of all that Mel Lyman has to say is a feeling of intense loneliness, an aching, inescapable longing to find some meaning in an apparently empty and futile universe. Throughout Avatar, this hopeless longing is expressed a hundred different ways, in a hundred different voices.

> *I keep grabbing at the rose trees*
> *As I tumble downhill;*
> *And the thorns pile up*
> *At the bottom*
> > *Dan*

Mel responds to this pain by teaching that only if he feels pain can a man really feel anything else. He answers the seeming emptiness of the universe with the teaching that God lies unrealized in every man. This God, divine spirit, or soul has come out in great men at their greatest moments, and he cites Abraham Lincoln, Ben Franklin, Clarence Darrow and others as examples. Mel himself is simply a man who is pure God. Any man can strive to find God in himself and meaning in his life, however. Before he can realize his soul, though, he must struggle, and work, and suffer until he has totally exhausted himself, wept so much that he has no more tears to cry and no more hope to lose. Then, when the man's self has been totally erased, when he has truly given himself up, there will be nothing left but his soul, and he will have found God. To live meaningfully, a man must spend every instant of his life in that search, he must believe that nothing is more important than to make his thought and action this moment, right now, as well as every other moment in his life, as true and as perfect as he possibly can. When he achieves this, he begins to live his life in a state of grace which knows neither hope nor disappointment, neither complacency nor impatience, only the constant struggle.

It is beautiful philosophy and it is probably clumsy and presumptuous of me to try either to explain or to interpret. A sense of it can only be felt by meeting the people of Fort Hill and listening to what they have to say, or perhaps by rereading the old Avatars. To even begin to understand it, and to see what it means to Mel Lyman and the people who live on Fort Hill, is a deeply moving, a humbling experience. For to them it is the absolute truth of life. We had been working that day at the old Milton Town Hall, salvaging pieces from the abandoned building to be used on Fort Hill. There was Randy, the dropout from Harvard who had driven out with me from the Hill in my red truck; he seemed to like me. Then there was Kurt, wearing his hard hat, business-like, and Rick, good-natured and amiable. Ned, also friendly and warm, with his long jaw and evenly-cut face; he seemed to be in authority there, with some competition from Eddie, tall, dark and powerful, an Army veteran with an ironic sense of humor and steely disposition. As they read this, they are all probably laughing at these descriptions, for I was only with them a very short time, only just long enough for them to judge me.

Each of them had his turn alone with me, his chance to hear me answer the same questions. Why had I come? What did I want on Fort Hill? What was I looking for? I would admit that I had come on a writing assignment, but I would also say that I had come for myself, to learn why the Lyman Family was the Lyman Family, to try to understand why they had turned their lives over to one man, to Mel Lyman, and to try and conceive of how they could believe that he is God.

They would nod to what I said, and then calmly explain that there was no way I could possibly understand. Even the fact that I was trying to understand—to fit their beliefs into some sort of concept—made it plain how hopeless it was for me.

I could only feel it if I came to need it as much as they did. Then perhaps I might see what Mel Lyman meant to them.

They had their chance to see me when we were all together as well. While we worked as a team on each of the day's separate projects, they were watching me closely, testing me.

Near the end of the day, as we loaded lights into the back of my truck, Kurt spoke to me again, asking the same questions and more, asking what writing meant to me, asking what this assignment meant to me and why I had been chosen for it. Then the calm fell from his face; he grew very serious and intense. He told me then that he could see that I was too young and inexperienced to write about Fort Hill, that there was more there than I could see or write about in years. He told me that others, many others, had come to Fort Hill and tried to write about it. Always they had thought they understood, tried to fit it into their own scheme of the world, and ended up simply exploiting it for their own trip. It hurt him, he said, for Fort Hill was his life, and to see it cheaply used was naturally a great and very personal pain for him. I answered lamely that I would do the best I could, that that was all I could ever do, but even as I was saying that, he had turned away and started back into the building.

Inside, Randy told me we were breaking work for the coffee and sandwiches we had brought from the Hill, and I followed him down into the basement of the building. There, amidst the broken cement and other debris we stood eating, our breath clouding in the unheated night winter air.

"Paul here says he's come to find out all about us. He's a writer," Kurt began, between mouthfuls.

"Well, what do you want to know, Paul?" Eddie asked. "What questions do you have? We'll answer 'em right now." His eyes were growing colder as he watched me.

"There's nothing I want to know."

"Oh. Well, if there's nothing you want to know, then you must think you already know everything, right? Maybe you're wrong," Eddie cut in.

"There's nothing that I want to know, really. And if there was, it isn't something I could put into a question for you to answer."

"What's that supposed to mean?" Eddie flashed. "I mean, you come here saying you're a writer and you want to know all about us . . now I give you a chance to ask us questions and you say you don't want to know anything after all. Now come on…"

"You know what he tells me, Eddie?" said Kurt. "He says that they sent him because the other writers they wanted to come were too scared. He was the only brave one."

"Are you the brave one, Paul, is that right? Tell me, what is it that those other writers were afraid of and you weren't, huh?" Eddie leered down at me.

It went on like that for about a half-hour. They didn't want to hurt me, though, and the only threat came when Eddie said that things could have been a lot worse than they were. When I asked him how, he said, "I could have broken you in half." He could have, too, but after I had admitted that I was afraid, and said some other things as well, they left me alone. I had known it was coming, having spoken with other people who had visited Fort Hill and gotten the identical treatment, with practically the same words used in the dialogue. Throughout it all, Randy and Ned sat silently, their heads bowed and their faces turned away. Kurt and Eddie did all the talking while the others looked on.

They wouldn't speak to me ever again after that, but as they left to take all of the things we had spent the day loading onto my truck off of it to send me on my way, Rick suddenly turned to face me, alone in the hallway, and said, "Can't you see? There's nothing that we can say to you. Can't you see that we don't even understand it ourselves?" and there were tears in his eyes.

I am going to fuck the world
I am going to fill it with hot sperm

Mmm mmm, I can't wait

I am a giant erection
I am ALL COCK
… and the world
is ALL CUNT

                Mel

What goes on in the mind of Mel Lyman? What does he dream about at night, and what is his first thought when he gets up in the morning? Does he really believe that he is God, or is this his own personal joke on the world? Could it be that he simply believes in an ideal society, and this is the best way of packaging his product to sell it to the world? Does he claim to be God as an elaborate publicity technique?

It is entirely too easy to dismiss Mel as insane. Psychology is a suspicious science at best. Many of its most distinguished proponents could be accused of being paranoid megalomaniacs themselves—and far more dangerous ones than Mel Lyman. In all likelihood, if Jesus Christ himself, the Son of God, did actually appear on this planet, he would be immediately regarded as a lunatic. All of this is overshadowed anyway by the fact that it must take at least a little insanity to have a vision of the world whose glory and illumination could make life worthwhile, and this is the vision that Mel Lyman has. If Mel is crazy, it is distinctly a most wonderful madness.

It is impossible to say what goes on in Mel Lyman's mind. This is one of his greatest strengths. By keeping himself as he does, completely isolated, he remains a mysterious and awesome figure. He is a dark, intriguing character, living alone on Fort Hill, cut off most of the time even from his own family, a complete recluse. He keeps the infrequent company only of his most devoted followers, and there is no way that anyone else can put a finger on who exactly Mel Lyman is.

Mel began to gather followers around himself during the mid-1960s. It was a time of outrage and confusion, a thousand new and amazing ideas, each challenging the others to be the truth. LSD began by taking faith in the intellect apart; a sudden political awakening to our country's horrific crimes lent righteousness to violence; all the regulation, security and beliefs of an entire generation—which had fought the world's most terrible war to defend them—were swept aside: worthless and worse, irrelevant. To answer this bold, irresistible disillusionment came a flood of new perspectives on the world: cosmic, fantastic, spiritual—breaking the law for grass is good—money is, after all, only evil—but living in the street loses its nobility. Does acid awaken you to God?

One man had a simple explanation of the conflicted world, and he could back it up in person. Mel Lyman is God. Looking up from pain and bewilderment to see him standing there confident and reassuring, his people believed. A philosophy and approach such as Mel makes works best on people who are lost in confusion, just after they have been bombarded by a thousand new ideas.

This philosophy is appealing largely because of its amazing and simple earthiness. It's hard to live a life of struggle with nothing but ideas for guidance. This is what has happened to many of the 1960s revolutionaries. Today they have found rioting and organizing to be a futile expression of their anger and an extravagant use of their lives. Mel offers the satisfaction of substance; his family doesn't simply fight all day for "freedom." They build their own homes, repair them, go on to build a studio, make a tape or a film. In the end they can stand back and see that they've created something new, and each construction is proof for them of the meaning in their lives.

In a sense the Lyman Family is a missionary group, bringing the Truth of Mel to the world. They are new American spiritualists. Their heroes are the great Americans, such as Lincoln, Emerson and Ben Franklin, and the attitudes of the Lyman Family are a sampling of what America may be after it has finally polarized. They believe in good, honest work and have nothing but contempt for hippies who live out their lives in a drugged stupor. When they're finished with the day's work, though, they'll enjoy a little grass and rap, and agree that the Establishment is bullshit. They denounce Nixon for the games he's playing with the American people, then back Ted Kennedy for president in '72. Mel Lyman was born an American, and while he may be God, or on a mission from another planet, he makes no move to deny his traditional, conservative American heritage.

The Lyman Family is true to American form in its reaction to criticism, as well. They become hostile and belligerent, closing any argument out of their minds. They are not alone in this country, either. In the years since the mid-1960s a number of experiments in communal living and expression of new spiritualism have developed into tightly knit, almost fascist communities who believe that one man, their leader, has all the answers and cannot be denied. Manson was only a well-advertised example. There are many more in California and strung out through the Southwest and other rural areas in this country. Each one is a little knot of righteousness, and their people live like members of an exclusive club. Visitors are informed that they have come across a community unlike any other in the world. They have the Key, the final meaning in the universe.

They, like the Lyman Family, have seen something beautiful in the middle of cheap, ugly existence and are no clinging to it for a meaningful survival. The great ideals are there, the love and the freedom, but frantic pursuit of them has turned liberation into an escape of dreams. When the destructive forces in America begin their sweep of the "subversive elements" they will find them like Manson, sandbagged behind the walls of their houses, determined not to see how quickly the sinking reality they have shunned will swallow them up.

But even without the U.S. doom that is stalking them, they are stepping heavily on their own ideals, crushing them. In the Lyman Family on Fort Hill, they have kept their goals fixed firmly in view, and their simple faith, even rugged determination. But they have also become smug, imperious and inflexible. It is a home of openness, innocence and compassion, but for the entire outside world there is suspicion, hostility, blind hatred. Melvin Lyman and his family have had a beautiful vision, a dream of ending the world's emptiness and loneliness, of filling it instead with love. ∎

THE MUD PEOPLE

by Nola Express, *Underground Press Syndicate, 1971*

Jacques says:

Duke was with a rock band called Rhinoceros when I first met him, when I was going to law school at Florida State. Duke, who I now consider my guru, invited me to go to Connecticut, where he split from Rhinoceros, and with my assistance formed the Mud People.

A bunch of people came to see us, and we narrowed down our possible cohorts to skilled people, and not just a trip for boys and girls. Our first destination was New Orleans.

We now have four musicians. A drummer, bass and two guitars. We also have a choir. Everyone in the Mud People sings. At first we sounded like a bunch of frogs. But with time and patience it came together. We're rehearsing now and we're about a month away from recording Papa Dukie's Mud People.

We have an electronics engineer, and that's a full-time job around the campsite. We have a Reverend with us who does wonders along the River Road. We have a mechanic who takes care of the engines. We have two buses and two generators. We have a carpenter.

■■■

Jack says:

I'm one of the musicians. I met the Mud People about a month after they arrived in Louisiana. I enjoyed them tremendously and had gone as far as I could in the Quarter. After I joined the Mud People I continued to play on Bourbon Street a short while but didn't have the time and gladly gave it all up.

The women's skills? One is an artist. One is a folk singer. What are some of the other positions women have? Most of the women came with men, came attached to the men. They take care of the children and take care of the kitchen. There are seven men, five women and three children. Our women take pride. You wince, but most of the problem is that men don't know how to compliment women. Our women dig being women and don't interfere with the men's trip. The women have their artistic side, one is a good singer, two or three of the women sew. They take care of the clothing. Our situation allows the women the chance to be women. It allows them to grow as women, to be able to sleep if they want to. If they want to know the details they can, but they don't want to know the details once trust is established.

What gives the Mud People strength is Duke's leadership. Duke's word is law, that's the first thing. It sounds like a heavy discipline to live under but when you have trust in someone there is no question of abuse. There's a four-man board elected by the Mud People. The board is the decision-making body of the group. It makes Duke's job easier. It gives the rest of the group some part of governing. The responsibility of the position doesn't leave time for the personal. Sometimes I'm sure Duke would like to go on vacation. Duke is a metaphysician, a master of yoga, a master of Zen Buddhism. It's so broad. He's done so much. He's a magician. He's an artist. A musician. He is an ancient historian. The Mud People is his concept. There's nothing to question; it's a matter of acceptance. He sees so clearly, it's unbelievable. I trust his vision.

Our laws let me give you the concept. One thought, one idea, one concept, all pulling toward the same goal. Our laws are universal laws. Everyone shared what they knew of the truth. It's like if you and I have been together long enough, when we see something, we see through the same set of eyes. After a while we begin to relate to things through the same experience. It doesn't matter which of the Mud People go somewhere. When I return I'll run down the questions that were asked, and I'll run down my answers so that everyone knows.

Our trip is the universal trip. It takes a hell of a lot of discipline to maintain it. Without discipline you fall prey to the influences of nature. The first thing one's confronted with when joining the Mud People is communal living doing away with the "mysies" (that's mine, that's mine!). To be subject to moods is natural. A mood is an influence. If you are subject to an influence and you go down, you'll take somebody with you. We stay in high spirits. It takes discipline. Pass on the little thing that irritates you, to grit your teeth is discipline.

We have a law separating fact from opinion. It keeps everyone on facts. Everyone can have all the opinions they want. Your trip is your trip. But we don't have time for opinion to be a major factor. When you're dealing with a group of people as large as us, you keep your opinions to yourself. It works. Everyone has become very good at it. What's the truth of the matter. It forces you to get your trip together.

We have a law dealing with results. We don't deal in excuses, explanations or methods. We deal with results. Nobody promises anybody anything.

We formulated our laws as the group went along. When there was a weakness, we made a law. There is a law against the picky-wicky scratch disease. It amounts to letting something about someone put you uptight. That the people involved get together and settle it before it's a major issue is the law. We have guest laws. All guests are to be treated excellently. Because they're the people and that's what we're about.

Drug laws? We have very heavy laws concerning dope.

Our sex law is whatever, whatever. You have the freedom to do a domestic trip if you want to. The trip is freedom, freedom, freedom.

Our laws aren't things that force us. It's the direction we're aiming at. We call them our laws because that's the way we organize things.

We hope we're a good example of the harmonious unit. The idea being to get our trip together to be of aid to others. One of the things we did over Christmas, we sold raffle tickets on a color TV and sold chances on matchboxes of money. We took them everywhere. We raised enough money to come to New Orleans a few days before Christmas to buy clothes, socks, pajamas, and we got these for kids who didn't have any of these things. On Christmas day the place was packed. The tent was filled. It was good for the head. The people on the River Road dug it because instead of words it was results. We've thrown barbeques for sick people to establish a trust relationship and to be of aid to the people.

Three hundred years ago, before Louisiana was in America, a black cat brought his family from Ethiopia. He would walk up and down the Mississippi looking for work. He ran across a white cat who had no money and paid him in land. He kept the work up and the white cat kept the deal up. They did this for two generations. It came out to 49 square miles. That came to be St. John the Baptist parish. The family has never felt the strong lash of segregation because they've owned their own land. The family has a seer, an old man. He is like the family uncle and Duke is his prince who will take over the job of seeing for the family when the time comes.

The religion they brought from Ethiopia was Islam. Their songs are Islamic mantras. When Christianity hit the South, it hit hard. Christianity replaced Islam but they kept the mantras and added Christian words. They create an unbelievable spirit.

For three days in April, we will present Calvary, a three-day gospel festival at the 2nd Ward Stadium in Vacherie. It'll be for all the people in River Road, New Orleans, Baton Rouge. All the local politicians have said right on, because it's for Jesus. We got the Five Blind Boys, we got 125 choirs from up and down the Road and New Orleans. We got 100 ministers who are going to do the Stations of the Cross. For the three days we're going to film it and record it. Warner Brothers is going to come and do it. And we'll make albums out of it. We're capturing a culture at its tail-end. ■

IN WARWICK WITH BROTHERHOOD OF THE SPIRIT

by Terry Mollner

"WE ARE SLEEPING, 9 A.M. TO 5 P.M." WAS THE FIRST INDICATION I had that I was coming upon the Brotherhood of the Spirit farm in Warwick, Mass. It was on a sign on a tree. I laughed figuring it meant something figuratively. However, in a few moments I was speaking to Scott who told me it was for real. "There is more positive energy present in the stillness of the night than in the harshness of the day, so all two hundred people now in the Brotherhood sleep during the day and move about by night."

The next thing my eyes fell on was a huge building that looked like an undecorated Bavarian lodge. It was four stories high including the basement and must have been 40 feet by 120 feet. A hundred yards from it, via a raised wooden walkway built to allow the grass to grow, is a large farmhouse with an extension on the back that used to be a large country restaurant. Scott took me inside the restaurant which is now the meeting room and dining area. It was 5:30 and all were just waking up and moving toward the meeting room to gather for a meeting.

Within moments of rapping to Scott I heard the words I was to hear over and over again from everyone during the two days I spent with the Brotherhood: "negative energy," "positive energy," "vibrations," and "spirit." On the ceiling above my head in the meeting room I could read the basic tenets of the Aquarian Gospel, their guiding light which gave me the context for understanding exactly what they meant when using those words.

Quietly all gathered. Someone began an "om" which flowed on powerfully for a good 10 minutes. After its death someone suggested reading from the Aquarian Gospel. A girl retrieved it and another read a passage from it. This was followed by different people sharing significant experiences, insights, and dreams that they had had. During most sharing Michael was quoted or referred to. It was clear that he was their leader. During a silence someone asked the visitors to leave. I later learned that this was done because the visitors seem to drag down the positive energy in the Brotherhood and it is bothersome.

A while later we returned to this room for a breakfast of Cream of Wheat, oatmeal, and molasses. (All but one of the meals I had while there were either the above or rice and vegetables. The exception was an evening meal of fish which we had one morning.) From the people I was eating with I discovered that there are now over 200 people in the Brotherhood. Beth Backman, a former instructor at Greenfield Community College, and her husband Bob have donated their house in Northfield, Mass. (a few miles away) to the Brotherhood where some are staying. They see themselves as learning to become one with the spirit, pure energy, as Michael is. They see him on the highest level of spirituality.

Michael Metelica is 20 years old, and although all refer to him as Michael and the "Spirit in Flesh" they balk at any reference to him as a Christ, Messiah, or such. However, my experience was that their words differ from their actions.

The second day I was there it was learned that Michael was coming to meet with them. All gathered in the meeting room. As they waited they sang songs full of energy and enthusiasm. When Michael arrived silence fell on all. All stared constantly at him as he stood at the entrance speaking with an older man, not of the commune, about something. Visitors were not allowed in. However, I wanted to hear what he was to say to them, so I went outside and stood by an open window and listened.

Michael sat above the crowd on some stairs that led to a balcony bedroom. He made all decisions and all agreed with his judgement on things. He had decided that another farm was needed and two straight-looking fellas were to start looking for one. Then many questions were asked of him concerning personal troubles people were having and he explained each for the questioner. Throughout there was a casual, happy yet intense atmosphere in the room.

The biggest burst of enthusiasm came when he said, "Wow, I've been going through something heavy." Midst the vocal mumblings of expectation people could be heard shouting, "Tell us, tell us…"

Michael told of a dream he had been having about one of his former lives when he was Ciaphus or some such name, a 23-year-old soldier that was made a general when his father died. At the age of 25 he led 35,000 men in battle against Hannibal and conquered him. Upon returning to Rome people hailed him as their leader. But some people saw him as doing it for the power and turned against him.

Then he told of another dream where he saw four people in the brotherhood, and he indicated to them, turn against him. Then he, being true to himself as he always is, left explaining that he does not fight. All in the brotherhood followed him and the four asked him to return.

He then explained that he had been a leader in all of his former lives but people turned against him because they were jealous and saw him as being after power. He explained that he has never wanted power. He has only wanted to fulfill his destiny to lead the world in the way of the spirit. He feels in his gut that he will do it in this life as a rock star. He told of his fear that some may turn against him as they have in the past when the album comes out and people begin treating him like a star.

With that the meeting broke. All left high as hell. He promised them that the record would be a hit and that they would be the guiding light to the new world. I found Bobby, a girl I had become friends with the night before, and told her that I found his words beautiful yet his actions contrary to them. She told me how "filled" she was after listening to Michael, filled with energy and beautiful vibrations. She explained to me that Michael does not want to be seen as a Christ or leader and that he is just fulfilling his destiny. He wants nothing for himself. He is pure love, energy, spirit.

From here Michael and the band members and all that wished to hear went to a nearby building to rehearse. I entered as Michael was cussing out the drummer from every angle and making him get in touch with the vibrations as he played the drums. When they broke a fella named Peter from New York City had told me earlier that he had come to get advice from Michael, ask him for advice. Michael swung around in a swivel chair for a few minutes contemplating. Then he told Peter exactly what was happening inside him in clear, direct language. Peter listened without saying a word and later informed me that it was fantastic and that Michael "sure was right." I have forgotten exactly what he said as I was sitting at a distance and unable to hear clearly, but I remember feeling it was rather general. Yet I marveled at his power.

The Brotherhood is full of energy and faith. Throughout the East Coast and beyond one will find posters made from their silkscreening presses in the attic of their huge lodge with Michael's picture and the words Spirit In Flesh. And I mean everywhere: walls, telephone poles, freeway bridges, construction sites, etc. A group even traveled to the New Mexico communes to bring the word but returned proclaiming, as one did to me, that there was "a lot of negative energy out there." This week (first week in July) their album is being released. Hundreds of copies are on order in the Amherst record shops. While I was there I helped them make some of the thousands of posters that will be included in the albums. I met a fella in the health food store the other day who has heard the album. He said that he didn't think it was really good but "man, was it intense."

To be a member of the Brotherhood you have to be willing to follow the 15 rules:

1. No drugs.
2. No alcohol.
3. No smoking.
4. No promiscuity.
5. Stay clean.
6. No overnight visitors.
7. All material in Michael's name.
8. Persons under 18 must have parental consent.
9. Pay off all debts before joining.
10. Prospective members must participate in all activities.
11. No relationships between members and prospective members.
12. Prospective members must stay two months before joining.

13. Group meeting before prospective member joins.
14. No prospective members on teaching trips.
15. Lifetime commitment to self and community

Their life is very austere. Money is never a problem. They believe that if you have faith it will be present when it is needed. Other than rule number 15 there are no demands on anyone to work. Yet much is accomplished.

Also, they have made many positive impressions on the community. . . and many negative ones also. One morning I took a walk and I was picked up on my way back by an old woman in her 60s whose husband had run off to the bar against her wishes. She was lonely and decided she would come out to the Brotherhood. I guess they had helped at her church once and invited her and all to come. She thought they were very helpful and fantastic people. On the other hand, the residents of Guilford, Vermont ran them off of what used to be the Johnson's Pastures commune last summer when they did things like dynamite when they couldn't dig into the hill to place the footings for the building they were going to build.

My final judgment of the Brotherhood is that Michael is someone who is badly needed by many. I was moved to type these symbols to you upon hearing the following words from the Hair album:

Where do I go?
Follow the river
Where do I go?
Follow the gulf
Where is the something?
Where is the someone?
That tells me why I live and die?

Michael is the answer to this plea. For someone who wishes to follow, he is the perfect parent replacement. He gives them answers; he gives them meaning. In return they must follow or meet the fate of the Johnson's Pastures people last summer and be rejected by him as negative energy that can do harm. He is the answer for a person in the counterculture or for a reactionary, for someone who still believes himself worthless and empty and in search of someone to give him worth, to fill his emptiness.

For me the Brotherhood message is beautiful, one happy world just as the Christian, the socialist, the communist, the capitalist, the humanist message is beautiful. However, their medium of leader-follower, rigid rules, rejection of those different, and dream of an ideology to be fulfilled is the same old shit that been causing our social ills for centuries.

My hope for the counterculture is that it become defined as the New Culture with each being "a light unto himself," as Krishnamurti has put it, and able to be "with" others viewing "contact as the appreciation of differences," as Fritz Perls has put it.

Yet there are many who seek the old way of liberation—from their misery, unable to walk alone or "with" others. They seek another parent man, ideal, belief to take care of them. Thus I anticipate that Michael and the Brotherhood shall continue to flourish. They just may be the next Beatles and much more. ■

THE BROTHERHOOD: MEDIA EXPOSURE

by Nick Tosches
Creem, *United Press Syndicate, Nov 1971*

AUGUST 3RD. HENNY YOUNGMAN UP THERE ON TEEVEE RAT-tat-tatting the David Frost Studio audience with old stand-up comic Thompson's Motif-Index of Folk-Literature rehashes. Rat-tat-tat the robber who went into the Chinese restaurant and said "give me all your money" and the little Chinese fella behind the counter says "to take out?" rat-tat-tat. Then there were the six rough-trade hippies who motorcycled up to a diner and went inside and started taunting this truck driver so the truck driver gets up and leaves and one of the hippies says to the counterman "he isn't much of a man, is he?" and the counterman says "he's not much of a truck driver either—he just backed up over six motorcycles."

Massachusetts, introduced by Frost in Copacabana voice of limousines and satin Times Square older than teevee.

Commercial. Piano player. Mike Metelica and Ronnie I forget his last name from the Brotherhood of the Spirit commune in Warwick, Massachusetts, introduced by Frost in some vague allusion to the pianist preceding them. Frost asks about the commune. Well, there are two hundred some odd people presently in the commune trying to grow with one another and to maintain contact with the forces of Creative Energy and to attune their lives to those forces.

Henny Youngman keeps interrupting with "How do you pay the rent? Where do you get your money from?"

Metelica won't give Youngman a straight answer, starts talking about "auras" and helping neighboring farmers. Reincarnation.

"Yeah, but how do you pay the rent?" Everybody in the audience is cracking up by now.

Station break cuts in on fading laughter and Metelica explaining that he'd like to talk more about reincarnation. After the station break, Frost assures him. After the station break, Frost introduces William B. Williams, who shares the rest of the airtime with Henny Youngman.

Hey, Man, What's All this 'Spirit' Shit?

The previous July 2nd, the day of the Frost Show taping, most of the Brotherhood of the Spirit commune had ventured down to New York City for a march up Fifth and Sixth Avenues that was to culminate at 1700 Broadway, where the Metromedia Records (Spirit In Flesh's label) offices are located. Everybody meets in Washington Square Park early that morning. There's a big pile of Spirit In

Flesh placards. The Spirit In Flesh mob are milling about. There're Spirit In Flesh balloons. (Practically the entire Spirit In Flesh publicity campaign has been completely the product of the Brotherhood of the Spirit commune. Months previous to the album's release, silkscreened posters with Metelica's dashing mug and the hand-lettered words "SPIRIT IN FLESH" had appeared miraculously glued to an unbelievable number of walls and street-lights around the metropolitan area. The commune had begun to flood radio stations with phone calls about Spirit In Flesh. They'd also taken to flooding Metromedia's switchboard with inquiries as to why the album wasn't being released yet, hunh? More of this matter anon.) David Peel is there hanging around. A few of the St. Marks Place alkies are there. Beautiful brown-haired woman slugging on the old Calvert's in the fantastic sunshine and an old black wino stumbling along, "What's all this 'spirit' shit?" Short, squat starry-eyes comes over and says "Hi," which I have since learned is the most commonly uttered expletive of the commune. "Hi." "Dija hear the Spirit In Flesh album?" Yup. Blah blah blah. Everyone in the commune has absolute undifferentiated faith that the Spirit In Flesh album will change the world. But what if it doesn't? I ask. "Oh, but it will." Yeah, but, you know, what if, by some gnarl in the stemma of manifest destiny, it doesn't? She looks at me in patronizing bewilderment. "It has to." This is the commune party line. No bouts about it, Spirit In Flesh is gonna change the world.

The march up Fifth Avenue was pretty neat. No incidents, though. A bunch of "Hi"s. They consume a lot of garbage, though, for people in touch with the highest energy force in the universe. I mean. Lemon ices. Orange "drinks." Sodas. If they really ever do make the big time, athletes might be in jeopardy of their soft-drink advertising monopoly. "... Hi, I'm in touch with the Highest Energy Force In The Universe. This? It's the Un-Cola..."

Upon reaching the main entrance to 1700 Broadway, they all converged in this big circle and began chanting a medley of Spirit In Flesh stuff. When I whipped out my cassette machine a series of pimply pusses assaulted, osculi agape, its meager microphone apparatus with rasping monosyllabic spiels of perpetual high and cosmic one-ness.

Upstairs, a little while later, I'm in a room with Michael Metelica and Ronnie Whatsizname, fresh from their David Frost taping. The trusty old tape recorder's on the desk in someone's unoccupied office. I'm nervous, Michael's wary. I start off by asking him about the consciousness level he refers to so often, can he describe it? Well, first let me say that Michael Metelica is one of the most mesmerizing, magnetic people I've ever come up against. Put him in a room and he'll beam openness and love into every brain-eye there. An amazing, amazing person. Now, I'm not being qualitative here, because, as far as I'm concerned, Michael may be just a unique psychotic. I'll bet my pretty blond locks, though, that he's absolutely sincere and beneficent in all his words and intentions. He just sort of pinned me with those eldritch fantastic baby-blues of his and told me that when he was very young, in a grade school classroom, he was on his way from his seat to sharpen his pencil at the pencil sharpener at the front of the room and Zomp! it hit him— fabulous eerie visions of lives past, future manifestations and total lovely flowing-ness of universal life/death continuum. Scared the shit out of me, he did. He told me things that he asked me not to reveal in print. They were about past life-form manifestations that he said might be construed as some kind of hype. He agreed that there were other auro-gangs emitting high levels of life-energy. They, though, themselves weren't in touch with the outermost sphere of consciousness as were Spirit In Flesh. In my own no-pushee no-shovee way, I'm trying to get him to ac-quiesce to Little Richard and Archie Shepp and their holy stature of godfuck and flow. Nothing doing. Spirit In Flesh is the centrifugal force of the contemporary ethnoastronomical universe in flux (they don't talk that neat, but I try to condense it and make it sound better). I ask the question for the umpteenth time that day. But what if Spirit In Flesh don't catch the human race by the midbrain? But it will. The old Socratic full-pitcher analogy. But it will. Echoes of 1966 peace/love time-loop Maharishi Mahesh Yogi trying to muzzle in on Mia Farrow's nookie and heroin Medicine Ball ("lots of naked girls...") Caravan radio commercials. But it will. Hence the amount of thryoxin produced may remain the same.

"Hi! Are You a Disc Jockey?"

On Saturday morning, July 31st, Metromedia bus'd a bunch of people out to the 90 Brotherhood of the Spirit commune in Warwick. Splendidly hungover from an all-nite debauch in the bowels of the lower West Side, the Air Raid Kid and myself boarded the rented bus parked in front of 1700 Broadway. Jon Tiven wore a green jumpsuit. Toby Mamis grinned. A few women from the commune served as host-esses. The long journey into the nether regions of Massachusetts was lightened by Mamis' spirited readings from The Quotations of Chairman Mao and the render-ing of Tiven, the 16 year-old editor of The New Haven Rock Press, into a state of public drunkenness, one of my favorite pastimes.

We disembarked the autobus to resounding cries of "Hi!" There were signs up on the trees. "No Drugs." "No Booze." And yes, "promiscuity" was a no-no, too. I was taken on a tour of the communal house (built by the commune themselves—nice job, too), had my decadence expounded upon. I had "a lot of potential," though.

Everybody asked, "Are you a disc jockey?" No one was asked less than say, 17 times, "Hi! Are you a disc jockey?" People started hiding behind shacks and shit to escape conversation. Within an hour, "Hi! Are you a disc jockey?" had developed into a running joke among the potato salad-scarfing conversation-refugees who chanced to meet in the more clandestine reaches of the commune grounds.

We didn't get to hear Spirit In Flesh perform that afternoon because we were supposed to go see the Dead in New Haven. Should have stayed. Anyway, upon leaving, I/we were accosted by the same woman who had acknowledged my "potential" earlier. "But you seemed to have so much potential, Nick." Yeah, I know, but I gotta go, my friends are leaving. "Well, then, go ahead, but you'll be sorry; you owe it to yourself to hear Spirit In Flesh." Don't make me feel guilty. "I can't make you feel guilty, only you can make you feel guilty." The car pulls away. Zomp! It's one of them at the wheel, and an hour-and-a-half ride ahead of us. Beautiful long red flowing hair. Glad I'm not in the front seat. We get to fallout rain pitter-patter on the windows in the back seat, Tiven up front talking to Mr. Energy.

Riverside Song

The Spirit In Flesh LP, Spirit In Flesh (Metromedia MD 1041), doesn't get much airplay on the radio, I don't think. Alex Bennett of WPLJ-FM in New York seems to have set the reactionary (technical sense, buddy) tone to their "publicity campaign" (flooding the station's switchboards and all that) by downmouthing them as "punks," with an aside to the effect that Metromedia Records (who'd almost gotten sued by the city for the communes' poster-posting orgy) shouldn't be held in responsibility for the group's punkness.

I like "Riverside Song," which I think is one super-fine aw-reet cut. The whole scam, though, is that Spirit In Flesh doesn't grid re musick, but, rather, in terms of literally turning around the course of civilization. Well, it's just Heraclitus and panta rei and if Heraclitus couldn't bend the carbon cycle scene in three thousand years, these guys sure aren't going to do it overnight.

I mean, it seems like a whole lot of naiveté for a bunch of kids who put restrictions on people (remember those signs I was telling you about?) and who don't even eat non-honko food to expect to change the monster divine. Universe, literally, when there are true red-line shifts by the likes of Jerry Lee Lewis, who's had one hand on a shot glass and the other hand on some Einsteinian dimensional warp for 15 years, and Archie Shepp, who could play 32 racks of 9-ball with Ra and come out on the money side every time, stalking this planet in overall unacknowledgement.

Last line: What we've got here is a cross between Jesus Christ and Florence Foster Jenkins and everybody knows Jesus sucks. ■

MODERN UT☯PIAN

A WAY OUT/ VOLUME 2 ISSUE No. 6 /75 CENTS

CHAPTER 9

group marriage communities

MAGIC FARM AND TALSEN

by Richard Fairfield

MAGIC FARM IS LOCATED IN A VALLEY OF ENCHANTED HIPPIES, or perhaps I should say an enchanted valley of hippies or a valley of hippies enchanted. Up and down Talma Road are the homes and communes of longhaired, dropped-out, ex-urban middle-class kids who are intent upon "doing their own thing" on the land, in the woods. Most of them return to the city or some other locale during those long, rainy winter months in Oregon, but settle back into the valley as soon as the sun begins to dry the rain-soaked soil. These people, along with a small but growing number living there year-round, may be considered permanent hippies, dedicated to the proposition that going back to the land will make them free, a dedication reinforced by experience.

The less dedicated ones, the more searching and confused types, come to the area in increasing numbers as the sun moves higher in the sky. By midsummer, the lakes and ponds in the valley are surrounded by travelers from all over the country—hippie vacationers who revel in singing, shouting, splashing, swimming, living in tents and bedrolls, eating dried fruit and cereals and nuts, drinking water and wine, smoking weed, dropping whatever pills and powders become available as people wander in and out of each other's lives.

Although a few die-hard storekeepers try to shelter behind signs in their windows such as "We Do Not Solicit Hippie Patronage," most of the local business people are cordial and friendly. One good reason for this is that permanent hippie residents provide good business. As the summer wears on and the transient population floods in, middle-class American businessmen get anxious and impatient with their carefree and unconventional patrons.

For all the gamboling hippie sprites along the way, the road leading in to Magic Farm is physically unimpressive. However, the parking expanse nestled among a grove of trees provides the visitor with a clue to the hidden loveliness of the area. Farther on, in a clearing beyond the parking area, stands the main house, a log-cabin-style frame structure that serves as kitchen, living room, and children's sleeping quarters. Two adjacent frame structures shaded by trees contain adult bedrooms, a workshop, and a kid's playroom.

Halfway between these structures and the parking area is the open-air communal outhouse, a semicircular, five-holed structure, partially covered by plastic sheeting as protection from the rain.

On the other side of the clearing near the main house is a garden, which, when I first saw it, was being watered by a member of the commune. And in a field beyond the bushes and a stream lay two more irrigated and well-tended gardens.

Slightly to the rear of the buildings and on a slight rise squats a massive table with long benches, the place where the community eats its meals during good weather. And farther back amid a clump of trees and next to the winding stream is the commune's large sauna bath.

Beyond all of these structures are beautiful meadows with tall grass and a magical forest. A few cabins and a large A-frame house are hidden among the trees. Some members sleep in these. But during the summer, most people prefer to sleep outdoors.

When I was there in June the commune had between 15 and 20 permanent residents. But this figure was expected to change. By August, it would probably increase to 30 or more. And months from now, in those dark, rainy winter months, it would probably drop to maybe 10, although the previous winter's residents had numbered only seven or eight. But changes such as these are normal in a commune. They are part of the rhythm of community life.

Some of the members of Magic Farm were no strangers to me, for I had known them in Berkeley before they had moved to Oregon to build this commune. I had gotten people together who were interested in forming communes. Magic Farm was one of the results.

Paul, Tom and Evelyn, Robert and John were the first to settle at Magic Farm. Their goal was to develop a self-sufficient agricultural commune in which all members shared equally and intimately.

Paul, a freelance gardener, was now the aggressive force behind the group, although he had attended the Berkeley meetings only intermittently and had not been an early member. Back in those days, his broad smile and his enthusiasm had made him well-liked and sought after in the group. He had developed both farming and manual skills, which gave him confidence about living on the land. When the Magic Farm property was discovered, Paul was ready to leave the city. Although Paul and I got along well, there was hostility beneath the surface of our relationship. Both of us were aggressive and competitive. As we were both too cowardly to get it all out in the open, we continued with the hugs and the façade of friendliness until we got to the snide remarks and the oh-too-hearty backslaps.

Reunion with Paul

When we met again at Magic Farm for the first time in two years, Paul and I managed to express some genuine friendliness. Our hair and beards were much longer. Paul said, "What are you doing here?"

"Oh, I just came by to visit for a while," was my first reply.

"You still doing that magazine about communes?" he asked.

"Oh, yes," I smiled.

"When are you going to stop writing about communes and start living in one?" he retorted, with a nervous laugh only barely concealing his hostility.

"Maybe never," I replied angrily. And then I continued in a more objective and friendly manner in an effort to conceal my anger. "You see, I don't think people should join a commune until they get themselves together, decide what they really want out of life. At present I want to travel and explore alternative lifestyles, not just communal ones. I do believe that the communal pattern is the best one but it has an infinite variety of forms. Another viable alternative is just being a hermit. Probably we all need to go through several lifestyles in our lifetimes rather than be stuck with just one. What about you, Paul? I hear you've moved to Talsen?"

"Yes, Magic Farm has become too open for me. I'm still interested in an intimate family-style commune. Magic Farm is too loosely structured, too open-ended. With new people coming in all the time, it's too difficult to really get to know them. People need to spend more time with each other to become an intimate family. It can't happen here. It's too open, not enough structure. This place is okay as a sort of halfway house. But if you're interested in a more intense communal life experience, you've got to get together with a fewer number of people and work through problems together to understand where each other is at."

Group Marriage at Talsen

Talsen was the group-marriage community nearby. It too had been formed from the group in Berkeley. Against the better judgment of those closely connected with them in the group, three couples, one single guy, and seven children left the San Francisco Bay Area for Oregon. Others promised to follow, but never did, except to visit. The people in the group had very little exposure to each other but nonetheless decided to live communally, sharing everything in common, including each other's spouses. One couple never really got into the sexual sharing and each of the two other marriages was on extremely shaky grounds.

Previously, they had carried on brutal suburban existences of pharmacist and housewife and college professor and housewife. The men frustrated and the women unfulfilled. The country, the land, intimate friendships: all these spelled liberation, freedom from the old unhappy pattern. They were desperate to start a newer and more fulfilling lifestyle. That desperation led them to move too quickly. Too many years of wrong habits could not be resolved so easily. Instead, seven desperate adults clung together, each shaking from the weight of his own lack of clarity. It was inevitable that that tiny group would be blown to bits.

Rob was one of that group. His wife Connie was also very close to Jim and growing closer to Joe. Rob turned to Mary, Joe's wife, and she to him. They were all together for a time. Then Mary left Joe, returned to Berkeley, and then went on to get a college degree. Rob and Connie also were divorced. Connie and Joe bought a house some distance away from the community. The second winter, only Jim remained at Talsen. Slowly others came. Rob advertised his plans for a community at Talsen through a Free University class in Berkeley. And more people became involved in developing Talsen.

Tom and Evelyn

In the beginning there had been only one couple at Magic Farm, Tom and Evelyn. They too had been in the original Berkeley group. Tom was a very calm, quiet guy. He always made me nervous, not only because he was so calm and I tended to be the opposite, but also because I felt it was a calmness always about ready to explode—so much held in, held back.

On the other hand, Evelyn was an aggressive and moody and very emotional girl. She was often bubbly and quite joyous. But at other times, she wandered around in tears and deep depression. Occasionally she could be a real bitch, someone to keep away from.

I don't know what really happened to Tom and Evelyn at Magic Farm, but they decided they couldn't hack it. So they moved to a neighboring town. Evelyn was pregnant. Tom cut his hair and got a job. They settled down into the domestic life.

Tom was at Magic Farm on the day I arrived. Evelyn was sick, he told me, to excuse the fact that he was alone. His eyes were filled with sadness. We talked briefly about the changes at Magic Farm. It had been a deeply disappointing experience for them. I wondered if they would ever again attempt an alternate communal experience. Tom's condition at that moment prevented me from asking that question.

Herb, who had found the commune only a few months ago, told me how a person got to become a member: "You come here; you make yourself at home; you gradually get to know the others. Anyone can ask anyone else to leave. Someone might ask you to leave; someone else might ask you to stay. We have regular meetings to deal with problems."

The only hostile member I encountered while at Magic Farm was a guy with blank staring eyes who looked at me and exclaimed, "Oh no, another one! There are more new people around here." The second time I saw him I got the same blank stare and the same hostile vibes, "Oh no, another one..." He was totally freaked. That time Jerry overheard and asked him to step into another room to talk for a second. The third time I saw the guy, I walked in a wide circle. I never did find out if Jerry's remarks did any good.

Big Robert, Little Robert, and Susan

I was walking on a path near the upper meadow, heading for the A-frame in the forest, when I recognized little Robert, all of six years old, in the distance. "Hi," I hollered. "Remember me?" I ran up to him and, catching his look of recognition, held him up and swung him high in the air.

In the meadow little Robert and I saw what looked like a moving black log. Then all of a sudden it stood up. It was big Robert, the boy's father, who had been meditating there sitting with his head bent down between his legs so that all we had seen was a big mass of hair that looked like a tree stump.

Of all the people in the Berkeley group, Robert and Little Robert were the two I had grown to love the most. The boy was his father's image. The man was quiet, kind, sincere, reliable, modest, and industrious. He was also overly idealistic and naive. His main problem was a lack of self-confidence in any area except his chosen work. He was a professional gardener and had had lots of experience farming on the East Coast. But he had had little experience with people.

He met Susan when she was 15 and he 26. For each of them it was a first love. She got pregnant and they got married. Soon after little Robert was born, big Robert's mother became very ill and Susan was left with the task of caring for both her mother-in-law and child. Making matters more burdensome, she became pregnant again. Robert worked long hours as a farm laborer in order to bring in enough money to support the family. After Robert's mother died, they returned to Oakland, California.

During those first four years of marriage, Susan's childish enthusiasm changed to resentment toward Robert. But perhaps that was no more than a very natural reaction to having had to carry an unbearable responsibility of being wife, mother, nurse, and mature woman at an age when she should have been going out on dates and to pajama parties.

Now, in the liberal Bay Area, with the two boys getting older and a father nearby who could babysit with them, Susan began to explore some avenues she had previously neglected. At the same time, Robert was weighed down by Susan's dissatisfaction and consequently allowed himself to suffer from enormous passivity and self-degradation.

The ideals of community and group marriage, sharing and returning to the land, appealed to them both. They were not happy leading isolated lives in the city, being without social contacts. So they advertised for others who might be interested in forming a group. As a result, they became faithful charter members of the group that I began in Berkeley and that group eventually set them free. And freedom also freed Susan and Robert from each other. Susan is still roaming the countryside living out her missed teenage years. Robert, however, has found a home at Magic Farm.

There in the upper meadow with his son, he seemed to have a greater confidence than before. He was more at peace. Still, he had not changed so much, even though his hair and beard were now long whereas before he had had short hair and no beard (much to Susan's distress). The two boys were on the farm and loved it. They too were at home in the forest and meadows, instead of having to make do with a cramped backyard and the concrete city streets. But they too had not changed much. Little Robert was still quiet and passive, being unable to defend himself against the onslaught of a cruel and aggressive six-year-old girl in the commune. And young Woody, like his mother, was jolly and active and nervous.

Magic Farm, it seemed, is a beautiful place to call home, to relax in, to find peace in. But it did not seem to require growth and balance. But then, few places do, for change is difficult. We are creatures of habit; change requires breaking those habits, but breaking them hurts as we seek comfort, not pain. Yet, paradoxically, we seek balance and equilibrium, and to obtain and sustain these is not at all comfortable.

For all my theorizing about comfort and growth, I knew from my brief renewed acquaintance with Robert that here at Magic Farm, an environment in which he was comfortable, he had gained a new self-confidence that could not help but be evident to those around him, thereby improving his social relationships and allowing others to see in him the kindness and beauty of his nature. How much dissatisfaction he now felt with his life at Magic Farm I could not observe, but I was sure it was much less than it had been in Berkeley.

Same Old Jean

When I walked up to the main house, Jean was sitting in the open side window talking with another woman.

"Hi, remember me?" I asked.

"Who are you?" she replied. "I don't know you. Go away. I'm busy now talking," she smiled and turned back to the conversation.

"She knows me," I said to a young fellow who was coming out the door. "She knows me," I continued to explain as we walked up the path toward the garden. Had my appearance really changed that much in two years, I asked myself in bewilderment? I guess maybe it had. My hair and beard were no longer carefully trimmed and I wore dungarees instead of pressed slacks.

Dear crazy Jean. I remembered that every time I had ever said hello to her she would break out in convulsive giggles, complete with half-closed eyes behind glasses and a wide smile. I had gotten to the point where I just wanted to give her a big smack across the face and tell her to snap out of it. But I never did.

Later that evening, when I saw her in the kitchen preparing dinner, she looked at me and said, "Are you Dick Fairfield? Are you Dick Fairfield? Well, I'll be darned." And she broke out in that convulsive laughter once again.

I just smiled and said, "Same old Jean, same old Jean."

Bob and Jean had been dropping out for years before Jean and her neurotic child came to Magic Farm. Bob and Jean were original members of a short-lived commune in Massachusetts in 1966 and moved to California in 1967. In Berkeley, Bob ran Free University classes, while trying to organize a community in his spare time. They both had joined the Wednesday Night Group, as my original group came to be called. And they too, like most of the other couples in the group, eventually split up.

Jean did not go to Magic Farm immediately after their breakup. She wanted to live alone for a while and get herself together. Meanwhile, Bob began visiting communes in New Mexico. Later he returned to Berkeley and Jean moved to Magic Farm to become one of its most stable members. Bob was supposed to be arriving at Magic Farm the night I was there, but he never showed up. He visited often, though, I was told.

Reunion for the Wednesday Night Group

It was a big day for meeting old friends of the Wednesday Night Group. Gary and Vickie, who lived nearby, came to visit the commune regularly. They had been traveling a great deal during the past year and had finally decided to live in that enchanted valley. Vickie was glad to see me. She and Gary had been fighting, I assumed, for her eyes were red and swollen. She explained that she was trying to adjust to living in the country. They didn't have many friends in the area. And as an artist, she disliked all the hippies around calling her work "groovy," which was what they called every piece of handmade craftwork. She yearned for more critical attention.

The last time I had seen her she had been dealing with five kids and a part-time job while Gary went to cooking school. The five kids were those of Gary's former wife, Joan, also an alumna of the Wednesday Night Group. Joan, like most of the other wives, was out trying to regain something that had been lost in marriage. But Vickie got stuck with all the kids, and only part of the welfare check (Joan got the rest). I had told Vickie to stop being a sucker. And I guess she had, because she and Gary were here and Joan and the kids were back in the city.

Vickie told me that they lived communally for a time in the former home of Robert and Susan. The place became a crash-pad, though, and they ended up throwing most of the people out, then leaving themselves.

I had always liked Gary, but that feeling had not always been reciprocated. When all the marriages in the Wednesday Night Group had been about to collapse, he believed that I was responsible, so he had resented me. Now, though, I felt he liked me too and I was pleased.

Finally, I met John again. In Berkeley he and his wife Laurie had been dropouts, just two young kids. At that time she still had some neurotic dreams of being a movie star (despite no training or talent) and he was trying to grow a beard. Laurie was an extremely attractive girl, who made every effort to capitalize on her good looks. The time came when she and John split up, with Bud moving in to take John's place.

After that, John wandered around the area living in an old Volkswagen bus that he had bought and repaired for $50. I saw him from time to time, but never really enjoyed talking with him. He'd ramble on and on about this or that experience, which I didn't have the slightest interest in, and then I would have to make a dozen excuses in order to leave. Then he'd be hurt because I never stopped to "get to know him."

I never had the guts to tell anyone I didn't want to get to know them. Instead, I was always in a hurry. And I wasn't lying. I made sure I was busy. I had a magazine to publish, mail to answer, full-time work in graduate school, a part-time job in a church, and domestic quarrels to contend with. And in addition to all this there was the Wednesday Night Group: I was in a hurry. Trouble is, I liked it that way—running so fast I missed a lot of the scenery. But I found out that eventually, if you aren't awfully careful and alert, the whole scene begins to blur and you keep running smack into walls. So if you don't want to knock out every tooth and both eyeballs, you just have to start slowing down.

John and I met that evening before I left the outdoor dinner table. His beard was really a beard now, and, what is more, he seemed more aware and mature. When he entered into the conversation during the evening meal, I no longer felt the strain of a high school student making all-too-obvious statements; rather, here was a person who spoke briefly and to the point. John had become a man at Magic Farm.

Only members of the "family" could attend the meeting that evening, so all visitors were asked to stay out. It was getting late as they began to gather for the meeting in the main house and so I made my way past that marvelous outhouse to my car.

The Magic Farm commune may not be magical, but at least it has produced some positive changes in the lives of the people who moved there after those traumatic times in Berkeley. True, communal living is no utopia, but it seems to me that for these hardy souls at Magic Farm life was certainly much better than before. Can we expect more? ■

HARRAD WEST
by Richard Fairfield

GROUP MARRIAGE CAN BE DEFINED AS A VOLUNTARY ASSOCIA-
tion to create a family group in which there is sexual sharing, consisting of four or
more adult members with at least two of each sex. Such a group-marriage community, called Harrad West, was started in Berkeley, California. I published their
public statement in The Modern Utopian magazine:

*Our basic idea at Harrad West is that perhaps six, eight or even a dozen or more adults
can form "marriage" relationships with each other as a means of attaining far more
than monogamous marriages can offer. (There are presently six adults, three male and
three female, plus three children living here.)*

The six adults at that time were Don, Barbara, Bill, Karen, Jack and Molly. I
had known all of them (except Molly) for some time before Harrad West, so I had
the chance to observe a group marriage in the making. But that sounds too objective and impersonal. As it happened, their lives and mine became interwoven, first
in a group meeting and then in a communal experiment I started.

The Evolution of a Group Marriage
It was back in 1968 that I organized a weekly meeting that lasted for about one
year and was known in the Bay Area simply as the Wednesday Night Group. The
name Harrad West is inspired by a book, The Harrad Experiment, written by
Robert Rimmer. Bob Rimmer is one of the foremost proponents for group marriage in the United States today. In addition to The Harrad Experiment which is
a fictitious account of college students who evolve a group marriage, Rimmer has
several other fiction and non-fiction books on the subject to his credit, including
The Rebellion of Yale Marrett, Proposition 31, You and I Searching for Tomorrow,
Harrad Letters.

The weekly meeting was intended for people interested in the possibility of
setting up one or more intentional communities. What I wanted to do was to get
a commune started with The Modern Utopian publication as the basic working
project. I too was personally interested in group marriage. It seemed like a positive
alternative to the unhappy marital situation in which I found myself at the time.

Don and Barbara began to come to the meetings regularly. At first there was
something about Don's behavior I didn't like. He seemed an insecure show-off.

Barbara was very thin and very quiet—I wasn't too impressed. It was two months before I learned from them that they too were interested in a group marriage. I was surprised: Barbara appeared unlikely to be that liberated or experimental. Don and Barbara had been married 14 years before deciding that a group-marriage community was right for them. They had tried and tired of the "swinging" scene and wanted relationships with more depth.

Eventually I rented a big old 12-room house in Berkeley and decided to live communally. Peter, a friend of mine, held the lease, but now he was splitting up with his wife and heading for the country. None of the other people living there were hip Berkeley types so they also decided to move.

I arranged for Don and Barbara to move into the house. Don, a commercial artist, was enthusiastic about the prospect of working on TMU magazine. He had dreams of quitting his regular job and working within the commune movement full-time. I had grown to like him and Barbara a great deal. We had driven to Iowa to visit Don's mother, so now I felt positive about having a stable family move into the house. Their three children—Lynn, 12, Ken, 10, and Joyce, 8—were very bright and also good company. They had been educated mostly in free schools. They were kind, cooperative kids, willing to help on the magazine or in decorating my room; I, in turn, enjoyed helping them with their schoolwork.

Soon, Don and Barbara had put their suburban house up for sale and were ready to move in. Meanwhile, three single friends—Andy, Walter, and Ruth—had taken the vacant rooms.

This was not really a life of togetherness yet. All of us, except Barbara, were scattered in different directions during the day and evenings. Don continued to work at his job in San Francisco. Andy worked nights, Ruth had an irregular schedule, Walter and I were going to theological school during the day and working with a Unitarian fellowship on some evenings. This commune was an example of what can easily occur in an urban area: too many outside diversions or commitments, too little internal commitment, no real task in common. Everyone had agreed to help on the magazine one night a week. As it turned out, though, only Don, Barbara and the kids could be counted on to do so regularly.

We did set up an effective housekeeping, dishwashing, and cooking schedule. Each of us cooked one communal meal a week and signed up for household chores. As Barbara was around the house most of the time, she ended up doing most of the work herself, out of habit acquired in those suburban days. None of us were particularly satisfied with these arrangements. True, it was inexpensive to live in one house together ($30 for rent plus $25 for food were the shared monthly expenses per adult). But that was not enough. Don and Barbara wanted a group marriage to get started. I preferred more communication through regular meetings, but these were impossible to set up. None of us communicated very well, nor were we very clear about what we really wanted or how we should accomplish it.

In December 1968, after a six-month marital separation, I had decided to see if there was any chance for reconciliation. When Jonathan Prince, a St. John's University (Minnesota) student, asked if he could come to live in the communal house for a month and learn how the magazine ran, I gave him my room and moved out on what I thought would be a temporary basis. In February 1969, I turned the lease over to Don and Barbara. I was divorced in March and subsequently I moved to Rohnert Park (near Sebastopol), where I became the minister of a small Unitarian church.

Don and family continued to work on the magazine with me one evening a week since I kept an office there as well. Now that I had moved, though, the possibility of our getting back together in a commune was left undiscussed until finally one day I opted to face the issue squarely.

"I really care a lot about you folks but I don't want to live with you," I said. "We should function independent of one another and yet try to cooperate in those areas where we can be of mutual benefit. I don't want to take advantage of you and I don't want you to put any expectations on me."

"Let me do you a favor," Don replied.

"That's just the point—I don't want you to do me any favors!" I exclaimed. And Don walked out of the room.

Bill and Karen moved into the Berkeley house soon after I moved out. Bill, an early advocate of group marriage, had been the principal founder of Walden House in Washington, D.C. back in 1965. After a group marriage failed to develop there, Bill eventually moved out. After that (April 1967), Bill started to compile a list of people around the country who were interested in experimental marriage systems. Many people contacted him because they had read his article entitled "A Utopian Answer: Walden House Plus Group Marriage," which I had run in the first issue of The Modern Utopian (September 1966). In October 1967, I published another article by him, "Utopian Ethics," which was an updated version of his ideas on group marriage. Bill described Utopian ethics as:

... positively reinforcing someone because he is a fellowman, not because he is a man of a particular type, but simply because he is part of all being... not a simple idealized love of all humanity, but the concrete positive reinforcement of the other real person... unconditional positive reinforcement...

Boiling down all Bill's verbiage, I came to believe that what he was really trying to say was: any girl whom I want to fuck should fuck me; any girl who wants me to fuck her, need only ask me. Bill's was a heterosexual approach. He hadn't extended his idea to all persons.

Committed to his ideals and ethics, Bill became interested in swinging, a phenomenon that was fast becoming a popular pastime for middle-class plastic America. When marital boredom sets in and your partner's eye begins to stray, how do you hold the marriage together? How do you keep mommy or daddy from abandoning you? The answer is: compartmentalize the "threat" of extramarital sex and conventionalize the rest of marriage; that is, become a swinger.

Bill, however, really did look upon swinging as the first major step toward group marriage. Many of the people he corresponded with had been swingers and were now interested in living communally.

Bill eventually met Karen and together they moved to California. In Berkeley, Bill and Karen appeared super-straight. I remember the first night they came to the house: Bill in his suit and tie, very stiff and formal, his words well guarded; Karen, in her best party dress, more conversational, but very proper. Even after several visits, they remained basically unchanged in their formality of dress and composure. Bill, especially, found it easier to join the Sexual Freedom League than to relax his manners.

The other two adult members of Harrad West were Jack and Molly. Jack was pushing 60, a past member of the Wednesday Night Group, separated from his black wife, and overly sensitive to the feelings of others ever since his mind-blowing encounter weekend at the Esalen Institute. He was a man who could be counted on: honest, sincere, no bullshit, anxious to be a friend.

Then there was Molly, recently separated from her husband, seeing her analyst, and wearing the gaudiest-colored dresses you can imagine. She joined the Sexual Freedom League and became the life of the orgy trying, trying to stay young, and doing quite well at it in a comic sort of way. Molly always made me feel a little uncomfortable, but perhaps it was only because of those lustful glances she used to give me.

The Credo of Harrad West

These were the six adults who started Harrad West in early 1969. And it was from the old 12-room house in Berkeley, now the home of Harrad West, that the group issued its credo which was part of the public statement mentioned earlier:

We feel that a larger number of concerned persons learning and growing together often can deal with stresses that would overwhelm two individuals. In addition, children in a group marriage can be more certain of the continued existence of their families and have more than two adults to rely on.

All adult members of Harrad West are considered married to all other adult members of the opposite sex. "Pair bond" relationships do exist since most of the members entered the community as couples, one with three children. These couples and those who have entered as singles do not demand exclusive rights with each other. Relationships are on all levels...

We believe that sex is vital in a successful marriage. We find that our more ample number of loving relationships helps us to become more affectionate persons. We feel our friendships deepened, our capacity for warmth and understanding increased, and our lives enriched as a result of this community. The development of this rational and agreeable means of helping fulfill our social and sexual nature has enabled us to become more honest with ourselves and others....

We share a certain number of possessions while reserving an ample amount of individual private property.... Most of us hold full- or part-time jobs and we pay monthly sums for housing and food expenses.

Since we are a growing community, we would welcome as new members those who share our aims... Couples who are unsure of how they feel about mate-sharing can find out by first "swinging" with other couples before applying to any group marriage community.

We sponsor weekly meetings in the Bay Area for those interested in exploring group marriage communes.... For those who join our community, these weekly meetings and other get-togethers are absolutely necessary. No one may move into Harrad West until we know each other very well.

In my opinion, the advice about swinging was very unsound, for it seemed to me that the Harrad West members' ability to relate had not been improved through mate-swapping. As I understand the notion about the swinger route to group marriage fulfillment, group marriage is an intimate personal relationship among people, while swinging is essentially sex among people. Now, if you don't know the difference, you're a swinger, and if you do, then maybe you're ready to go from swinging with others to living with them.

Their advice, I think, is like telling a person that if he wants to be sexually free, he should have sex with a donkey; the only thing that happens to the person who follows such advice is that he gets a piece of ass. Swingers and sexual freedom leaguers I've met do not appear more free than others, often quite the opposite: controlled and reserved. Sexual freedom is determined, I believe, by an attitude, an emotional state, rather than by a person's ability to "freely" couple in a room full of couplers.

Two people accepted by Harrad West were Sam and Jean, a married couple. However, this apparently did not work out well, for Sam and Jean left Harrad West within a month of having joined. Subsequently, they went to live at Crow, up in Oregon. It was there that I met them and had a chance to find out what had been happening back in Berkeley.

"They used to write little notes to themselves," Sam began. "Saved up all their complaints and hostilities for the Sunday night encounter session, going around all week with that tension inside, unwilling to say anything waiting for that Sunday evening meeting. The vibes were very heavy there."

"And that woman who ran the encounter sessions," Jean joined in, "a professional therapist, yes, but I don't know if she handled things very well. Don had some serious problems. You knew he quit his job, didn't you?"

"No, I haven't been in contact with them for quite some time now," I replied.

"Well, he quit his job and then locked himself in a closet for two weeks," Jean continued. "They ended up taking him to the mental ward at Herrick Hospital."

"And the whole thing has split up now," Sam concluded.

"Back up a bit. Why did he lock himself in a closet?" I asked.

"You know Don was having some pretty heavy experiences in that house, in those encounter sessions," Sam said. "There was an aspect of himself he just wasn't willing to face, and that whole experience just got too much for him. Especially after quitting his job."

"Yeah, the job was a kind of escape, a crutch which he needed. Then, because he was always so busy doing his clown act for kids on weekends, and writing little notes to people, the pressure was on to spend more time relating to others," Jean added.

"So he figured if he quit his job he'd have more time," Sam noted.

"And then he locked himself in a closet! Whew, heavy… that's heavy, man," I exclaimed. "How come everyone split? Who's left?"

"Bill and Karen moved out. And Molly, too. Jack stayed with Barbara and the kids," said Jean.

"Bill was pretty tight," Sam interjected. "He was always pushing for everything to be on a schedule. They had this elaborate rotating-partners schedule. You had to sleep with whomever you were assigned on the list, whether you felt like it or not that particular night. Bill liked this system. He was afraid if it were done more freely, he might get left out."

"Still, I think Bill opened up a great deal as a result of that experience," I came to Bill's defense. "When he first came to Berkeley, he wasn't very social. He softened some, let down his guard and became much more human and likable."

"Yes, that's true, but he didn't like doing the dirty work very well—house-cleaning or anything like that," Jean added.

"Didn't he, Don and Jack do the evening dishes?" I asked. "When I was there last, they decided the women preferred to cook and cooked better than the men so the men did the cleaning up."

It was sometime later that I received a letter from Don, bringing me up to date with his group marriage:

We are doing rather well now. Barbara went down and ripped off some welfare for us. And now I'm beginning to get some commercial art to do.

Molly and Bill have both moved. We have stopped having Wednesday evening meetings too. Now we have people over if they really seem interested (and interesting). I have talked at a few places too. The idea is to get the whole Harrad West thing out of the house.

Meanwhile the members of Harrad West had prepared a new public statement, which was duly distributed as a flyer to the world:

Harrad West is a group of half dozen adults and several children who live together in a big old Berkeley house. We function as a family; joyful, angry, helpful, turned on and turned off. Our children are cared for, we care for each other.

Physical needs that are provided for as a family include housing, food, some recreation and a variety of things related to the home. Our economic structure is similar to that of a cooperative. While employment, transportation and most other things are individual responsibilities, there is a great deal of non-structured (spontaneous) sharing within the family. We do not see ourselves as a commune.

Emotional needs are met (much of the time) in ways that make us different from ordinary families for we believe in multilateral relationships between adults. Our shared ideals include a belief in openness and honesty between people, responsibility for one's own feelings and concern for others. Our family has had regular group therapy sessions within the house and most of us have been involved with individual therapy.

If you are interested in multilateral relationships, we suggest reading Robert Rimmer's books, The Harrad Experiment and Proposition 31, as well as Stranger in a Strange Land and The Moon is a Harsh Mistress by Robert Heinlein. These books each contain fictional accounts of multilateral marriages. An excellent series of articles, based on information gathered from existing multilateral marriages, has been written by Larry and Joan Constantine, 23 Mohegan Road, Acton, Mass. 01720. Send a stamped envelope for information. Two good books on therapy are Gestalt Therapy Verbatim by Fritz Perls and Don't Push the River by Barry Stevens.

In two years we have come up with an alternate to the existing family structure. It isn't exactly what we planned, but it is us. If you think something similar might fit you we would like to hear from you. We have no big organization to join. We are just humans who want to know and enjoy other humans.

Many groups do not consider themselves a commune by their own definition of that word. They might, for instance, define "commune" as a group which shares all things in common with no private property or private space, etc. and oppose this idea. The term is used loosely by myself and others who do not care to deal in precise definitions. Harrad West's new statement reveals a yawning chasm between reality and fantasy, public propaganda and private practice, posture and perception.

Translating ideals into actuality is damned hard. Read all the science fiction you want, read all the articles on multilateral marriages and gestalt therapy and modern utopias. But just forget about doing your thing until you've got enough self-awareness and courage to be able to deal with revealing your failings as well as your successes. Pep talks and propaganda have no place in positive interpersonal relations, for they sell only products or images, not human beings.

By telling only the best part of the story or pretending that utopia is finally a reality, how many people will believe you? I'll bet the only people attracted to such a story will be those who love to fool themselves. These are the people who, when confronted with the problems of attempting to actually live their ideals, either run into the closet (seek refuge in beliefs) or run out of the house (escape from reality).

Until these people can face the ugly as well as the beautiful, the cycle will simply keep repeating itself in another broken marriage, another dose of incompatibility, and another load of blame dumped on somebody else for one's own failings.

I hadn't been back to visit Harrad West for quite some time when that mythic manifesto appeared. I felt that if they had been more frank and more honest, especially with themselves, their statement would have begun something like this:

"We are attempting to be a group marriage but it's not easy. Each of us is fucked-up as a result of our previous conditioning and hang-ups, which we cling to like grim death. But despite the pain and the difficulty of sharing and growing toward a new family structure, we keep at it. Why the compulsion, why the need? Lots of reasons. But what's really important is that, whatever the reasons, we have made the choice to go ahead in this direction. We know there are no absolutes and that group marriage isn't the ultimate answer to anything. But group marriage is what we're attempting to explore now...."

I realize that these words can be dismissed as verbiage. In the long run the best thing to say is nothing. However, words are a valued part of our cultural heritage hang-up, so the alternative may be to say everything. That, of course, ends up being nothing and everything and so forth.

The way we say something is important, though, because it will attract the kind of people who dig it. And if we don't dig the kind of people we're attracting, we've just got to try saying it another way...

Harrad West is still functioning and living in the same place. I'll bet (and hope) they've come a long way as a result of their early experiences. ■

THE CRO RESEARCH ORGANIZATION
by Richard Fairfield

BEFORE I VISITED THE CRO RESEARCH ORGANIZATION IN OR-
egon, commonly known simply as Crow, I heard at least a dozen rumors about the
place. Seven of them, just to give you an idea, were as follows:

"There are about 50 people who eat, sleep, and work inside a gigantic dome-
like structure."

"Everything is shared totally, including sex. There is no private space. It's just
one big open dome."

"It's mainly an agricultural commune, with lots of land and a large herd of
cattle."

"There are actually two groups with two differing lifestyles living on the land.
They keep separate but are friendly and cooperative. They're encouraging other
groups to come there and settle."

"Don't go to Crow. They have a lot of interpersonal tension to work out and
aren't open to visitors now."

"CRO Research Organization. Yes, I know about them. They just got burned
out. Had a big fire over there. I think everyone has left now."

"A fire burned down one of the houses near the road. All that remains of it is a
big stone chimney. They have another house back up the road."

Then there was the information I received directly from the group. According
to a prospectus I received from Crow:

*CRO represents a radical new experiment in "total involvement" living... Its over-
riding goal is to create a total immersion community in a rural environment that
combines creatively the advantages of farm living with those usually associated with
the urban setting.*

I visited Crow to find out for myself. At Crow, I learned, the members are not
the slow, pondering, easygoing ranch types. Rather, they are active, aggressive, and
forward. They tend to impose themselves on the land, rather than blend with it.
They earn enough money to make the $1,200 monthly payments on their 65-
acre farm site. Most of the cash income is derived from outside contractual jobs,
such as crop picking, house painting, and other short-term projects. By hustling,
this 28-member commune has an income and expenses that balance out at approximately $3,000 per month. This does not prevent these people from eating

well. The night I visited, for instance, dinner consisted of steak, mashed potatoes, asparagus, lima beans, salad, and various assorted drinks.

Crow has several head of beef cattle (not a herd, as reported in one of the quotes) grazing in pasture. They hope to add more cattle gradually. They had purchased a pregnant dairy cow, Bessie, two weeks before my arrival. One of the women, Lillian, was made responsible for Bessie's care. She explained in some detail what this chore entailed. While most women at Crow are happy in the kitchen and the nursery performing traditional female roles, Lillian finds greater satisfaction in minding the cows and also in learning to be a midwife. She is studying with a woman doctor and hopes to learn midwifery well enough to be able to travel from commune to commune helping pregnant mothers deliver at home.

A worthy service, I thought. Yet, somehow, I looked at that pregnant cow contentedly chewing her cud and felt sure that in this day most expectant mothers were about as dumb as she, especially those who were working on their second or third "calf." I could forgive the cow. Her mental and emotional capacity is limited. Pregnant women, on the other hand, are capable of understanding the dangers of overpopulation.

According to the CRO prospectus,

Communication among members, children and adults, must be established at all levels, verbal and nonverbal, to an extent far beyond that usually deemed "acceptable" in conventional society. This means that the traditional "right to privacy" is consciously and voluntarily surrendered by all members.

I was told soon after I arrived that this is a radical experiment in community living. There is no right to privacy. Although each member has his own sleeping area and space for personal property (clothes, toothbrush, and the like), anyone can occupy that space, at any time, day or night. No rooms are private. In practice, though, this is not always the case, much to the dismay of some and the relief of others.

Actually, there are two houses at Crow, and correspondingly, two major opposing lifestyles. The larger house is not a dome, but a dormered two-story structure, which serves as a communal kitchen and provides space for dining, living, sleeping, and recreation. Adjacent to the living room are the children's sleeping quarters. Besides bunk beds, this room contained two or three boxes of toys. Upstairs there were two large bedrooms. One of these has an alcove, which serves as an office where correspondence is handled and the commune's business and financial records are kept. An annex to this building holds the large communal washer and dryer, the deep freeze, and bags and cans of food bought in bulk.

When I was there, the living arrangements in the large house were as follows. Two couples shared a downstairs bedroom: one couple was unmarried and flexible in their sexual relations with other commune members; the second couple was married and preferred remaining strictly monogamous. One of the two large upstairs bedrooms (the one with the alcove) was shared by two females and three males, who all slept together in one large mattressed bed. The other upstairs bedroom, known as the "men's dormitory," accommodated five males. These men, the excess after all available women in the community had been matched up, occupied this room with varying degrees of dissatisfaction or resignation. None of the members with whom I spoke felt this to be a very happy arrangement—neither for the five men who were without sleeping partners, nor for the three "liberated" females who were being continuously propositioned. The other house resembles a prefabricated one-story bungalow yanked straight out of the middle of suburbia. It is a white frame building situated on the hillside overlooking the large house. When I was there, the couples who lived in its four bedrooms were all monogamous and quite traditional in family structure. There was no formal attempt to communally rear the children with all adults acting as parents. This was espoused as an ideal but the reality of the situation was that the biological parents retained primary responsibility for their own children.

Some time before I visited Crow, the commune had undergone a major ideological division. Although the commune began with a definite set of ideals, the male/female relations and sex roles were not clearly defined. As new members arrived with ideas of their own, a division was inevitable; this is not an uncommon experience in new communes. It was a split that ran right down the middle, between those who favored communism of persons as well as property, and those who wished to pursue a more traditional family style within a communal structure. When the confrontation over group marriage arose, differences were so strong that the proponents threatened to leave. This did not influence the opponents, who would neither leave nor change their attitude. Two women who favored group marriage did, in fact, move out, but only as far as a neighboring city where they set up their own commune. Meanwhile, the remaining five group marriage proponents stayed on. They, even more than their opponents, had an investment in Crow amounting to many thousands of dollars and a great deal of time and energy. In staying on, these five hoped that in time the others would be persuaded to share more totally as relationships within the commune deepened.

When there, I did not see any signs of progress in this matter. The people in each house still tended to communicate among themselves rather than with those in the other faction (house). There were two separate communes, eating together and sometimes working together, but essentially distinct—one living in the large brown house, the other in the small white one. Thus Crow, for all its espousal of radical experimentation, was on one level a communal economic venture, but on another level was simply a cautious social and personal project.

Even those who favored group marriage were not clear in their definitions of family roles. They still felt that it was permissible for women to do the bulk, if not all, of the housework, while the men did the outside jobs and the so-called heavy work—building construction and repairs, tractor and vehicle operations, etc. But true communism means more than everyone balling everyone else. It requires an obliteration of rigid or habitual role behavior. It requires that no person be restricted to one set of economic tasks and social roles, that no person should have to repeat actions so much so that his or her behavior becomes categorized and defined.

While I was at Crow, the meals were prepared mainly by the tradition-oriented females, while cleanup jobs (doing dishes, mopping floors, etc.) were the work of the more "liberated" ones. After dinner, I recall, the men retired to the living room or sat leisurely around the huge dining room table, but the women who had done the cooking seemed to disappear. The following morning, though, those women were almost the only people around. The reason was that in the morning, most of the men went off to work, some to outside jobs, some going to their own fields in order to cut and bale hay, one or two staying around the barns helping to care for the chickens and pigs and cattle. They had just butchered a 250-pound hog the day I arrived.

The Crow people hold no meetings as a group. Each person is responsible for creating and maintaining whatever relationship he or she has with another person. Meetings, I was told, accomplished nothing. No one is interested in heavy encounter scenes. They feel free to speak up to another person to express a gripe or a desire on a one-to-one basis without the need for a group. If a person does not speak up, then that's his tough luck.

"This is a commune for aggressive-type people," Lillian admitted. "If a person is passive or slow, he probably will feel very uncomfortable here. You have to be pretty forward and make your need known."

Despite this admission and despite the fact that these are active, hardworking, aggressive types, a lot of feelings are obviously not communicated and many relationships, even if cordial, tend to be superficial.

All of the men are required to work on weekdays. Most of them had their own special jobs. A few, mainly the newer members, help the others. They leave at varying times in the morning and return at dinnertime, five or six p.m.

Mike, a new member, explained it to me this way: "Yeah, it's kind of a drag sometimes. Today we're haying and I don't like it, but sometimes I work with Sam on the truck and I like that better. Some days I don't feel like working at all so I just try to look like I'm working."

Bill, another member, said, "By the time I get home at night from working all day, I don't have the energy to try to relate to everyone on a one-to-one basis, if that were possible. I'm not interested in playing all the games required to get to take a girl to bed."

Later when I was talking with Jean and Sam, one of the couples in the group marriage, Jean told me: "I don't like guys to play games. If a guy wants to make out with me I just wish he'd come right out and say so. Some of the guys around here think they have to go through all kinds of maneuvers to get a girl to bed."

"Well, that's a pretty standard expectation, isn't it?" I asked.

Sam, Jean's husband, added, "Yeah, all a guy really has to do is say 'Have you got 20 minutes to spare?' Then she can say "yes" or "no." Simple as that. I think too many guys fear rejection, as though it was some sort of putdown to him personally. It may be she just doesn't feel like it at the moment."

Jean continued, "We need more women now. I could spend all my time in bed. Especially when most of the women here won't sleep with anyone besides their mates."

"Like Marian, for example," Sam said, pointing to a dark-haired girl who was putting food in the deep freeze. "She won't even undress in front of anyone. 'Fraid we might see her body!" Sam added, partly to cover up his resentment, "She does a lot of good things around the place, though; she's the treasurer and I trust her with the money more than if I were handling it myself."

Now, I'm one of those rare birds who likes to wash dishes, so after dinner I volunteered. "You must have visited communes before," one member commented, noticeably pleased with my contribution. I replied, "Oh, I like to do dishes." An hour later I remarked, "Man, there sure are a lot of dishes. You need a dishwasher. You sure there was only 40 people for dinner? I've washed at least 100 plates."

And then came the pots and pans. Hell, I really do like to wash dishes. But in moderation, man, in moderation.

Jack was in a jolly mood. He came up to Lillian and began to make pelvic gestures against her buttocks. "I'm hot! I'm hot!" he exclaimed. Then he rushed over to Jean, repeated the performance, and moaned. Shortly thereafter, he went upstairs to the men's dormitory, read for a while, and went to sleep.

Henry and Susan, the monogamous couple who lived in the larger house, came into the dining area where several of us were talking. Henry was in a bright velvet robe, preparing for bed. He and Bill joked for a bit and then Henry exclaimed, "Presto, chango!" and threw his robe open to expose his naked torso.

Everyone laughed. "Encore, encore," several shouted. Henry turned toward his audience and repeated his performance. "Bravo, bravo." Henry laughed and then made his exit. "Good night," he said.

Along with other aspects of Crow life, the rumors I'd heard about their treatment of visitors turned out to be less than accurate. Visitors are asked to make a donation of $3 for each day they stay. They are provided with meals and, in general, are told to make themselves at home. On the other hand, if visitors are not welcome (say because of overcrowding or any other circumstance), there is no reservation about turning them away. On one occasion, I was told, a fellow showed up and announced to all that he had come to live at Crow permanently. When gentle persuasion did not result in his leaving, three of the more husky men in the commune threw him to the ground and physically and verbally scared him so badly that he immediately got his belongings together and left.

In former times, visitors (those of them made welcome, that is) stayed in a third house closer to the highway. But that building, part of which had served as the communal school, had been lost in the fire, a rumor, for once, being at least partially correct. The commune members, I learned, had decided not to rebuild at that location, as it was too far from the other houses. At that distance, the school had tended to be a separate entity; also, visitors staying at the third building had been little inclined to participate in the primary activities of the community. The members now feel that the school and visitors' quarters alike should be an integral part of the main community complex. They want visitors to involve themselves as totally as possible in and with the community.

A unique opportunity for such involvement came my way the day after Henry's torso performance. An eight-year-old boy standing near the shed with a shovel asked me to help bury the hog's head. "Well, ahhh ..." I said. "Let me see..." Backing off smartly, I rushed indoors, got a whiff and a taste of some yeasty home-made bread for breakfast, and then drove off in the flashing sunshine to find still another glorious commune. ■

THE FAMILY
by Richard Fairfield

WE HEADED FOR THE NORTHERN PART OF NEW MEXICO HIGH mountains, cooler weather, more greenery, less dryness and desert. We were on our way to Taos, once the Hippie Mecca, but now, according to the roundup of late state news, no longer congenial to longhairs. Two hitchhikers whom we picked up along the way told us of a hip general store and information center in Taos that would provide us with a map of all the communes in the vicinity. It was mid-afternoon and we had only eaten a few handfuls of raisins since breakfast and hunger was catching up with us. Also, I had a headache from a need to shit. So we decided to get the information on the communes and then find a convenient restaurant and restroom.

It was such a relief to see a large, well-stocked, hip general store complete with health foods that I completely forgot about my physical discomfort. After wandering around the store and buying some sunflower seeds, we went next door to the information center, which also published a local hip paper, The Fountain of Light.

We could get little information about communes because, apparently, the communes got upset about the center giving out directions on how to reach them. Too many tourists. So there were no more maps.

We were encouraged to meet Lord Buckley, who was, I guessed, the editor of a commune magazine which was being prepared. With some sketchy directions on how to get to Hog Farm and New Buffalo, we offered a ride to the new magazine's typist. She was going to the local free school, where we could probably find Lord Buckley.

We were ushered into the spacious living room of a large and elegant house in the center of town. This large room had to be the free school, for its crates, toys, playpen, plants, and general appearance strongly suggested that lots of kids had been there recently. Our typist, whose name I had missed up to this point, disappeared into another room. Shortly after that, a young guy in his early 20s with rosy cheeks and lips appeared. He told us about the school, that it was attended by the commune children and a few kids belonging to local hip types, and that the commune members took turns running the school.

Our typist entered the room with a radiant guy sporting a red beret and a broad grin. "Hello," he said, "I'm Lord Buckley."

We were led to the back of the house, where Lord Buckley seated himself behind a desk while we took chairs in front. Our rosy-cheeked friend Dave and two other guys joined us.

"We're a commune of about 50 people and we live in a four-room house together," Lord Buckley began…

There they were—four guys and a girl at a free school, sitting in a small room discussing the beautiful life of a turned-on service commune consisting of 23 girls, 22 guys and nine kids in a two-bedroom bungalow and a school bus.

"How did you hear about us?" Lord Buckley asked.

"Oh, just now. We were at the information center inquiring about communes and agreed to give her a ride here," Consuelo said, gesturing toward the typist.

I added, "We're really interested in knowing more about your commune, though."

"One thing—you publish a magazine about communes, right? Are you planning to write about us? We aren't interested in publicity that'll bring more people into this area. There are too many already. Some of us are even thinking about moving and setting up a branch elsewhere."

"Of course I want to write about you and let people know of alternative possibilities," I replied. "If you don't want publicity, I won't give out your address. The main thing is to let others know. I personally think people should do the commune thing where they are anyway, rather than visiting or joining others."

I talked much too long about my good intentions instead of letting them begin to explain their lifestyle. All five of them were proud, enthusiastic, and excited as they started to tell us what some 50 people were doing.

Crowded? A key to their success was having to deal with impossible situations. They deliberately chose the crowdedness. It required them to be together. "We are people-oriented, growth-oriented," they said. "We are flexible, we have no elaborate structure, rules, requirements; such organization evolves as the group evolves."

"Today," Lord Buckley mentioned, "I'm editor. Tomorrow it may be someone else, or one person in the morning, someone else in the afternoon. Inefficient? Time-consuming? That doesn't matter. We've got plenty of time. It's people that count."

Lord Buckley: We've tried every type of decision-making method except democracy (majority rule) and the method changes from situation to situation. An individual may write an article for our new magazine, but he reads it to the whole family and, maybe, to others individually for criticism and suggestions for improvement. Then he may rewrite it. But it's still his article.

Lady Jane (the typist): Music? When we did have records at the house and someone didn't like what record was playing, or if it was too loud, he would just turn it off, change it, or whatever he felt like doing.

Dick: And if someone else objected?

Lady Jane: Well, then, he objected. He did whatever seemed right to him at the time. We don't have a phonograph at the house anymore. We used to, but we moved it to the store.

Lord John: Yeah, someone broke John Wesley Harding. Sure wish it hadn't been that, but it's only a record. I was too hung up on that record anyway. One of our basic tenets is no hang-ups on material possessions. When someone joins, they come in with all their personal property. If we think they're too attached to something, they have to give it up.

Lord Jim: Like the girl who loved her down sleeping bag so much. Or like if someone is reading too much, someone will point it out. "Hey man, what's with you?" We're a product of a thing-oriented culture. To live with people you have to get over that hang-up. That's why we have the rule. It's better to break records, even John Wesley Harding, than to break up people.

Lady Jane: Sure, I've been hit a few times. If someone feels the liberty and is open enough to give me a good wallop, I feel like we're really communicating. I probably deserve it anyway. I can act like an ass sometimes.

Lord Buckley: So what we're saying is that anything that interferes with people communicating with each other gets the axe. We don't use drugs any more, either. Up until a few months ago we smoked marijuana and occasionally used LSD or mescaline or stuff like that. But we found it interfered with communication. Now we have a no-drug rule.

Dick: You're not talking about alcohol, wine or beer, right?

Lord Buckley: No, but we don't bother with liquor much. Money? Our attitude toward it is to turn it over—spend it, put it back into the system as quickly as possible. We just finished making a movie about the communes in this area. It's going to get mass distribution and we expect to make a million dollars with it. Two of us are in Hollywood finalizing distribution plans right now. It's not a short, but a full-length film. We had rented cameras and film provided to us by a corporation and we'll split the profits 50-50. With rented equipment we don't have any possession hang-ups regarding what to do with it now that the film is completed.

With the money from the film, which we made collectively, we plan to set up a research foundation. It will explore extrasensory perception, dreams, psychic phenomena, that sort of thing. We are open to new members. But frankly, we have reached our limit here. Some of us may move to a city in the Northeast. There was a branch in Michigan, but last winter they broke up and a few of them moved in with us. Most of the hippie communes around here think us a little weird. They can't believe what we're doing, either. It does sound fantastic but it's real.

Lord Jim: Sometimes I wake up in the morning and just lie there in amazement. This is the greatest, most unbelievable experience in the world.

Lord Earl: Hordes of people aren't flocking to join us, not because we've been secretive (although we don't advertise ourselves) but because most people aren't willing to go along with the situation.

Lord John: Like sleeping 44 in four rooms. And a guy would have to cut off his long hair. We decided a few weeks ago that the long hair had to go. Too much importance was being placed on it. Now that eliminates most of the hip types right there, especially with the no-drug rule.

Lord Buckley: What holds us together is a collective urge toward individual growth and self-realization. This is best achieved through others being mirrors for us. The idea that the individual gets submerged in the group or has to conform to group pressure is hogwash. I feel like more of an individual, with more freedom, than ever before in my life.

Lord Jim: Privacy? Another silly notion. Who needs it? I've never once felt the need for what is termed "privacy." Privacy, or the view that the human needs to be physically and completely alone without anyone else present, has no validity. Privacy is in your head. You can have "privacy" in a crowded room if you like. What if you want to be alone in your head and someone is jostling your body? Maybe you need to be jostled. It depends on the circumstances. Are you communicating or withdrawing, spending too much time or too little time in your own thoughts?

Lord Buckley: Meditation? Not much now. Used to. Now we're into movement dance as a way of communicating feeling, of expressing ourselves. We have a movement class once a week.

Lady Jane: We used to have encounter sessions every night but it's not as frequent now.

Lord John: We have business meetings whenever they're necessary. Anyone can call one if there's something important to discuss.

Lord Earl: Our ages range from a new birth to about 35.

Dick: What do you do about the tendency to couple? (Laughter)

Lord Buckley: There's a whole lot of coupling. We encourage it. (More laughter.)

Dick: I can dig it, but what I meant was the tendency for a guy and girl to pair off and get possessive and jealous of each other, you know. (But I wasn't sure they did for a moment.)

Lady Jane: Oh, we had a problem with that a while back but it worked itself out okay.

Lord Jim: Yeah, every now and then. But our specific goal is to eliminate possessiveness and unhealthy attachments. Everyone has that in mind and so we work at it.

Lady Jane: I have six husbands here. There are a few others that I relate to fairly well. As time goes by, these relationships and others will develop even further. (Lady, incidentally, was full of child, about five months' worth.) We're a group marriage.

Dick: Group marriage, what does that mean?

Lord Buckley: Oh, it's just a term we've latched onto in the last week or so to describe ourselves. Next week it might be something else.

Lady Jane: Once we were all going around talking about being "mystical." A few days later it was another term we liked.

Lord Buckley: Again, you see, we don't want to get hung up on words. They're only tools we use to communicate. Inadequate ones at that. That's why we're into movement classes. Bodily control, movement exercise has been emphasized by Sufi masters and other teachers for ages.

It was easy to see that the commune handled the quantitative aspect of human relationships pretty well. But what about that elusive thing called quality? My own relationship with Consuelo has so much depth and meaning for me that I was suspicious and doubtful of the possibilities of that kind of involvement other than on a one-to-one basis.

"Are there any people in the group that came into it as a married couple, with a history of a monogamous relationship?" I asked.

Lord Buckley said that he had been married previously. The others had difficulty remembering who had come in married and who hadn't. Recently they had all married each other symbolically. And the quality of their relationships? The question is difficult to answer. Each person felt good about his particular set of relationships, and different people related in different ways, in different degrees.

Buckley expanded on this: "If someone is not willing or able to relate to someone else, the group encourages them to spend more time together. Usually, they are not relating for a reason, which, if discovered, will aid their personal growth and break down the barriers between them. What you don't like in someone else may be something you don't like in yourself, but fail to admit it.

"If Joe, for instance, can't stand Jane, we might ask him to sleep with her for a few nights. We mean sleep. They don't have to make love. Usually that solves the problem. By the second night they might want to make love. Physical intimacy then would enhance other aspects of the relationship.

"Somehow I still believe that you have to give up something in order to get something else. You have to pay a price for all this but I can't for the life of me figure out what it is."

"I think you only give up what you don't want anyway," Lord Jim added.

"We may not have material possessions, new cars, fancy clothes," said Lord John. "But we don't want them. That's no price to pay."

I was still skeptical. "There's a law in physics that for every action there is an equal and opposite reaction, which I believe applies to the realm of human and all living matter, as well as the inanimate."

"Maybe so," Lord Buckley said reflectively, "but if a reaction is created which we expect, anticipate, even want anyway, there is no loss—right? We think we've got the right formula. Things work out the way we want them to—it's not all wine and roses. That's not what I mean, not what we want in fact. The struggle, the conflicts, are part of the whole, which moves us closer together as a group and makes us stronger and more fulfilled human beings."

The Family, as they called themselves, got its start in Berkeley, California, in early 1968, when five men and women from an encounter group decided to live together. In the encounter group they had learned to utilize various techniques, including ideas from the writings of Gurdjieff and Ouspensky. One of the five was considered the leader, a sort of guru to the group.

With only $100 between them, they set off for Las Vegas where they took their chances at gambling, and subsequently won several thousand dollars. With this large sum they moved to southern New Mexico and settled in for the winter. There they picked up additional members. And before long the money ran out. Throughout the spring and summer, they obtained their food and other basic necessities on a precarious day-to-day basis. When food was needed, several of them (by now a group of 20 or more) would go out and sell newspapers to earn enough money to buy the evening meal, or they would check with local supermarkets for free spoiled food, part of which might be edible. Their emphasis was always and fanatically on interpersonal relations—on each other's growth rather than on possessions. They had seemingly instinctual awareness that acquiring possessions and object attachments would cause disruptions within the group.

Their zeal for opposing such attachments was and is unbounded. As a result, they moved around a lot. In the first two years of their experience together, more than a thousand people related to the group in one form or another. Some of these people stayed for only a few days, unable to adjust to an environment of such material austerity and interpersonal passion. Finally the family settled in Taos, where they began helping to run a health food store, medical clinic, and information center for local residents. They soon began a free school and then went on to make that full-length movie about other communes in the area. As of 1970, they were confidently hoping to eventually distribute 40,000 copies of the film. Perhaps they will, for not only are their plans ambitious, but their enthusiasm and optimism are at a peak.

Home is a Bungalow and School Bus, Under Guard

The commune's relations with the town (when I was there) seemed precarious. True, they were on excellent terms with the fire department because members of the group had helped the department set up a shortwave radio system. But the police were, at best, medium cool and the residents were suspicious, though not overtly hostile.

The recent shootouts and hassles from local rednecks of other communes in the area (a Hog Farm school bus had been dynamited and two longhairs were wounded by gunfire while sitting on their front porch one evening) had made the Family extremely cautious. At night windows in their free school had been broken and someone had fired bullets through the general store window.

"It's going to get dark pretty soon," Lord Buckley began. "We better close up and get out of here. I'll call the house. Will you stay for dinner?" he asked us.

We accepted as it slowly dawned on us that the free school was not the commune's living quarters. (The school in fact turned out to be larger than the bungalow where they all lived together.) Lord Buckley and one of the other fellows went to a front room, from which the chatter and buzz of a shortwave radio came back to us. When they returned they announced that the house was notified that we were coming and that someone would be sent here to the school to stand guard after dark. Windows had already been broken; and they now feared someone might try to burn or bomb it.

Shortwave radios were in operation at the information center, the house, and the free school, as well as in several of the commune's vehicles. This radio network provided swift communications for emergencies and also for the daily routine. So, when people at school wanted to return to the house, they simply called and asked for someone to drive over to pick them up.

In this case, though, we all piled into the Plymouth station wagon, the two girls up front with me and the four guys in the back.

"I hope it's not too crowded back there," I yelled. Then I laughed at my own remark and added, "Guess you're used to it, huh?"

We drove several miles before turning onto a winding dirt road that took us to the top of a hill, from which we could look down over the town in the distance. Then we turned right, down a one-lane driveway that led to the house.

"Blink your lights a couple of times when we get close," one of the fellows instructed.

There at the foot of the drive, in a small clearing, was an equally small building with several parked cars in front, an old school bus to one side, and what appeared to be two or three old sheds on the other side. I parked in the first available space and we all piled out. The entrance to the house was on the side near the bus and it led directly into the kitchen, where several women were bustling about preparing dinner. Two little kids, aged five or six, were running about underfoot while several people were standing around, just talking.

Consuelo and I were left to make it on our own as our original hosts disappeared into other rooms. We stood there somewhat awkwardly and I began reading a bulletin board which listed the names of current residents. Most of the people were Lord this or Lady that, but some of them did not have any such illustrious prefix by their names. One guy, who looked like a cross between Mickey

Rooney and Mickey Spillane, was standing nearby so I asked him what Lady and Lord meant and how come all the names didn't bear these titles. He smiled brightly and remarked cheerfully that he didn't know and couldn't care less; it was just fun and games. And he added that his name, Mickey, was one of those who was Lordless. Mickey went on to say that he had only lived with the group for four days. I surmised that a certain length of residence was required before a member could assume a title.

At that point I knew better than to ask if my assumption was correct. No title or rule was so rigid or absolute as to warrant a fixed answer. The few exceptions to this generalization appeared to be the following: (1) no drugs; (2) no attachments to material possessions; (3) no long hair on men; and (4) required individual flexibility and openness to group demands (if the group felt that an individual was hung up about one thing or another, that individual should be willing to change his behavior). Finally, I looked into the next room. It was rather small, about the size of a double hallway. But the room was crowded, buzzing with the noise of conversation. In one corner three or four people were talking together. Nearby, a few people sat quietly on the couch or floor. Everyone seemed in good spirits—the vibrations were very high. We entered the room and sat down on the couch. The open doorway to the front room revealed more people sitting on bunks and standing while engaged in conversation.

I noticed that one mother was nursing her child. Lady Jane sat down next to us and I asked her about women's liberation, as it seemed to me that the women here were playing pretty traditional roles cooking, doing other household work, caring for children, and having babies.

Lady Jane explained: "We get help from the men sometimes in the kitchen and with the children. It's just that I don't want to chop the wood or do the heavy work and the other women don't either. We could if we wanted to. We feel liberated, and that's what counts, isn't it?"

"I'm not so sure," I replied. "Most Americans would think us insane if we told them they are not free. They feel free. But what is the freedom to discuss and argue over tons of misinformation disseminated to us by the government, the military, big business, financial and advertising interests, all using the communication media of radio, TV and mass-circulation newspapers."

"Anyhow, what about overpopulation?" I added. "I think there should be some sort of moratorium on having kids until we provide a minimum health-care standard for everyone who's already alive. What's your rationale for having a kid?"

"Well," she replied, "we think any woman who wants the experience of having a child should be able to have it. This is going to be my first and I'm excited about it. If a woman wants more than one child, well, that depends on the circumstances, I think."

307

"Will it be a natural childbirth at home or will you go to the hospital?"

"Oh, I'll use the Lamaze method and have the baby in the local hospital. We are on very good terms with the hospital. One of the girls had her baby there just a few months ago and the fathers were all able to watch. They're getting used to our coming in like that. We believe everyone should have the opportunity to witness the birth of a child."

"Like Aldous Huxley recommended in his utopian novel, Island, huh?"

"Exactly!" she exclaimed. Our meal looked simple but nourishing—a bowl of hot potato soup and a sort of egg-roll burrito. Famished, I started to eat. Lady politely stopped me saying, "No one is supposed to begin eating until everyone is served."

Somehow, although hungry, I was pleased with that rule of courtesy. It was immensely reasonable, almost ritualistic, for a group that large, seated as they were on chairs, on the floor, on couches and beds. Before we ate, I happened to go out to the car. Through lighted windows I could see the front room and a portion of the first bedroom. These were crowded with two and three-tiered bunk beds. So that is how 44 people could sleep in four rooms!

After dinner, a brief meeting was held. A map of the house and surrounding grounds was shown, indicating the angle at which rifle shots could enter the house if hostile outsiders staged an ambush. In the event of such an emergency, a warning alarm would sound and people would be expected to immediately take shelter according to the prearranged plan. A practice drill was to take place that evening.

Because of the fear of harassment, the commune had begun posting guards to watch over the house at night, taking turns in two-hour shifts. One or two women were also among the volunteers.

Gazing around the room during the meeting, I was struck by several things about the people present. None were too fat or too skinny; indeed, a few were physically beautiful. Most of them seemed in good spirits, though one girl with a furrowed brow and an angry look to her kept me from feeling that everything was a billowy cushion of love. One fellow whom we had sat next to on the couch before dinner had moved to the other side of the room, but I didn't feel any bad vibes from him; of course, it may have been that I was too hungry and too distracted by other things there for me to pay close attention to him.

On the whole, the atmosphere there made us high. And when it was time for us to leave, we excused ourselves reluctantly. Dave, who had greeted us initially at the free school, said goodbye to us at the car. As we drove away, our headlights paused momentarily on two of the family's members walking up the road, rifles in hand, to stand guard on the hilltop that overlooked that amazing 44-member, bungalow-and-bus commune. ■

service communities

There are a number of service-oriented communities active in the United States. Privately financed, self-supporting, or associated with some large organization, they exist in order to provide certain services for various segments of society. Inevitably they all involve some form or other of communitarianism sharing among those who serve, sharing among those served, sharing by all within the community. This particular characteristic makes them part of the world of the commune although some of them in practice do not care to actually be called communes.

CAMPHILL VILLAGE

Camphill Village, located in Copake, New York, considers itself to be part of a movement rather than a single community, for it serves and receives support from a much larger and widespread population than resides at its own location at any given time.

The Camphill Movement, begun in Scotland by Karl Koenig, is based on the work with mentally retarded adults that was done by Rudolf Steiner (1861–1925), the founder of anthroposophy. Steiner's ideas about what he called Curative Education are based mainly on the principle of accepting the retarded person as an individual, caring for him as a total person, body, soul, and spirit, and concentrating on his potentialities (rather than his liabilities), however limited they may be.

Camphill Village, which was established in 1955, provides a warm and supportive environment in which the handicapped can work and support themselves as much as possible, thereby increasing their self-confidence and self-respect. For young people between the ages of 18 and 21 the community also provides a progressive education program.

The community, which has a population of approximately 150 (as of early 1969), is divided into families. Each family consists of a staff member, his own immediate family, and five to nine retarded adults. Each family, which lives in one house, manages its own finances in order to encourage a maximum of shared responsibilities and the greatest degree of individual flexibility.

There is a wide variety of both workshops and occupations available to the villagers. The people work in teams on the farm, in the bakery, and at construction and such crafts as doll-making, woodworking, and making enamelware. In addition, the villagers are expected to do the usual tasks of housekeeping and taking care of the grounds.

In order to qualify for admittance, applicants must be able to take care of their personal needs; that is, they must be able to wash and dress themselves as well as not require constant medical supervision. They must also have both the ability to work under guidance and the incapacity to earn their living in the outside world. In addition, their families, if they can afford it, are required to pay as much as $200 per month. This cash income, together with that derived from the output of the farm and workshops, is responsible for the community being almost self-supporting.

Recently the U.S. Government has offered the community a $20,000 grant on a matching basis. If the community can raise an equal amount from private sources, it will qualify for the grant. And that will enable the Camphill Movement to expand its facilities and perhaps even to develop new community locations to accommodate the applicants on its long waiting list.

There is also another Camphill community in the United States. Called Beaver Run, it is a community that specializes in the treatment of retarded children. It is located in Glenmoore, Pennsylvania. ■

THE CATHOLIC WORKER FARM

The Catholic Worker Movement originated in New York City in 1933 during the depths of the Depression. When begun by Dorothy Day, it consisted solely of The Catholic Worker, a radical pacifist newspaper. Soon after that a House of Hospitality was opened in the city to help feed and clothe the poor and un-employed. And in 1936 the movement bought a farm at Tivoli, in the Hudson Valley, New York, in order to start a Catholic Worker community. It was only the first. By 1941, there were well over 25 Catholic Worker rural farms, most of them connected with hospitality houses in various cities. The Catholic Worker's circulation climbed to more than 100,000, but Pearl Harbor made pacifism immensely unpopular throughout the country and the paper's circulation subsequently decreased to 35,000.

Today, The Catholic Worker and the New York City House of Hospitality are still flourishing. So is the Tivoli farm, where Martin J. Corbin co-edits the paper with Dorothy Day. In addition, several other autonomous CW farms and hospitality houses still operate in various other places throughout the country.

In December 1970 I paid my first visit to the Tivoli farm, which represents the Catholic Worker Movement's principal rural effort. I found that the farm consists of a 90-acre tract of land, most of which is left uncultivated. There are three main buildings, which provide space for sleeping quarters, kitchen, dining room, chapels, and library. The community's population is between 25 and 35 people in winter, and a good many more during the warmer months. In the summer the farm also serves as a center for conferences, which can mean the presence of as many as 150 people on a weekend. The farm depends primarily on donations for support. All able-bodied members share in the routine maintenance and repair work there. In spite of its title and origins, the Catholic Worker farm houses people of all sorts of religious persuasions, including not a few unbelievers. The purpose of the Farm itself is still, as it has always been, to provide a home away from the city for the poor and needy regardless of religion, race or creed. Work and facilities are shared in common, without structure, and with most members having the privacy of their own room when needed.

Among the people I had a chance to talk to about the Catholic Worker Movement was Stanley Vishnewski, who had been one of the movement's early members. The following is a transcript of part of my conversation with Stanley:

Stanley: Running the paper is our main work, see. Communities like Twin Oaks, they make hammocks. Other communities, they make organic foods. Our main work is the paper. After we started the newspaper back during the Depression, people came to us for help. A woman came to see us and said, "I heard you people write this paper and I'm out of a job. What are you going to do with me?" So Dorothy says, "Well, the only thing we can do is rent a house." We rented a small apartment and we were able to take care of about 12 ladies in our first House of Hospitality. The paper's circulation increased to 20,000 and our staff slowly increased. Then we moved to Charles Street; we got a bigger house. We got this bigger house because our staff increased.

The third part of our program was to establish communities. This seems to be a much more popular idea now than then. When The Catholic Worker movement started it was completely, well … utopian, looked down upon, crazy. "How are you going to work it?" People put up all kinds of objections. None of them were valid. None of them were actually the kind of problem you actually met, you know. It's funny, because the problems that you do meet are altogether different from what people think you're going to meet. It wasn't until we got a staff of people who had skills that we were able to start our first farming commune.

Dick: Have you personally been involved in the city mostly or did you spend most of your time in the country?

Stanley: I worked a lot in the city through the Depression. I always had a love for the land, so when we got the farm I worked there a lot. But we alternated back and forth, because we actually were one unit, the farm and the city house. We were one staff and so we'd alternate back and forth. We had the ideal of a beautiful farming commune but we were always taking care of lots of sick people. We were always sort of a house of hospitality on the land, more than the ideal farming community that we envisioned. We had to face reality, you know, that's the one thing you can't escape. You have to realize that you're living here, now, and if a man comes to you in need, what can you do? It's only a matter of space. There's always food for people, you can always share food, but space… that's the problem. Summertime, people can sleep on the ground, with their sleeping bags, but it's wintertime now. And also, you can't overcrowd a commune because people's nerves, they get on edge; people need space. Privacy is very important in a commune; that's one of the very important things in order to establish a successful commune.

Another mistake people make is they think all they have to do is get a group together, go out on the land, and start a farming community. They fail within nine months, unless they have an underlying principle. People have to have a reason for their existence. Not only a reason for their existence, but also they have to realize that in the beginning they have to sacrifice more than they would if they were working at a regular job. They have to give up creature comfort. They can't expect creature comforts in the beginning; they're working toward a better life. If they're willing to sacrifice, then eventually they will get together. It won't be forced. You see, you can't force a commune. You just can't take 12 families from the city and say, "There's a house." It's not going to work. My advice to people who want to start a commune is to get together for about 12 months in a city, meet twice a week, and have common meals. Pool your interests, go out for walks, and maybe have a trial run by renting an old abandoned farmhouse and spending a vacation up there for one month. And then see.

My own experience, and I have been 35 years with the Catholic Worker movement, is that communes based on a religious motivation seem to succeed, whereas the ones based on a purely economic motive fail. Because a man who's got talent suddenly realizes: "What the heck am I doing here? I could be getting $150 or $200 a week with my skills, and this other guy here is just living on my work, he's not contributing half as much." So he leaves. In a group with a religious motivation, there's a common reason for being together. It works out that way.

Our farm here is not really like a farming commune because we work so closely with our city place. We take care of a lot of sick people; I have joined the list now. And for the first time, I tell you, I came to realize the value of community when I got sick with this heart disease; I mean, people take care of me. They cook my meals for me, they see my bed is made, that I'm comfortable. Suppose I had been living in the city? Making money, all unhappy, stuck in an abandoned old room, social worker to see you once a week? A community has its blessings which far outweigh its faults, but people have to sacrifice for that in the beginning and have to work toward that goal.

Dick: You don't get something for nothing.

Stanley: Oh no, you don't get something for nothing. You have to do it because you want to do it, and then you really will have a beautiful commune. As a way of life it's very rich and very rewarding and satisfying.

While visiting the farm at Tivoli, I also interviewed Marty Corbin (co-editor of The Catholic Worker) and Marjorie Hughes (one of the central figures at the Farm).

Martin: During World War II there wasn't much opposition to war, only on the part of pacifists and Trotskyists.

Marjorie: It was a very uncomfortable boat to be in, you know.

Dick: Your philosophy is also anarchist, I believe. Is there any easy definition of anarchism?

Martin: Yes. The basic idea is that it's a movement which calls for the abolition of the state and its replacement by a federation of communities. This federation would gradually usurp the function of the state and perform the same functions the state does now, but on a decentralized basis. Of course, there are other schools of anarchism, but this is the one we subscribe to. Some anarchists are syndicalists, for example, the IWW. They favor the idea of one big union which would perform the function of the federation of communities.

Dick: That idea has gone down the tubes with the "one big union" almost a reality today.

Martin: Yeah, although it's funny, there's a revival of the IWW among many people at the University of Chicago. There have also been extreme individualist anarchists based philosophically around Max Stirner who wrote a book called Ego And His Own. Marx wrote a couple hundred pages attacking him. Stirner's anarchism was that you don't accept any law outside yourself.

Dick: I'd like to change the subject to what's going on here. You've started to have meetings on Monday nights, I hear.

Martin: We don't have formal community meetings. We're very informal. We have little talks once a month on Sunday afternoon. We invite a guest to speak. For example, tomorrow a priest from India will be here. These aren't really concerned with community problems, just information. Mostly the decisions are arrived at quite informally. Plus, Dorothy Day is the leading person who has most of the say about both the paper and the farm. She just returned from Africa, India, and Australia. She was also just out in the Midwest on a speaking tour. She divides her time between traveling, the House of Hospitality in New York City on the Lower East Side, and here.

Dick: Are you taking all the people that get sent up from the city?

Marjorie: No. We take in people that arrive on our doorstep. Very often the ones who didn't bother to call are the ones to get taken in 'cause we don't have anything else to do with them. We get a lot of visiting kids in the warm weather, even in the winter. It's surprising how many turn up with their sleeping bags. That's never a real problem because they'll sleep anyplace, you know, and they'll eat whatever's there. If they don't show up for meals they'll eat bread and peanut butter and not complain. The real terrible thing is the families. We get so many calls from families that have no place to live and that are being evicted, or that have a run of bad luck, and we just don't have any place to house them. All summer long, there were families on the move, and not all poor either. Many were middle-class, college-educated people who'll go back to their jobs in the fall if they don't find what they're looking for. On the move with their children, looking for a community.

Dick: A lot of people who subscribe to The Modern Utopian are the type of people who read about communities and get interested in them that way. Many younger people tend to get into communes more experientially while older people get into them more intellectually. I get a lot of white-collar, professional-type people writing and asking, "Where is there a community I can join, I can't stand my present situation." Like one time there was a doctor with 10 children. His wife had already left them a couple of years before. And he said it's time for him to do it. But I thought to myself: Where is he going to find a place that'll take 10 children? Ten children! You have people here of all ages and types. Don't you have any hassles with such diverse people coming in?

Marjorie: We do from time to time, but generally speaking, if you're patient and wait, people who don't really fit in will take themselves off—maybe not as soon as you'd, like them to, but eventually. Or else they'll change. Once in a great while you get somebody you can't cope with at all. That doesn't happen often.

Martin: We've only had two people who could be really violent. Both psychotics, I would say, but psychotics given to physical violence. Boy, that's a really sticky problem, because you have your children to think of and you're opposed to calling in the police, at least in principle. We have occasionally called the state police to take people to a mental hospital, people whom we couldn't capture and take care of ourselves when they really freaked out. But then, they'd come back when they were over that, so… so far, we haven't had any serious violence; we had a couple of close calls.

Marjorie: We have a lot of conflict but it generally stays at the level of shouting and grumbling and doors slamming.

Dick: What is it that makes you who have been here these last six years willing to tolerate that conflict?

Marjorie: Well, I don't know about Marty, but I know there have been many times when if I had had the money I would have gone. At the same time, I can say it's lucky for a person if he can't leave, because there's so much to be gained if he can stick it through. You learn so much. One thing I've learned is that conflict is inevitable and not to duck it. Conflict can be creative if you don't let it be completely destructive. For me that's a big lesson, because I tend to just walk away from things. The more aggressive people learn to simmer down a little bit and learn that other people have legitimate points of view. But it's hard. It's terribly hard. We are a community of need here, we're not an intentional community. Which means that we avoid some problems but we also get problems that could be avoided by weeding people out. The other thing is that we don't support ourselves from the land, and that makes a big difference. Many communities fold because the economic problem is too much. I still think it's desirable to support yourself, because I don't think it's a very real experiment as long as you're having outside support. ∎

SYNANON

Perhaps the best-known service community in America is Synanon. Although there was only one to begin with (in California), Synanon is now a collective name covering the several Synanon communities that exist in various parts of the country. Synanon began as a communal approach in treating drug addicts. As a result of its subsequent overwhelming success, Synanon expanded its therapy program (the core of which is the Synanon Game) to include alienated middle-class Americans.

The Synanon Game is not unlike the Twin Oaks (Oneida) practice of mutual criticism, but it is geared to expressing more overtly and passionately one's hostile feelings toward others. From these beginnings have developed the present Synanon community complexes which, although still very middle-class and comfortable, are highly communal in their organization and operation. Within each complex there are separate facilities for children, communal dining and recreation activities, and the pooling of income. Adults, though, do have private rooms. Synanon has a sort of tribal structure, patriarchal, with Charles Dietrich, its founder, as head chief. The main criticism I have heard of Synanon is that it takes a person off hard drugs and makes him dependent on Synanon. This criticism sounds too much like a rationalization which allows the critic to dismiss the group's value in order to smugly continue old biases and attitudes. Certainly even the critic who reflected ever so slightly would have to admit that the Synanon alternative to drug addiction is no worse than dependency on a methadone program and far better than continued addiction. When it comes to some of the middle-class addictions which are dispelled through Synanon, the critic might very well feel his case was stronger, but then he would perhaps be defending his own addiction. Nevertheless, it is the patriarchal, somewhat less than democratic, structure of Synanon which is worth a most deserving critical reflection. ■

GOULD FARM

A community that specializes in serving the emotionally disturbed is Gould Farm, which is located near Great Barrington in the hills of western Massachusetts. Gould Farm's objective is to help people through their period of emotional stress and then return them to the mainstream of society. The staff that runs the place is paid, which is a somewhat rare phenomenon among communities. But then, Gould Farm's board of directors does not consider the place a "community." ∎

PEACE ACTION FARM/AMMON HENNACY

Another place that more readily lends itself to being called a community (and doesn't object) is Ammon Hennacy, or Peace Action Farm, which is situated in upstate New York. This place is cooperatively owned by three member-families. Its principal activities and interests are in providing a place for disadvantaged urban children who come for summer vacations and in attempting to provide accommodations for the families of conscientious objectors who are in jail.

Among the hundreds of thousands of young Americans who are experimenting with cooperative and communal living ventures, there are not only the somewhat stereotyped, dropped-out hippies, but also the degree-seeking college students as well as the more conservative young professionals and working secretaries and typists. Even people who previously restricted their sharing to an apartment in the city (and this because of exorbitant rents) are now experimenting with an increased degree of sharing, both of living quarters and household expenses. Still more radical changes have taken place in attitude. Instead of such unspoken agreements as "I keep out of your way, you keep out of mine" or "You help me and I'll help you," the trend has been toward a commitment perhaps best expressed in the phrase, "From each according to his ability, to each according to his need." This saying is hardly new, having long served as the slogan of an effete Communist ideology, but what is new is that it has become a basic and widespread humanitarian consideration. Mainstream America, or at least its youth division, is edging rapidly toward alternative lifestyles. ∎

what happened to the communes

by Timothy Miller

SO WHAT HAPPENED TO THE COMMUNES? THERE WAS A HUGE
burst of communal energy in the late 1960s and early 1970s, and then communes
pretty much fell from public consciousness. Most Americans must think they were
like Roman candles, burning brilliantly for a moment and then disappearing. But
that's far from the actual story.

It's true that many of the communes did not make it past 1975 or thereabouts,
but a great many of them did survive. The Farm, in Tennessee, is still there, with
hundreds of residents and many of its original ideals intact. Twin Oaks, in Virginia, is doing just fine. Tolstoy Farm remains an open-land commune and has
several homesteads nearly half a century after its founding. The list of surviving
communes could easily run to several hundred.

One reason the survivors are as nearly invisible as they are is that they tend to
avoid publicity. During the optimistic heyday of the counterculture, the air was
full of peace and love and exuberant openness, but that sometimes led to problems. One serious problem for many of the communes was that of deadbeats and
the walking wounded—people who would join and then not work, psychological
cases that needed tending, and sometimes outright criminals who stole and even
killed. A commune that did not need new members and had had trouble with
problem cases in the past could easily conclude that it had no need to publicize
itself, and indeed sometimes tried hard to stay out of public view.

Another problem that got worse as years went by was zoning. Once upon a
time zoning was unheard of in the United States, and by the time the 1960s-era
communes erupted, it was still unusual in many rural parts of the United States.
A lack of zoning laws meant that people could do pretty much anything with the
land the owner wanted to and could let any number of people live there. Gradually, however, zoning has become stricter, in some cases because upstanding local
citizens were horrified at the countercultural invasion they experienced. Zoning

laws not only limit land uses, but are often coupled with building codes, ensuring that simple structures cannot legally be constructed, and often specify occupancy limits—often as few as three or four unrelated persons in a given building or on a given piece of land. That kind of restriction inhibits communal living severely, and more than a few of the continuing communes keep very low profiles since publicity might disclose their noncompliance with zoning laws.

So that's part of the after-story: the communes quietly continue, sometimes nearly invisibly. But thousands of new communities have come along since then as well. The same kind of idealism that fired the 1960s-era counterculturists is present in many of the intentional communities that are founded each year in the United States. The old values of self-sufficiency, dissent from prevailing cultural patterns, and cooperation continue to motivate communal founders today.

Over the last three or four decades two forms have marked much of American intentional-community building: ecovillages and cohousing. Of the two types, the ecovillages probably more closely carry on the vision of the 1960s era, but both types are vital, ongoing links in the American communal tradition.

Ecovillage residents take a serious and thoughtful approach to minimizing their environmental impact and creating sustainable ways of life. They build highly efficient buildings, often of straw bale or cob construction. They are often off the electrical grid, getting such power as they use from solar, wind, and water sources, but more generally just using a lot less of it than the average American does. Composting toilets are standard in ecovillages, at least where local codes allow them. (One ecovillage on the West Coast has even outlawed toilet paper, replacing it with a water-cleaning routine, just as the 1960s-era commune called Wooden Shoe Farm had done dozens of years earlier.) Ecovillagers minimize their driving, using bicycles and public transportation extensively, and in several cases operate motor vehicles on discarded cooking oil. Sewage is treated in lagoons that contribute to biodiversity. And, of course, organic gardens are the norm as ecovillagers seek self-sufficiency in food.

Cohousing tends to be a bit more mainstream and upscale than ecovillages, but the overlap between the two forms is considerable. Sometimes cohousing and ecovillages are combined, and in most cases there is a bit of the ecovillage spirit in a cohousing project. Although cohousing typically involves new construction and is often located in suburban or even rural locations, the buildings are usually built to standards of high energy efficiency, and the per-capita impact of the residents is nearly always less than that of persons and families who live in single-family houses. Cohousing involves small living spaces (because many common facilities, such as laundries and workshops and guest rooms, are shared), and members in most cases recycle and compost and cultivate organic gardens.

In their own ways, ecovillages and cohousing tell us not only that intentional communities continue in American life, but that themes from the countercultural

1960s continue to shape American life much more broadly as well. Today organic food has reached conventional supermarkets, casual and comfortable clothing is much more widely accepted than it once was, and sexual behavior once considered "deviant" (homosexuality and nonmarital sex, for example) has achieved more widespread acceptance than anyone would have thought possible half a century ago. Concern for the environment has become mainstream. Socially responsible businesses and investments continue to grow. Decriminalization and even legalization of marijuana progresses, slowly but seemingly inevitably. And communal living continues to have a following.

In short, the seemingly radical social innovations of the 1960s era don't seem so radical any more, and more of the spirit of the 1960s survives than most of us consciously realize. The experiments that Richard Fairfield chronicled in the late 1960s seemed marginal, even bizarre, at the time. But they pointed toward the future, as social experiments often do. The countercultural roots of much of modern life richly deserve to be remembered. ▪

RIGHT: MOBILE HOME, OLOMPOLAI RANCH (NORTHERN CALIFORNIA)

PREVIOUS SPREAD: THE SOURCE FAMILY, SANTA MONICA, CA

Process Media
1240 W. Sims Way Suite 124
Port Townsend, WA 98368
www.ProcessMediaInc.com

Design by Bill Smith

about Richard Fairfield

RICHARD FAIRFIELD WAS BORN IN GARDNER, MAINE, IN 1937. His extremely varied education included work in Japanese, psychology, English literature, creative writing, and Mandarin Chinese, which he learned in connection with his military service. After establishing and operating his own insurance agency, he went on to study religion at Tufts University in Massachusetts and to serve as student minister in two Massachusetts churches. He received his Bachelor of Divinity degree at Starr King for the Ministry in Berkeley, California, and served as the Unitarian minister in Santa Rosa until 1970.

From 1966-1971, Fairfield edited and published The Modern Utopian, which he founded to report on the developing communal movement in the United States. Articles in the Modern Utopian were contributed by Fairfield, insiders in the communal scene, or underground journalists whose features were published through The Underground Press Syndicate (UPS). In 1970, Fairfield visited communes in England, France, Holland, Denmark, Germany, Switzerland, and Japan, and soon after wrote, edited and published three oversized, heavily-illustrated books: *Communes Europe, Communes Japan,* and *Communes USA.* Penguin published a revised paperback edition of *Communes USA* in 1972.

Richard continued to self-publish books, magazines, and newsletters until the mid-1970s. He also continued his graduate studies at the Union Graduate School and the United States International University. He was employed as an instructor and academic advisor at the University of California, Santa Cruz for 17 years.

He moved to Southwest Florida in 1992 where he currently resides. Today he works as a realtor but his passion is still writing. He publishes a monthly review of films (moviereviews1.com) and has begun to document his diverse life experiences on his website (mylifeinprocess.com), including information on the evolution of *The Modern Utopian.* ∎